RESEARCH IN THE SOCIOLOGY OF WORK

RESEARCH IN THE SOCIOLOGY OF WORK

Series Editor: Volume 28: Lisa A. Keister
Volume 29 onwards: Steven Vallas

RESEARCH IN THE SOCIOLOGY OF WORK

EDITED BY

STEVEN VALLAS
Northeastern University, USA

United Kingdom – North America – Japan
India – Malaysia – China

Emerald Group Publishing Limited
Howard House, Wagon Lane, Bingley BD16 1WA, UK

First edition 2016

British Library Cataloguing in Publication Data
A catalogue record for this book is available from the British Library

ISBN: 978-1-78635-406-8
ISSN: 0277-2833 (Series)

ISOQAR certified
Management System,
awarded to Emerald
for adherence to
Environmental
standard
ISO 14001:2004.

Certificate Number 1985
ISO 14001

INVESTOR IN PEOPLE

CONTENTS

PART III
GENDER, SEXUALITY AND PRECARITY

EDITORIAL ADVISORY BOARD

LIST OF CONTRIBUTORS

Kathryn Freeman Anderson	Department of Sociology, University of Houston, TX, USA
Andrew S. Fullerton	Department of Sociology, Oklahoma State University at Stillwater, OK, USA
C. Elizabeth Hirsh	Department of Sociology, University of British Columbia, Vancouver, Canada
Julie A. Kmec	Department of Sociology, Washington State University, Pullman, WA, USA
Robin Leidner	Department of Sociology, University of Pennsylvania, Philadelphia, PA, USA
Amanda E. Lewis	Department of Sociology, University of Illinois at Chicago, Chicago, IL, USA
Michael A. Long	Department of Social Sciences and Languages, Newcastle upon Tyne, UK
Jennifer L. Nelson	Department of Sociology, Emory University, Atlanta, GA, USA
David Orzechowicz	Department of Sociology, University of California, Davis, CA, USA
Brian Ott	Department of Sociology, University of Oregon, Eugene, OR, USA
Vincent J. Roscigno	Department of Sociology, Ohio State University, Columbus, OH, USA
Michael L. Siciliano	Department of Sociology, University of California, Los Angeles, CA, USA
Sheryl Skaggs	School of Social Sciences, University of Texas, Dallas, TX, USA

Eli Wilson   Department of Sociology, University of
                           California, Los Angeles, CA, USA

George Wilson   Department of Sociology, University of
                           Miami, Miami, FL, USA

THE CHANGING FIELD OF WORKPLACE SOCIOLOGY: AN INTRODUCTION TO VOLUME 29

Earlier this year, as the incoming editor of *Research in the Sociology of Work*, I was handling submissions and reviews when I happened upon Weber's (1949/1904) "Objectivity in Social Science," written as Weber himself became editor of *Archiv fur Sozialwissenschaft und Socialpolitik*. Weber raised the question of the "ideal values" and moral concerns that motivate the members of any scholarly community as they carry out their research. His words resonated:

> A journal which has come into existence under the influence of a general interest in a concrete problem will always include among its contributors persons who are personally interested in these problems because certain concrete situations seem to be incompatible with, or seem to threaten, the realization of certain ideal values in which they believe. A bond of similar ideals will hold this circle of contributors together and it will be the basis of a further recruitment. This in turn will tend to give the journal ... a certain *"character"*. (1949/1904, p. 61, Weber's emphasis)

Weber's ruminations are worth posing with respect to *RSW* at this juncture in its history. What precisely *are* the "ideal values" that our academic community holds dear? What is the *"character"* of our field and of the journal that bears its name?

To answer these questions, a bit of down and dirty intellectual history is helpful. In the United States, the sociological approach toward workplace life found its first incarnation in the form of "industrial sociology," as embodied in the work of Alvin Gouldner, Donald Roy, and Ely Chinoy. The trade union movement was at its zenith, and what we now call the Fordist model was taken for granted. This arrangement allowed scholars to view work *as* a society in its own right — a view we can attribute to Roy (1952) and Gouldner (1954) — or else to view work *in* society, as in the work of Chinoy (1955; see Tausky, 1984). Though there were certainly marked divisions among this generation of scholars, the field itself was relatively unified — a state not destined to last.

A centrifugal tendency took root, spinning out a number of divergent subfields that in many cases led scholars to form separate literatures, conceptual languages, journals, and even professional associations. First to break away was the sociology of occupations and the professions (see Abbott, 1988; Dingwall, 2008; Johnson, 1972). By the 1960s, the sociology of organizations had formed its own domain, which by the 1970s had generated distinct paradigms − mainly neo-institutionalism and theories of population ecology − enabling it to become an analytical domain in its own right (Perrow, 1979). What then arose was a loosely organized array of competing schools of thought, each with its own conceptual tool-kit, each gaining momentum for a time but then falling into disuse. The new structuralism, along with theories of economic segmentation, emerged as potent challenges to human capital theory (Kalleberg & Berg, 1987), but then seemed to wither away − ironically at the very moment when economic dualism was becoming highly pronounced. The labor process school arose in the work of Braverman (1974) and Burawoy (1979, 1985) but by the late 1980s lost most of its support in the United States − not surprisingly perhaps, given the legacy of Reaganism and the rise of a neo-liberal orthodoxy. Theorists of a more managerial persuasion began to hold sway (Heckscher & Donnellon, 1994; Womack, Jones, & Roos, 1992), at least on this side of the Atlantic.

At least some of this uncertainty stems from institutional changes reshaping sociologists' employment contexts. In the United States and Europe, a growing proportion of sociologists has found employment within Schools of Business, Management Science, and Organization Studies.[1] Although this trend is international, it has had disparate consequences on opposite sides of the Atlantic. In the United States, the result has been an increased focus on the legal, political and normative environments of the corporation and a decreased focus on the meanings and activities found among workers within the workplace itself. So pronounced has this tendency been, in fact, that scholars have repeatedly felt compelled to ask "where have the workers gone?" (Simpson, 1989), or to insist on "bringing work back" into the analysis (Barley & Kunda, 2001). This effort to repopulate the workplace with actual workers has also found expression in Hallett and Ventresca's (2006) "inhabited institutionalism" and in Kellogg's (2011) "micro-institutionalism" (see Bechky, 2003).

Interestingly, in the European countries, the absorption of sociological analysis by business schools has had a different effect. It has expanded critical analysis focused on a blind spot within much American research − the nature of power and domination within work organizations − in effect, extending the concerns of the labor process school beyond American shores. What has resulted has been a richer conception of organizational discourse, worker identity, and the nature of worker resistance (see Ackroyd & Thompson, 1995; Beck, 2000; Alvesson & Willmott, 2002; Fleming & Sturdy, 2011). A key issue in much European literature – how entrepreneurial ideology has reconfigured the work experience (Du Gay, 1996; Vallas & Cummins, 2015; Williams & Connell, 2010) – has received remarkably little emphasis on this side of the Atlantic.

There are of course counter-tendencies. Key has been the steady growth of research on organizational inequalities, which has built on the early work of Kanter (1977) and then Acker (1990) and has traced the relation between organizational structures and processes on the one hand and the uneven distribution of job rewards along racial and gender lines on the other (Browne & Misra, 2003; Castilla & Benard, 2010; Tomaskovic-Devey, 1993; Williams, 1992; Wingfield, 2009). More recently, this literature has sought to understand how "inequality regimes" have been shaped by the ebb and flow of social and political movements, legal reforms, and shifts in the public arena more broadly (Acker, 2006; Stainback & Tomaskovic-Devey, 2012). Yet even this school of thought, which has shown sustained growth and momentum, has been marked by a profound gap between its macro-oriented approach, focused on shifts in the demographic composition of privileged occupations, and the micro-level of analysis – the social relations that underpin such inequality regimes (Berrey, 2015; Reskin, 2003; Vallas & Cummins, 2014).

This thumbnail sketch of the field's evolution is a story of one step forward, two steps back. Alongside increasing sophistication and much insight are notable omissions and systematic oversights that have slowed the growth of our knowledge of workplace life. Especially troubling has been the boundary between American and European literatures on such key issues as workplace diversity (Dobbin, Schrage, & Kalev, 2015; Kalev, Dobbin, & Kelley, 2006) and precarious employment (Hatton, 2011; Kalleberg, 2011; Padavic, 2005). American studies of diversity have made important gains but have shown little willingness to draw on the European school known as "critical diversity studies" (Benschop, 2001; Zanoni, 2010; Zanoni & Janssens, 2004), much to the field's detriment. And while US-based analysis of precarious employment has grown enormously in recent years, American scholars have yet to consult the European literature on enterprise culture and the employment regimes that have emerged in response to neo-liberal capitalism (Boltanski & Chiapello, 2005; Du Gay, 1996; Gallie, 2007; Vidal, 2013). When important theories cannot flow freely across international lines, or when "structural holes" emerge that impede theoretical innovation (Burt, 2004), the result can only impose stark limits on the field. Important questions go unasked, scholars are distracted from important trends and explanations for them, and useful concepts go unused. What's a scholar to do?

It is here that *Research in the Sociology of Work* enters the picture. For nearly three decades, *RSW* has functioned as a research annual whose contents were devoted to a given theme each year. This design enabled each guest editor to collect a set of papers that stood at the cutting edge of a particular facet of the literature. Yet as the complexity of the terrain has increased, the tasks that confront members of this academic community have expanded exponentially. Needed then is a shift in the structure of *RSW*, the better to support a more ambitious approach – one capable of fostering scholarly debates that cut across the balkanized terrain that the field has become.

As of this volume, *RSW* has begun to move in this direction, adopting the features that characterize any peer-reviewed specialty journal of note. First, *RSW* will now appear with greater frequency (twice annually). Second, its contents will be open to the full range of topics and themes that exist at any point in time, the better to accommodate the field in all its breadth. Third, the inclusion of articles will be more fully subject to the sobering ordeal of peer review. Fourth, a distinguished Editorial Advisory Board has been assembled (whose members are listed elsewhere in this issue). Finally, *RSW* will now be formally sponsored by the Occupations, Organizations, and Work section of the American Sociological Association, the better to anchor itself in the field.

But the question must be asked: What is the "character" of *RSW* and the intellectual community that *RSW* aims to represent? What ideals does it hold dear? How does it define its birthright jurisdiction, especially given the unruly nature of the field? To state the obvious perhaps, the key concern that members of this community share is a determination to capture some aspect of the work situation that workers encounter in their everyday lives. By implication, this means that the fate of *workers* must figure prominently in the analysis. By implication, the coordinates of the field can be said to encompass the *meanings* that work assumes, whether historically or in the contemporary world; the *authority relations* that govern work and that define the employment relationship; the conditions under which *boundaries* are drawn among workers, privileging the members of some groups while depriving "others" of valued job rewards. And it must include the institutional and political conditions that shape the employment relationship, whether within or across particular nation-states – a matter of particular urgency, as globalization erodes long-standing conceptions of the wage-labor relationship (Bronfenbrenner & Luce, 2004; Collins, 2003; Vallas, 2012, chapter 6).

What of the "ideal values" that members of this disparate intellectual community are likely to hold dear? Here, there may be no overarching moral consensus, given how the field is riven by differences in methodology, level of analysis, and conceptual frameworks. Yet, in the spirit of Weber, it seems incumbent on us to articulate the moral precepts that lead scholars to participate in this academic community. Of course, some are driven by sheer curiosity or the compulsion to extend the boundaries of our knowledge of workplace life. For others, motivation derives from a political commitment to defend the interests of vulnerable groups. This motivation may include a hope for the pursuit of worker control, or at least, some greater version of autonomy than corporate domination has allowed, or merely for the defense of the worker's dignity – an issue foregrounded by the late Hodson (2001), himself a long-time editor of *RSW*. The moral purpose for some might also encompass a commitment to the rights of historically excluded groups to full and equal inclusion in workplace life: women, racial minorities, members of the LGBT community.

The present issue constitutes a down payment on *RSW*'s obligation to its readers. The issue's contents address three important domains that lie squarely within the field's coordinates: worker identity, workplace authority, and the gendered nature of workers' labor market positions. The literature on work and identity has a long and honored history, reaching back to Marx's own work and that of Hughes (1951/1994; cf. Snow & Anderson, 1987), to feminist scholarship on gender identity (Lee, 1998; Salzinger, 2003), and to European schools of thought based on Foucauldian analysis (Alvesson & Willmott, 2002; see also Anteby, 2008a, 2008b). Though literature has often been polarized between structural and agentic approaches, the papers in this issue try to disentangle the structure/agency relation, doing so by examining how workers respond to structurally based threats to their identity *as* workers. Thus, Robin Leidner's article provides a sensitive, moving analysis how actors struggle to cope with the symbolic assaults their occupation routinely imposes on them as they soldier on in their "survival" gigs, performance of which provides daily evidence of their inability to "be" that which they insist they *are*. The paper by Jennifer L. Nelson and Amanda E. Lewis extends this foray into the structural/identity relation, examining early-childhood educators in four organizational contexts. The take-away concerns the duality of structure – a theme first developed by Giddens (1979, pp. 81–85), by feminists such as Hossfeld (1990), and then by Hodson (1995, 2001), all of whom have viewed structures as both constraining and enabling the actions and identities of subordinate groups. As Nelson and Lewis note, structural contexts not only pose identity threats; duly redefined, they also furnish the resources with which workers can resist threats to their identities as well.

The paper by George Wilson and Vincent J. Roscigno asks how the exercise of authority shapes those who wield it. Their point of departure is a long-standing one: the assumption that one's position in the organization of production (broadly conceived) has consequences for workers' world views; surprisingly, little research that examines this assumption empirically. Seeking to fill this gap, they show how the assumption of supervisory power reshapes political views. Using GSS data, they show that supervisors seem to become more inclined to limit the provision of social support than non-supervisory workers, while also adopting more functionalist conceptions of stratification (Davis and Moore live, it seems). These effects are especially pronounced among whites – a point that raises questions about the intersection of class, race, and political action.

If Wilson and Roscigno are concerned with the consequences of authority relations structures for political attitudes, the other papers in this section target managerial systems of authority and control in their own right. On this score, a rich and vibrant literature has opened up, from studies of the normative controls that come to be inscribed within organizational cultures to (most recently) the "just be yourself" managerial style (Fleming & Sturdy, 2011). The paper by Eli Wilson identifies a beguiling expression of the latter type of regime, examining the case of an upscale California restaurant where workers are selected, trained, and evaluated according to their ability to shed the subservient frame typical of food servers in favor of a "we're equals and even friends" style of comportment. This style – which in effect obscures the unequal nature of the server/customer relation – epitomizes what Bourdieu routinely termed "misrecognition," a form of alchemy that construes economic transactions as personal interactions. This paper can be viewed as linking labor process literature to studies in economic sociology, such as those of Viviana Zelizer (e.g., 1994). It broadens our understanding of the discursive acrobatics employers can seek to have employees perform.

The structure of control is also problematized by Michael Siciliano, whose study fastens on routine analytics workers – workers in the high-tech field who labor without the heroics that system architects can be expected to display – and thereby exhibit interesting contradictions. Their work — essentially equivalent to the production of Nielsen ratings — exhibits a fascinating combination of the often enthralling nature of analytic work on the one hand, and the "acute frustrations" it fosters on the other. The frustrations, the author makes clear, stem from the infrastructural coupling that has grown up in the high-tech sector: the operations of these firms has come to rely on technologies that spill over the boundaries of the firm, and thus trouble existing understandings of the links between work, skill, and technology. Needed then is research that is able to grasp the complexities that result when workplace technology fails to correspond to the boundaries of the firm as traditionally conceived. Such research might be viewed as an extension of Harrison's (1994) argument about capital's "concentration without centralization." It also prompts us to think about networked firms in more nuanced ways.

The last paper in this section is Brian Ott's analysis of the service relation, again examining food service workers (though in a more downscale sector of the service economy). Here, we see a collision between the organizational demand for conformity and the quotidian requirement of performativity in everyday life. The question Ott poses is how workers navigate the intersection of their employer's formal expectations while *also* adhering to the commonsense norms that govern interaction with their fellow human beings (Leidner, 1993). What, Ott asks, are the limits of control via scripting? What happens when stores employ "mystery shoppers" — an industry in its own right — to enforce the routinized regime they have devised? The answers show us the savvy that workers amass, the skill they must exercise in detecting the spaces in which they work, and how they juggle the competing demands they face in what Marek Korczynski (2009) has termed the "customer-centered bureaucracy."

The third section of this volume engages one of the most lively and provocative lines of analysis in the sociology of work, exploring how the contemporary workplace exhibits not only gender-based inequalities that render women vulnerable to harassment and precarious employment, but also those stemming from heteronormative conceptions of employee identity. On this last score, David Orzechowicz extends the utility of spatial metaphors (glass ceilings, escalators, cliffs, etc.), showing us an organizational setting in which gay men seem to have escaped the closet, but in fact have simply rendered it more comfortable. Here, in a seemingly gay-friendly context, the performance of a gay identity is almost a job requirement, even to the point that the girlfriends of straight men begin to worry about their boyfriends' "catching" a homosexual identity. Yet, as the author shows, all that has unfolded in this case is the development of an idioculture, to use Fine's (2006) concept, which has enlarged the space in which gay men are confined: Dealing with the public, or assuming "serious" managerial duties, requires that these men conceal their gay identity and instead act as if they were straight. Orzechowicz has used this setting to help identify the conditions that reproduce closeted norms – and, by implication, might lead beyond so oppressive a state.

The last two contributions to this volume both highlight the vulnerabilities that women continue to confront in the sphere of paid employment. The paper by Julie A. Kmec, C. Elizabeth Hirsh, and Sheryl Skaggs uses a novel data set that combines for the first time data showing the efficacy of federal versus state legal protections against sexual harassment. Key here is the authors' effort to trace the determinants of not simply the *presence* of a sexual harassment but also its level of *codification* (in a sense, the degree of effort that firms invest in preventing sexual harassment). Though based on a relatively small sample, their study opens the way for larger and more elaborate analyses that lead beyond the customary fixation on federal policy – legislation, judicial rulings, and EEOC interventions – now encompassing legal and political influences at the subsidiary, state level. If states are indeed social laboratories –and indeed, that seems to be the case in this domain – then our research designs must adjust. What the authors' findings portend for the future, given the proliferation of reactionary legislation at the level of the states, is a matter for additional research.

The paper by Andrew S. Fullerton, Michael A. Long, and Kathryn Freeman Anderson extends previous research on the health consequences of precarious employment in two important ways: first, by exploring how these links are gendered, and second, by drawing a link to workers' dependence on illegal substances. In keeping with previous research (Gottfried & Graham, 1993; Hatton, 2011; Williams, 2013), Fullerton et al. find that the burden of labor market uncertainty weighs most heavily on women – so heavily, in fact, that women workers stand at particular risk of drug dependency over time. Their analysis is all the more timely because it points to a link between public health concerns over drug addiction and the transformation of work underway for several decades. This study comes at a time of not only rising concern over deaths from overdoses but also of rising levels of mortality, drug addiction, alcoholism and suicide among working class whites, many of whom are being left behind by economic trends (Case & Deaton, 2015). Clearly, much remains to be known about the link between the transformation of work, gender, and worker well-being.

Much more work remains to be done *on* work. It is an exciting era in which to study work and workers, and I hope that *RSW* will furnish the site for creating provocative connections among schools of thought that might otherwise have languished. I look forward to readers' comments and submissions as we together seek to produce compelling research in the sociology of work.

Steven Vallas
Editor

NOTE

1. See the panel discussion of this development at https://workinprogress. oowsection.org/2014/10/30/does-organizational-sociology-have-a-future/ (accessed April 12, 2016).

REFERENCES

Abbott, A. (1988). The System of Professions.

Acker, J. (1990). Hierarchies, jobs, bodies: A theory of gendered organizations. *Gender and Society, 4*, 139–158.

Acker, J. (2006). Inequality regimes: Gender, class, and race in organizations. *Gender and Society, 20*, 441–464.

Ackroyd, S., & Thompson, P. (1995). All quiet on the workplace front? A critique of recent trends in British industrial sociology. *Sociology, 29*(4), 615–633.

Alvesson, M., & Willmott, H. (2002). Identity regulation as organizational control: Producing the appropriate individual. *Journal of Management Studies, 39*, 619–644.

Anteby, M. (2008a). Identity incentives as an engaging form of control: Revisiting leniencies in an aeronautic plant. *Organization Science, 19*(2), 202–220.

Anteby, M. (2008b). *Moral gray zones: Side productions, identity, and regulation in an aeronautic plant.* Princeton, NJ: Princeton University Press.

Barley, S., & Kunda, G. (2001). Bringing work back in. *Organization Science, 12*(1), 76–95.

Bechky, B. A. (2003). Sharing meaning across occupational communities: The transformation of understanding on a production floor. *Organization Science, 14*(3), 312–330.

Beck, U. (2000). *Brave new world of work.* London: Polity.

Benschop, Y. (2001). Pride, prejudice and performance: Relations between HRM, diversity, and performance. *The International Journal of Human Resource Management, 12*(7), 1166–1181.

Berrey, E. (2015). *The enigma of diversity.* Chicago, IL: University of Chicago Press.

Boltanski, L., & Chiapello, E. (2005). *The new spirit of capitalism.* London: Verso.

Braverman, H. (1974). *Labor and monopoly capital.* New York, NY: Monthly Review.

Bronfenbrenner, K., & Luce, S. (2004). Offshoring: The evolving profile of corporate global restructuring. *Multinational Monitor, 25*(12), 26–29.

Browne, I., & Misra, J. (2003). The intersection of gender and race in labor markets. *Annual Review of Sociology, 29*, 487–513.

Burawoy, M. (1979). *Manufacturing consent: The labor process under monopoly capitalism.* Chicago, IL: University of Chicago Press.

Burawoy, M. (1985). *The politics of production.* London: Verso.

Burt, R. (2004). Structural holes and good ideas. *American Journal of Sociology, 110*(2), 349–399.

Case, A., & Deaton, A. (2015). Rising morbidity and mortality in midlife among white non-Hispanic Americans in the 21st century. *Proceedings of the National Academy of Sciences, 112*(49), 15078–15083.

Castilla, E., & Benard, S. (2010). The paradox of meritocracy in organizations. *Administrative Science Quarterly, 55*(4), 543–676.

Chinoy, E.. (1955). *Automobile workers and the American dream.* Boston, MA: Beacon.

Collins, J. (2003). *Threads: Gender, labor, and power in the global apparel industry.* Chicago, IL: University of Chicago Press.

Dingwall, R. (2008). *Essays on professions.* Aldershot: Ashgate.

Dobbin, F., Schrage, D., & Kalev, A. (2015). Rage against the Iron cage: The varied effects of bureaucratic personnel reforms on diversity. *American Sociological Review, 80*(5), 1014–1044.

Du Gay, P. (1996). *Consumption and identity at work.* Thousand Oaks, CA: Sage.

Fine, G. A. (2006). Shopfloor cultures: The idioculture of production in operational meteorology. *Sociological Quarterly, 47*(1), 1–19.

Fleming, P., & Sturdy, A. (2011). Being yourself in the electronic sweatshop: New forms of normative control. *Human Relations, 64*, 177–200.

Gallie, D. (2007). *Employment regimes and the quality of work.* Oxford: Oxford University Press.

Giddens, A. (1979). *Central problems in social theory: Action, structure and contradiction in social analysis.* Berkeley, CA: University of California Press.

Gottfried, H., & Graham, L. (1993). Constructing difference: The making of gendered subcultures in a Japanese automobile assembly plant. *Sociology, 27*(4), 11–628.

Gouldner, A. (1954). *Patterns of industrial bureaucracy.* Glencoe, IL: Free Press.

Hallett, T., & Ventresca, M. J. (2006). Inhabited institutions: Social interactions and organizational forms in Gouldner's 'patterns of industrial bureaucracy'. *Theory and Society, 35*(2), 213–236.

Harrison, B. (1994). *Lean and mean: The changing landscape of corporate power in an age of flexibility.* New York, NY: Basic.

Hatton, E. (2011). *The temp economy: From kelly girls to permatemps in postwar America.* Philadelphia, PA: Temple University Press.

Heckscher, C., & Donnellon, A. (1994). Defining the post-bureaucratic type. In C. Heckscher & A. Donnellon (Eds.), *The post-bureaucratic organization* (pp. 14–62). Thousand Oaks, CA: Sage.

Hodson, R. (1995). Worker resistance: An underdeveloped concept in the sociology of work. *Economic and Industrial Democracy, 16*, 79–110.

Hodson, R. (2001). *Dignity at work.* Cambridge: Cambridge University Press.

Hossfeld, K. (1990). 'Their logic against them': Contradictions in sex, race and class in Silicon Valley. In K. Ward (Ed.), *Women workers and global restructuring.* Ithaca, NY: ILR Press.

Hughes, E. C. (1951/1994). Work and self. In L. Coser (Ed.), *On work, race, and the sociological imagination* (pp. 57–66). Chicago: University of Chicago Press.

Johnson, T. (1972). *Professions and power*. New York, NY: Palgrave MacMillan.

Kalev, A., Dobbin, F., & Kelly, E. (2006). Best practices or best guesses? Assessing the efficacy of corporate affirmative action and diversity policies. *American Sociological Review, 71*, 589–617.

Kalleberg, A. (2011). *Good jobs, bad jobs: The rise of polarized and precarious employment systems in the United States, 1970s–2000s*. New York, NY: Russell Sage Foundation.

Kalleberg, A., & Berg, I. (1987). *Work and industry: Structures, markets, processes*. New York: Plenum.

Kanter, R. M. (1977). *Men and women of the corporation*. New York, NY: Basic Books.

Kellogg, K. (2011). *Challenging operations: Medical reform and resistance in surgery*. Chicago, IL: University of Chicago Press.

Korczynski, M. (2009). Understanding contradictions within the lived experience of service workers: The customer-oriented bureaucracy. In M. Korczynski & C. Macdonald (Eds.), *Service work: Critical perspectives* (pp. 73–90). New York, NY: Routledge.

Lee, C. K. (1998). *Gender and the South China miracle: Two worlds of factory women*. Berkeley, CA: University of California Press.

Leidner, R. (1993). *Fast food and fast talk*. Berkeley, CA: University of California Press.

Padavic, I. (2005). Laboring under uncertainty. Identity renegotiation among contingent workers. *Symbolic Interaction, 28*(1), 111–134.

Perrow, C. (1979). *Complex organizations: A critical essay*. New York, NY: Random.

Reskin, B. (2003). Including mechanisms in our models of ascriptive inequality. *American Sociological Review, 68*, 1–21.

Roy, D. (1952). Quota restriction and goldbricking in a machine shop. *American Journal of Sociology, 67*(2), 427–442.

Salzinger, L. (2003). *Genders in production*. Berkeley, CA: University of California Press.

Simpson, I. H. (1989). The sociology of work: Where have the workers gone? *Social Forces, 67*(3), 563–581.

Snow, D. A., & Anderson, L. (1987). Identity work among the homeless: The verbal construction and avowal of personal identities. *American Journal of Sociology, 92*(6), 1336–1371.

Stainback, K., & Tomaskovic-Devey, D. (2012). *Documenting desegregation: Racial and gender segregation in private-sector employment since the civil rights act*. New York, NY: Russell Sage Foundation.

Tausky, C. (1984). *Work and society: An introduction to industrial sociology*. New York, NY: Peacock.

Tomaskovic-Devey, D. (1993). *Gender and racial inequality at work*. Ithaca, NY: Cornell/ILR.

Vallas, S. P. (2012). *Work: A critique*. Cambridge: Polity.

Vallas, S. P., & Cummins, E. (2014). Relational models of organizational inequalities: Emerging approaches and conceptual dilemmas. *American Behavioral Scientist, 58*(2), 228–255.

Vallas, S. P., & Cummins, E. R. (2015). Personal branding and identity norms in the popular business press: Enterprise culture in an age of precarity. *Organization Studies, 36*(3), 293–319.

Vidal, M. (2013). Postfordism as a dysfunctional accumulation regime: A comparative analysis of the USA, the UK and Germany. *Work, Employment, and Society, 27*(3), 451–471.

Weber, M. (1949/1904). *The methodology of the social sciences*. New York, NY: Free Press.

Williams, C. (1992). The glass escalator: Hidden advantages for men in the "female" professions. *Social Problems, 39*(3), 253–267.

Williams, C. (2013). The glass escalator revisited: Gender inequality in neo-liberal times. *Gender & Society June, 27*(5), 609–629.

Williams, C., & Connell, C. (2010). Looking good and sounding right: Aesthetic labor and social inequality in the retail industry. *Work and Occupations, 37*(3), 349–377.

Wingfield, A. H. (2009). Racializing the glass escalator: Reconsidering men's experiences with women's work. *Gender and Society, 23*(1), 5–26.

Womack, J. P., Jones, D. T., & Roos, D. (1992). *The machine that changed the world.* New York: Free Press.

Zanoni, P. (2010). Diversity in the lean automobile factory: Doing class through gender, disability and age. *Organization, 18*(1), 105–127.

Zanoni, P., & Janssens, M. (2004). Deconstructing difference: The rhetoric of human resource managers' diversity discourses. *Organization Studies, 25*(1), 55–74.

Zelizer, V. (1994). *The social meaning of money.* New York: Basic.

PART I
IDENTITY WORK

WORK IDENTITY WITHOUT STEADY WORK: LESSONS FROM STAGE ACTORS

Robin Leidner

ABSTRACT

Work has historically been an important basis of identity, but the sharp decline in the availability of stable attachments to jobs, organizations, or occupations jeopardizes paid work's capacity to sustain identity. If available work opportunities are increasingly precarious and short-term, can the same be said for identities? Analysis of the efforts of members of an unusual occupational group — stage actors — to support an identity based on unstable work provides insights into the variability and indeterminacy of responses to structural employment uncertainty. Despite manifold identity threats, actors struggle to maintain identity as actors both in others' eyes and in their own.

Keywords: Actors; work; identity; arts; precarious; contingent

Many sociologists have considered how workers in low-status jobs try to minimize the significance of their work for their personal identities. Janitors, domestic servants, McDonald's workers, temporary clerical workers

Research in the Sociology of Work, Volume 29, 3–35
ISSN: 0277-2833/doi:10.1108/S0277-283320160000029008

(Hughes, 1984 [1951]; Leidner, 1993; Rogers, 2000; Rollins, 1985): all have reason to seek to establish role distance (Goffman, 1961) from their jobs. Some workers, though, are in the opposite position: they identify strongly with an occupation, or wish to, but their entitlement to the concomitant work identity is uncertain. Contingent faculty, lawyers doing temporary work, and artists of many kinds who earn little or nothing for their work may all find that their entitlement to claim the status associated with their occupations is subject to question (Lingo & Tepper, 2013; Rogers, 2000; Schneirov, 2003). Asserting these identities leaves them open to challenge. Goffman (1952, p. 452) goes so far as to speak of "a cardinal social sin – the sin of defining oneself in terms of a status while lacking the qualifications which an incumbent of that status is supposed to possess." What these workers lack is not professional qualifications but regular employment.

This paper examines the difficulties of claiming an occupational status in the context of precarious work by focusing on the experiences of stage actors. Like other artists (see Caves, 2000; Menger, 1999, 2006; Throsby & Zednik, 2011), many of these actors are unable to support themselves through artistic work. Based on interviews with actors in two cities, I describe the institutional factors that make it so difficult to support oneself through acting, identify the numerous threats to their identities as actors, and characterize the "identity work" (Snow & Anderson, 1987) they do to sustain their commitment and their sense of self.

WORK IDENTITY, CONTINGENT WORK, AND ARTISTIC WORK

Traditionally, work identity has been essential to the self-understanding of large numbers of people. Generations of sociologists and other social theorists have analyzed the significance of work for identity and critiqued the social and economic arrangements that structure what possibilities work provides for establishing a stable sense of self, developing one's abilities, attaining material well-being, and achieving moral standing (see Leidner, 2006).

Work can bolster identity in a number of ways. Merely holding a job has typically been key to establishing stature as a competent adult capable of meeting responsibilities, especially for men. Many occupations and professions have strong cultures that shape jobholders as members of a community of shared norms and traditions as well as skills, and often link workers into broader class-based identifications (see Leidner, 2010). For much of the twentieth century, large numbers of people developed work-based identities based on the organization that employed them rather than on their occupations, identities that were manipulated by employers but nevertheless meaningful, if only as something to resist (Edwards, 1979; Kunda, 1992; Margolis, 1979). Most jobs and occupations immerse people in webs of relationships of various sorts and provide order and predictability to their lives, as well as providing the material resources necessary to support oneself and perhaps one's family, all of which can be central anchors of identity. Ideally, the experience of work itself can provide a sense of mastery, an arena for self-development, challenge, accomplishment, and collaboration that makes labor meaningful and provides a work identity of which one can be proud.

Of course, it would be a gross over-simplification to argue that work necessarily provides such benefits. For one thing, it is by no means the case that steady, secure work has been available to everyone in the past. Moreover, for many people, work prompts not pride but self-recrimination or listless indifference, resentment, or even rage. People have every reason to resist identifying with work when it is structured in ways that deny them autonomy, negate their intelligence, pay them poorly, or enforce subservience (Rollins, 1985; Sennett & Cobb, 1973). But even such work can allow jobholders the dignity of knowing that they are earning a living, living up to their responsibilities, and pulling their weight in a way that makes them deserving of rights and respect (Lamont, 2000).

However, much sociological research and theorizing on work identity has been concerned with the degree to which employers have laid claim to employees' subjectivity, for example through "concertive control" (Barker, 1993), the imposition of emotion work (Hochschild, 1983), or the requirement that workers become "enterprising subjects" (DuGay, 1996). Alvesson and Willmott (2002, p. 621) argue that "identity regulation is a significant ... and increasingly important modality of organizational control" and Brown and Lewis (2011) illustrate how organizations discipline professional identities. Nonetheless, employers do not necessarily succeed in conjuring the work identities they aim to produce. Collinson (2003), focusing on the impact of workplace surveillance systems, argues that while workers may develop "conformist selves," they may also produce manipulative "dramaturgical selves" or "resistant selves."

As these varied responses suggest, the meanings people assign to their work and the ways they accommodate their identities to their work are by no means fixed. Research on service workers has shown how workers strive to interpret their interactions with customers and clients in ways that allow them to maintain self-respect even when forced to enact behavior that they would wish to distance themselves from, either reinterpreting behavior in ways that are not demeaning or establishing role distance (Goffman, 1961) to show that their behavior on the job is distinct from their real selves (e.g., Leidner, 1993; Otis, 2012; Sherman, 2007). Workers in a broad range of jobs use similar techniques of neutralization (Matza, 1964) to protect their sense of self from work that makes them act like people they don't want to be or in which they are treated like people they don't want to be, disclaiming the implications of their work for their identity.

However, changes in employment relations have called into question whether work will continue to be an important basis of identity. Recent analyses of changing conditions of capitalist enterprise emphasize a sharp decline in the possibilities for forming stable attachments to jobs, organizations, or even occupations, with some theorists arguing that job insecurity is becoming the prototypical experience. Beck (2000) describes "a political economy of insecurity" which sharply undercuts the capacity of people to build an identity based on work. Gorz (1999, p. 53) writes that:

> [T]he central figure of our society – and the "normal" condition within ... society – is no longer (or is tending no longer to be) that of the "worker." It is becoming, rather, the figure of the insecure worker, who at times "works" and at times does not "work," practices many different trades without any of them actually being a trade, has no identifiable profession ... and cannot therefore identify with his/her work.

This insecure worker, he says, "is unable to identify with work" and tends to regard as "his/her 'true' activity the one he/she devotes himself to in the gaps between ... paid 'work'." Some contemporary theorists argue that consumption has replaced production as the basis for building an identity (Baudrillard, 1998 [1970]; Bauman, 1998; Smart, 2003), but without a secure income opportunities for consumer choice are obviously limited.

One might assume that the increasing prevalence of contingent employment relations (Kalleberg, 2011) would loosen the hold of employers on workers' sense of self and that workers would maintain some distance from a potentially stigmatizing work situation. Research on workers in insecure positions has painted a more complicated picture. Smith (2001) found that workers in temporary jobs at a highly desirable employer identified with that prestigious company despite their lack of job security. Padavic (2005) found that while contingent workers sometimes provided cover stories explaining why their insecure work did not define them, they generally adopted "the managerial ideology" and prided themselves on being hard workers. Pugh (2015) similarly demonstrates that even those in insecure jobs emphasize their commitment to dutiful hard work, regardless of whether their employers have any commitment to them.

Some workers' identities are bound up with a particular occupation rather than with an organization or workplace. We would expect such identity commitment to be especially staunch for those who have devoted years to occupational training, including both professionals and tradespeople who have served apprenticeships. For people in these occupations and others with strong cultures (see Leidner, 2010), work may be central to the sense of self. Artists, who frequently must struggle to assert and defend an identity as a professional rather than an amateur (despite irregular pay, if any), face distinctive difficulties.

The level of competition is perhaps the major problem facing those seeking an artistic career. Menger (1999, p. 566) comments, "The oversupply of artists has been underscored nearly as often as sociologists, economists, and historians have dealt with artistic labor markets." That oversupply has been explained by a number of factors, including "the low barriers to entry (e.g., no license or degree required to practice), the lure of autonomy and freedom, and a chronic underestimation of the risk involved and chances of success" (Lingo & Tepper, 2013, p. 338). Among those who do find work or buyers for their artwork, earnings are extremely unevenly distributed (Caves, 2000; Menger, 2006). Pinheiro and Dowd (2009, p. 490) note succinctly that among creative personnel, "relatively few obtain ongoing success, while many enjoy fleeting (if any) success."

Artistic work varies considerably in the number of collaborators required, though Becker (1982) has shown that even practitioners of apparently solitary arts rely on an array of participants in an "art world." Artistic communities are important both for the development of artists as individuals and for the creation of communal resources (Bain & McLean, 2013; Cornfield, 2015; Umney & Kretsos, 2014). Artists are drawn to large cities for this and other reasons, summarized by Lingo and Tepper (2013, p. 346):

> they provide a more robust arts market, with a larger and more educated audience; they exhibit agglomeration effects, where a dense networks of cultural producers and project-based work make it easier for artists to piece together employment; and historically, core cities – that is, Vienna, Paris, New York, Los Angeles, and London – both develop reputations as artistic hubs and serve as magnets for artists seeking the aura and status of the city as sources of validation (e.g., "you're not a real artist unless you've made it in New York").

In many arts, work is organized as projects rather than as long-term employment. The perennial need to find the next project makes social capital especially important (see Anheier, Gerhards, & Romo, 1995). The uncertainty of employment also means that many, if not most, artists are unable to support themselves solely through their artistic work. Throsby and Zednik (2011, p. 9) note that:

> artists allocate their working time between three types of jobs, corresponding to three separate labour markets: the market for their creative work (including time spent on all preparation, practice, rehearsal, research related to their creative work etc.); the market for arts-related work that is not part of their core creative output but that uses their artistic skills in areas such as teaching in their art form (especially relevant to visual artists, instrumental musicians, singers and dancers); and the non-arts labour market (for actors this seems inevitably to involve work as a taxi-driver or a waiter in a restaurant, a time actors generally describe as being "between jobs").[1]

Work in all three categories is often precarious, either short-term or part-time or both.

Several authors have examined how cultural workers, including artists, manage the precarity of their work lives. Lloyd (2010) has argued that the trope of bohemian life allows "starving artists" to interpret their economic vulnerability positively as a rejection of bourgeois respectability. Umney and Kretsos (2015, p. 317) found that jazz musicians in London — at least those with some economic privilege — "often embraced labor market precarity," foregoing stable but unchallenging work in favor of pursuing their artistic passion. In addition to the practical problems of living with uncertainty and economic vulnerability, Lingo and Tepper (2013, p. 338) point out, artists must also engage in symbolic work "to build reputations, convince others of their legitimacy as artists and professionals, and, importantly, to make sense of their precarious existence, find worth in what they do, and persist in spite of daunting personal and professional challenges."

Hesmondhalgh and Baker (2010, p. 4) briefly summarize research on artistic work this way: "artists tend to hold multiple jobs; there is a predominance of self-employed or freelance workers; work is irregular, contracts are shorter-term, and there is little job protection; career prospects are uncertain; earnings are very unequal; artists are younger than other workers; and the workforce appears to be growing." The workforce is growing because to many people, work in the arts is a "labor of love" (Freidson, 1990), a passion that makes the economic risks seem worthwhile.

Understandably perhaps, research on artistic careers has tended to focus on the structural factors that make artistic work so precarious. As a consequence, though, this has meant that much less attention has been paid to the experiential dimension of pursuing a career in the arts. What sacrifices does commitment to a labor of love entail and how do artists justify enduring them? How do they hold on to a deeply meaningful occupational identity in the face of manifold challenges to their self-conceptions? And what can we learn about the experience of living with work precarity by examining an extreme case? To address these questions, this paper takes up the case of stage actors, for whom precarity is a virtually chronic state of being, and who "might be expected to experience, or at least to have to fend off, more crises of confidence in their way of life than others who enjoy more stable and integrated occupations" (Taylor & Williams, 1971, p. 188). Yet actors do not concede that the absence of steady employment means that they are not "really" actors. Rather, most struggle to maintain their self-identification as actors, to present that identity as plausible to others, and to cope with frequent challenges to their preferred identity. What can actors teach us about the preservation of identity and pride in precarious work?

This paper begins by outlining the structural conditions that threaten identification as an actor and details the identity work actors engage in to shore it up. It then extends this structural concern by exploring the ways in which actors experience and justify their commitment to an occupation that routinely exposes them to painfully high levels of uncertainty. In this respect, my concerns focus mainly on the "identity work" in which actors engage, that is, "the range of activities individuals engage in to create, present, and sustain personal identities that are congruent with and supportive of the self-concept" (Snow & Anderson, 1987, p. 1348). Actors' identity work includes their practical efforts to succeed as well as their interactional practices and their internal struggles to maintain their desired self-definition.

In what follows, I demonstrate the salience of identity issues to actors and then describe the data on which my analysis is based. I lay out the labor market conditions that make it so difficult to maintain one's identity as an actor, contrasting New York and Philadelphia as theatrical arenas. After detailing the challenges actors face in maintaining their occupational identities and the sacrifices they make to persist despite the discouraging odds, I turn to their efforts to sustain their identities as actors and the factors that support them in those efforts. I conclude by considering the relevance of the actors' experiences to broader discussions of precarious work.

Acting the Part

"Sometimes," Goffman tells us, "the individual will act in a thoroughly calculating manner, expressing himself in a given way solely in order to give the kind of impression to others that is likely to evoke from them a specific response he is concerned to obtain" (Goffman, 1959, p. 6). For stage actors, this account of everyday behavior could serve as a job description. Indeed, rehearsals of plays are intended to allow the actor to develop ways to induce particular responses in audience members. Often, audiences are asked to suspend disbelief, to ignore their knowledge that the actors are not really the characters being portrayed, and to allow their emotions to be manipulated by the performers.

However, the large majority of those seeking careers in theater seldom have the opportunity to do this persuasive work for pay: most are unable to find regular acting work. Are they able to use their dramatic skill in taking on a character and making it believable to others to support their chosen identity? If they are to continue to pursue acting work they must make efforts to hold on to the belief that they really are actors despite the discouraging reality that they are not earning their living as actors. And, like all of us, they must look for confirmation from others to uphold the self they claim (Goffman, 1959). They must engage in identity work to counter the numerous identity threats that challenge their belief in themselves.

For many actors, then, how to hold on to the identity of actor is an everyday concern. It is a cherished identity, one that is continually threatened, but also a prerequisite to keep going in the face of disappointments and frustrations. Some even argue that deep commitment to that identity is required to perform the work successfully, as in this passage from one of the many books about how to make a career as an actor, a book that is largely devoted to practical information and advice:

> You may have substantial doubts about your long-term career success, but you must never doubt that you "*are*" an actor. That belief must be in your bones, sustaining itself through every interview and every audition, so that it shows even though you make no effort to show it. This belief is your authority. It gives you a power that allows you to galvanize every aspect of your personality and every bit of training and experience into an exciting and apparently artless performance. (Cohen, 2004, p. 12)

The passage bears a resemblance to Weber's discussion of the psychological necessity Puritans felt to consider themselves one of the Elect: "an absolute duty to consider oneself as chosen, and to combat all doubts as temptations of the devil" (Weber, 1958 [1904–1905], p. 111). In both cases, doubt itself is taken as a sign of undeservingness.

But doubts are all too common among actors, given the many threats to that identification. As one told me, "I think we all think of ourselves as only as good as our last gig, and 'Are you working?'"

The basic conditions of work in theater that make careers so precarious are, first, the dramatic oversupply of labor, and, second, the organization of work in short-term projects – plays that run for a limited time – hence the constant need to look for work (see Menger, 1999, 2006). These factors mean that very few stage actors can earn a living by acting. To support themselves, they typically seek out the kinds of temporary, insecure, part-time jobs that we would expect to be least amenable to supporting a work-based identity. Actors choose these jobs primarily because they make it possible for them to continue to search for temporary, insecure, performance work.

Because of such challenges, actors are unusually conscious of the problem of maintaining an identity. Unlike most of us, they are aware, sometimes acutely aware, that various kinds of effort go into maintaining an identity. One might say they are natural Goffmanians. In looking for work and in exercising their craft they must concern themselves with how others perceive them, but they are also attuned to the importance of managing their self-perceptions so as to sustain their identity as actors and to enhance their likelihood of success. They therefore carefully monitor and manipulate their own feelings, attitudes, motivations, and self-presentations in efforts to get work, to do the work effectively, and also to persist in the struggle to live out their chosen professional identity.

Data

This paper draws on interviews I conducted with a convenience sample of 49 actors in New York and Philadelphia, two cities with markedly different theater scenes and labor markets, as described below. As Lingo and Tepper (2013, pp. 346–347) point out, "research on creative workers in the United States has disproportionately focused on core cities – New York, Chicago, Los Angeles," although "understanding the labor market dynamics of ... second-tier or off-center cities is critical to understanding artistic workers in the 21st century."

I found respondents in a variety of ways. Starting with personal contacts, I requested interviews with friends of friends. I attended two large combined auditions in Philadelphia and asked auditioners to sign up for interviews. In New York, I solicited interviews from attendees at an introductory session of an Actors Fund program called "Actors Work" (now called the Career Center) that is aimed at those seeking ways to support themselves without giving up acting. I interviewed multiple cast members of two Philadelphia productions that included both New York and Philadelphia actors and I directly requested interviews with other actors whose performances I attended. In all cases I asked respondents to refer me to friends who might be willing to be interviewed. I conducted a group interview at one of the combined auditions and did two double interviews. I asked the respondents for copies of their résumés, which guided some of the questioning. The interviews focused on career trajectories, definitions of success, and maintaining an identity as an actor when not employed as one. They took place in various locations, including a hotel where auditions were being held, my apartment, respondents' homes, coffee shops, and backstage at a Broadway theater. Most interviews lasted between an hour and an hour and a half, though some were substantially longer. They were audio recorded and transcribed. To understand the workings of theatrical employment better, I also interviewed 14 other theater professionals, including directors, casting directors, an agent, a union official, a career counselor, and others.

The actors I interviewed worked primarily on the stage, though most of them would have been delighted to perform in television, film, or commercials, and some had done so. Twenty-three of the actors were men and 26 were women. Twenty-five of them were currently based in or near New York and three more had previously lived there, including one who had recently decided to give up her struggle for a career in theater. Twenty-one lived in or near Philadelphia, one more had previously lived there, and one lived in Washington, DC. I interviewed 33 white actors, eight African American actors and one Caribbean, four Asian or Asian American, one Latino, and three biracial or multiracial actors. My respondents ranged in age from their mid-twenties to perhaps sixty, with the majority apparently in their twenties or early thirties. The respondents varied widely in how much success they had so far achieved onstage, with some at the very beginning of their careers, some working steadily, and some worrying about whether earlier success could be revived. Some supported themselves with acting work while others had earned virtually nothing. Despite the variation in their experience, all of them recognized that maintaining an identity as an actor is an ongoing struggle for most people in their line of work.

My analysis is based on repeated readings of the transcribed interviews, which I coded by hand as I searched for dominant themes.

I am an Actor

Rather than distancing themselves from an identity based on unpredictable, temporary, low-paid work, actors passionately embrace it. Most of the people I interviewed were deeply committed to an identity as an actor before they even began seeking professional work, let alone getting it. Many respondents told me that they have always been performers, that they have wanted to be on the stage since early childhood, that they never wanted any other kind of career, and that they could not imagine themselves not being actors. The actors had gone through extensive socialization, garnered positive feedback from family, friends, and instructors, and developed ties to others active in theater. The large majority of my interviewees had committed themselves to a career in performance early enough and seriously enough to devote their college or university years to training in drama, music, dance, or all three, and some had attended prestigious graduate programs in theater. Through experiences of performance, education, and participation in peer groups with shared passions, they became increasingly persuaded that they *were* actors and that they could build their lives around that reality – or at least that it was worth a try.

Actors' preoccupation with identity issues and their training and experience in discussing them make them excellent informants. But although they are well aware of the effort that goes into sustaining their own work identity, they typically validate that effort by asserting the existence of a core self that is immutably an actor, an artist, a performer. Many have cherished this self-conception since childhood. In explaining why they were committed to a kind of work that demanded great sacrifice, the actors gave only a few kinds of answers: this is who I am. This is what I love. This is what I was meant to do. One actor told me, "Even if I'm an unemployed actor, I'm still an actor living in New York City. And that's a big part of who I am."

My respondents cherished not just the identity of actor, but also the work of acting. One who was actually quite discouraged about his career told me, "Well, the overriding joy of doing the work is the main thing of what it's all about to me. I cannot describe what a powerful force that is." Another told me, "It's all I ever wanted to do ... I've always been comfortable in a performance. ... I feel at home. I feel like I can breathe." A different actor also spoke of home:

> When I'm in the middle of work [that is collaborative] – That's where you feel most like home. Just in the midst of the work. It's like a home to me. It just feels – Wow, I can't even believe I'm saying this, but it's a sense of everything in the universe is in this play. And when you see yourself being able to contribute to a product, you're contributing to the development of a character, where a playwright is changing things based on what you're contributing to it, then yeah. I think those moments – you feel like you're part of history. Yeah, it's moments like that where I feel like, "I'm meant to do this. Because this couldn't have happened without me."

As Layder (1984, p. 153) notes, the exhilaration actors experience in performance recharges their commitment to their art.

Other kinds of artists commonly share the idea that they are called to do their work. They also often share the belief that fulfilling that calling will require sacrifices in a world that is not guided by artistic values, so struggling to live as an artist in the face of disparagement or setbacks can be seen as both test and proof of commitment.[2] Nonetheless, actors are considerably more dependent on others to validate their identities than are many other kinds of artists. After all, one can write or paint all alone in a room and consider oneself a writer or painter, whether or not others recognize the worth of the work. But actors cannot be actors all alone. Their work is usually collaborative, and at the very least it requires an audience. As a rule, someone must give an actor an opportunity to act by casting her or him in a performance. In this dependence, actors are like most other kinds of workers, who need to be hired in order to work. For most actors, finding paid opportunities to confirm their identities by acting is tremendously challenging.

Challenges to Identity

Prospects for Making a Living

In the United States there is minimal government support for the arts in general or for theater in particular. There is no national theater, there are no civic theater companies, and the amount of government funding to non-profit arts organization is extremely low.

The commercial theater world, centered on New York's Broadway, relies on private investors who hope to recoup their investments and to make a profit from ticket sales and other revenue. Most theater, however, is produced non-commercially, both in New York and around the country. Some not-for-profit theater companies are well established, producing regular seasons of plays with money from private foundations, individual donors, government grants, and ticket sales. Much other theater work is produced on a shoestring by smaller companies or *ad hoc* groups, which may pay performers little or nothing. Even well-established companies normally do not support a permanent or long-term troupe of actors. Instead, they hire actors on a per show basis. Resident theater companies are almost non-existent, so most actors are constantly looking for work and even relatively successful ones often cannot count on steady work.

Wages and working conditions for much theatrical work are determined by agreements negotiated with Actors Equity, the union of professional actors. Actors can join the union only if they meet fairly restrictive criteria, and my informants include both union and non-union actors. Whether or not an actor is a union member determines her or his eligibility for various jobs: union membership both opens up possibilities for better-paid work and rules out many work opportunities, since by no means all theater work is covered by union contracts. Pay scales for union work vary considerably. The highest wages by far are for work on Broadway and on national touring productions of Broadway musicals. These, along with less lucrative commercial productions, are the only theater jobs that offer the possibility of open-ended, long-term employment, though they also carry the risk of sudden unemployment if the show is a commercial failure. Other jobs, whether union or not, are generally for a specified number of performances or weeks of employment. At the bottom of the pay scale − actually, off the bottom of the pay scale − are union-permitted workshops and readings that may pay only transportation costs (frequently subway fares) and those non-union productions that pay actors nothing. Even further off the scale are apprenticeships and internships that charge aspiring theater professionals for the privilege of working.[3]

Poorly paid actors and those who are chronically out of work − that is, most of them − cannot rely on government subsidies to make ends meet and therefore must seek other kinds of jobs, unless they have a partner or parents able and willing to provide financial support. The main form of government support for individual actors is Unemployment Insurance, which provides time-limited financial payments to eligible unemployed workers. Benefit levels are determined by earnings in the previous eighteen months, but if you have not worked enough weeks and earned enough money to meet the eligibility thresholds, you are not entitled to any benefits. For this reason, one actor told me that at the beginning of her career, "My idea of success was to be eligible for Unemployment." Many, many actors do not qualify for Unemployment, and at best it is a short-term and not very generous form of support. Members of Actors Equity do have access to health insurance, but must work a minimum of 12 weeks per year for union wages to remain eligible for it.

While these eligibility requirements may not seem stringent, many actors do not meet them, since very few actors work consistently for pay or earn much when they do work. Given the dramatic oversupply of actors, there is often intense competition for even the most poorly paid work. In 2014−2015, fewer than half of the members of Actors Equity (41.8%) worked on the stage at all, and in any given week only 13.3% were employed (DiPaola, 2015, p. 2). Of union members who worked onstage at all that year, more than two-thirds earned no more than $15,000 and median earnings were $7,548 (DiPaola, 2015, pp. 12, 17). On average non-union actors probably earned even less. Since almost all acting work is short-term, ranging from one day to a few months, actors are always looking for work and most experience periods of unemployment between jobs. They frequently must accept non-acting work in order to support themselves, but the range of jobs they can take without sharply diminishing their opportunities to look for theater work is quite limited because most auditions take place during the day, frequently with little notice.

The oversupply of actors is especially extreme in New York, which is the center of all kinds of theatrical work, ranging from highly commercialized musicals intended for the tourist market to *avant garde* work aimed at a limited audience of cognoscenti. Young actors and singers and dancers pour into New York every year from conservatories, universities, and other training programs. Others who have been working in other parts of the country or world come to try their luck in New York. Some without prior training or experience come too, seeking training in New York or hoping to establish themselves without it on the strength of their talent and looks.[4]

An actor who moves to New York soon discovers that because of the huge number of aspiring actors, people compete not only for roles but also for the opportunity to be considered for roles. Often, casting decisions are made even before auditions are held based on decision makers' prior experience with an actor or familiarity with that actor's work. Access to auditions for the remaining roles is controlled by union rules, by all sorts of informal networks, by casting directors, and in New York, by agents. Some auditions, especially for unpaid, low-paid, or non-prestigious work, are open to anyone. Productions operating under union agreements must hold some open auditions at which any union member can sign up to be seen. But much casting is done through auditions held by appointment to which actors are invited based on some connection, such as a casting director's knowledge of their work or, particularly in New York, on their agents' efforts to present them as suitable candidates for a given role. Many New York actors are therefore preoccupied with getting an agent, or getting a better agent, or persuading their agent to submit them for more roles or different kinds of roles.

Two Philadelphia actors who had previously lived in New York reflected on how important and how difficult finding representation could be. One, looking back with dismay on his years in New York, described some exhilarating acting experiences and went on:

Here's the crushing thing though: After each of these experiences, the way I measured whether or not it was successful was whether an agent called. And if an agent didn't call me because of it, if I didn't get an interview, I wrote it off. It was like it was a failure. Because I hadn't advanced up this rat-race ladder that I was on. And people were pulling me aside and saying, "That was so great what you did!" But it didn't matter because an agent hadn't called me.

The second, an elegant woman from Louisville with an MFA from a top program and a résumé that includes major Shakespearean roles, described a relationship with an agent that didn't pan out:

I had one meeting in particular with sort of a small potatoes agent who was more optimistic than anyone else I had met about getting me some work, but then I never heard from him, I never heard from him, I never heard from him, and finally when I'd sort of forgotten all about it, he did call, not with an actual audition but with a possible audition ... He said, "I really feel good about it. It's right up your alley because they're all Kentucky hicks." I went, [sigh] "This partnership isn't gonna go anywhere either."

Several other cities in the United States have substantial populations of theater artists and support a broad range of theater companies; other locations have a single important non-profit theater company. Non-profit regional theaters have become the main locations for developing and premiering new works as the costs of mounting full-scale New York productions have become prohibitive. Some of these regional theaters are quite prestigious, pay well, and produce high quality work, and many actors based in New York work primarily out of town, traveling to different parts of the country for weeks at a time. Nevertheless, New York remains the center of the American theater world, with the largest pool of theater artists. Therefore, theater companies based elsewhere in the country often hold auditions in New York.[5] No other city provides anything like the volume of audition listings that New York does, so actors who wish to achieve fame on the stage or just to gain access to the largest number of auditions in the widest range of prestigious venues move to New York. Although many of them gladly accept work out of town, those work opportunities have the cost of making the actors unavailable for audition opportunities that may come up in New York.

An intrinsic characteristic of theater magnifies the importance of New York. Unlike film and television work, theatrical performance is inherently ephemeral and place-specific. For stage actors, then, being seen is a crucial concern, central to their prospects for employment. Many accept low-paid work or participate in unpaid workshops or showcases in the hopes that their performances will be seen by agents and other influential members of the theater community, which will enhance their chances of being

represented by an agent, being invited to auditions, and being hired. Work
in well-regarded regional theaters has many attractive features, but a major
drawback for New York-based actors is that such work will not be seen by
key decision makers in New York. One actor described a "triumph" in a
musical at the Guthrie, a prestigious theater in Minneapolis. He went on,

> I wasn't seen in New York in this terrific comic role. I'd had enormous successes out of
> town, in a lot of different parts, I mean I hate to – not meaning to slur Boston and
> Honolulu, you know, but for as far as New York is concerned, those places are out of
> town ... And, you know, I always said, "My God, if I could have played this part in
> New York, you know, I'd be a star."

In short, New York is a magnet for actors because no other city has the
same visibility and prestige or as many casting opportunities, but the oversupply of actors makes finding work tremendously challenging. The city
is therefore home to myriad actors working at other jobs while trying
to preserve their identity as actors. The aspiring actor waiting tables is
such a stock figure that restaurant patrons sometimes ask waiters
whether they're actors:

> I had a waiter friend, who used to work at the same restaurant, and when he would get
> asked this question, "Are you an actor?," he would say, "Are you a casting director?"
> And the person would usually say, "No, I'm not." And he's say, "Well, then I'm just
> your waiter tonight, thanks." Which is a little snotty, but at least that's what he said
> he said.

Not all aspiring professional stage actors head to New York. My
respondents based in Philadelphia face quite a different set of circumstances. Philadelphia has a lively and fairly diverse theater scene. The city
has a number of well-established theater companies with Equity agreements, some of which are quite well respected, if not among the most prestigious nationally. Several Philadelphia theater companies regularly
commission or develop new works, which sometimes go on to be produced
at other regional theaters or in New York. Local audiences have options
including well-established companies with their own theaters and regular
seasons of new and classic plays, more experimental companies that devise
productions rather than use scripted plays, a large non-profit theater
devoted to crowd-pleasing musicals and plays, a Shakespeare company, a
company presenting only comedies, numerous small non-union companies
with varied missions, and touring companies of Broadway shows that
appear in one of the city's large commercial theaters.

Some of the larger companies there routinely hire actors from
New York, but Philadelphia has a pool of talented actors, some of whom

work a great deal more regularly than most New York actors do. In fact, a New York casting director told me that "the acting pool in Philadelphia is incredibly well developed and they are good. And it is one of the few places in the country where an actor can make a living not being in New York." Few actors decide to head to Philadelphia to embark on a career in theater, but the area is home to a number of universities that provide training in theater, and some graduates of these programs choose to stay and work in the city.[6] The acting pool also includes people who grew up locally or moved to the area for other reasons, as well as a small number who moved after finding the local theater scene to their liking. Philadelphia offers far fewer opportunities for work in television, film, or commercials than New York does, and theater work generally pays less, though the cost of living is substantially lower as well. Because the supply of labor is much smaller, agents are not involved in the casting process in Philadelphia. Casting directors or directors of particular plays invite actors to audition directly. Open auditions are rare, so personal networks are crucial. While there are far fewer roles available in Philadelphia than in New York, the competition is considerably less. A small number of exceptional actors are able to work steadily in a comparatively broad range of roles and some have even had company leaders choose plays based on their availability. It is also easier for gifted newcomers to be noticed than it is in New York.

Nonetheless, in both cities, as elsewhere, the likelihood that an actor will make a consistent, full-time living from work in the theater is small. Virtually all actors know that the odds are against them, yet thousands decide to try to establish themselves as professional actors. In order to persist in their efforts, they must hold on to the belief that they are indeed actors, whether or not they are employed as such.

Identity Threats

While my respondents spoke with great conviction about their identity as actors, most also regarded that identification as potentially precarious, certain to be tested. Even those who had not yet experienced it firsthand knew that acting is a profession in which one is likely to experience much more rejection than acceptance in the never-ending process of seeking work and that periodic unemployment is to be expected. Yet few understood in advance just how varied and difficult the challenges the profession posed to their identities would be.

The most obvious challenge my respondents faced to their identity as actors was that they frequently were not acting. The relatively well-positioned ones were auditioning regularly, though even they were turned

down more often than not. Less lucky ones struggled even to be noticed by
agents, casting directors, and others with influence over audition opportunities, hoping to be invited to audition. The experience of repeated rejection, no matter how widely shared, threatens to undermine confidence
and optimism.

Without the usual supports for occupational identity − immersion in the
work itself, a workday routine, a set of co-workers, and so on − it is easy
to lose hold of the identity and of one's self-regard. Doubts about whether
or not one will make it in the business are not limited to newcomers who
are first trying to establish themselves. Many of my respondents, including
those who had some measure of success, admitted that it is hard to maintain one's confidence while out of work. One Philadelphia actor, now unusual in being steadily employed, recalled the pain and depression he felt
during a long period of unemployment:

> You [felt] like [you'd] accomplished something, you know, you learned a skill and
> you're good at something ... And if you're not allowed to do it, you can't prove to
> yourself and the world that you're good at it. So what good are you?

A New York actor told me, "You feel like you're on top of the world when
you're working, and you feel when you're not working that you are barely
hanging on."

Many who were out of work or doing unpaid acting work had to take
paying jobs, which, of course, they did not wish to consider definitive of
who they were. The career counselor at Actors Work called jobs that led
nowhere and were unfulfilling but paid the rent "survival jobs." The most
common ones were waiting on tables, bartending, and temporary office
work. These jobs demand little commitment and some have night shifts,
allowing actors to attend auditions as necessary and to quit if an acting job
comes up. Most respondents were able to maintain role distance (Goffman,
1961) from such jobs relatively easily. Those who enjoyed these jobs sometimes found that threatening − they did not want to be lured into investing
much of themselves in a job that might contradict their preferred
identity − while others intensely resented being in low-status jobs that
undermined their self-regard. Several respondents who were working as
waiters mentioned that they found it particularly disheartening that their
lives were a cliché. Persuading oneself and others that these paying jobs did
not represent the self in a meaningful way could be difficult, especially as
years went by.

Interacting with outsiders to the theater world was a common occasion
of identity threat. I asked my respondents how they answered when asked,

"What do you do?" Almost all of them recognized this situation as emotionally fraught and potentially hazardous. The challenge was to answer in a way that did not feel like a misidentification or a betrayal of oneself, but that did not leave one open to inquiries that would be discouraging or discrediting (Goffman, 1963). Those with substantial theater credits usually identified themselves as actors, while some who were not working steadily did not quite have the nerve to answer, "I'm an actor," feeling almost as though that would be claiming an honor they did not deserve. Some said they were an actor, but also mentioned their day job to preempt dubious reactions. Others felt that any answer other than "actor" would be untruthful and, moreover, would undermine their own belief in that identity.

Sometimes identifying as an actor would provoke an admiring response, and several respondents who were open about being actors at their day jobs reported that co-workers were supportive and enthusiastic, eager to attend performances. On the other hand, virtually everyone knew that all too often saying one was an actor would prompt discomforting responses. Some people questioned the validity of the identification, asking (whether dismissively or sympathetically) "So that means you're a waiter, right?" Others, accepting the claim of being an actor, showed their interest by asking, "What movies have you made?" or "What have I seen you in?" or "What are you working on now?" Actors found it hard to avoid feeling defensive in the face of such responses, since most had made no movies, many had performed exclusively in low-visibility productions (which, for interlocutors who associated acting only with movies and television, included all stage work), and a large number were out of work altogether. Questions like these could deflate the self-regard of actors who had been feeling buoyed by having received a call-back (a request for a second audition) though they had not been cast, or who were doing work that was meaningful to them though unpaid or seen by tiny audiences, or who were doing work that was prestigious within the theater world but invisible to the broader culture. Even actors who felt reasonably secure in their own professional identity could be annoyed by responses that made it plain that outsiders saw them as deluded or simply as failures, while those feeling more vulnerable found the questions undermining or infuriating. Some spoke of the decision to declare themselves an actor regardless of the risks as an important turning point in their professional life and emotional health: "I used to have a harder time saying it. I might have said, 'Well, I'm trying to act' or something like that. But now I say, 'I'm an actor'." The career counselor at the Actors Work program was used to hearing about the problem of dealing with uncomprehending or dismissive responses. She helped actors develop upbeat, self-respecting, and educative accounts of what they were doing with their lives:

> I say, "Okay, let's practice that. What could you say that would represent you and also give information to the general public about what it is to embark on a career that you're embarking on." ... So it's a way of casting it ... of saying, you know, if you're a new grad and you just left drama school, "I'm working on an interesting manuscript with a friend of mine who's a playwright or we're doing this film together and to make money while I'm doing this, I'm looking for some kind of office support work, ideally dealing something to do with kids or an educational setting because I really care about that too." ... And if they [say], "What if you don't make it as an actor?" Your answer is, "Well, I don't know that yet, but I have a wide range of interests and I have to give acting all that I can, that's my first priority, but it doesn't stop me from pursuing other things as well." ... I like to get in with the young people because they're saying, "Well, I guess I could say that. That's not a real betrayal."

Even actors who had had some measure of success often found it hard to maintain confidence in their identity while out of work. One told me that separating who you are from whether or not you have a job is "the hardest thing an actor has to do." He illustrated his point by voicing both parts of a "what do you do?" dialogue:

> "I'm an actor."

> "Are you working?"

> "No, but I'm an actor." You know, not just when I'm working am I an actor, but even when I'm not working I'm an actor .... The down times are really hard because you lose your identity. Just because of the way that this world identifies your job with who you are.

It is important to note that early success was no guarantee of ongoing employment. As actors age, they typically become unsuitable for the kinds of roles they had been playing or hoped to play — some spoke longingly of particular roles they would never get to play — and might not be employable for some time, if at all, in another category of roles. This problem was especially severe for women, for whom there are fewer roles to begin with and whose opportunities generally diminish as they age.

To maintain one's determination and faith in the face of repeated experiences of rejection and dismissal requires a strong set of social supports and emotional defenses. One experienced actor pointed out, however, that in this line of work emotional defenses pose their own risks:

> You have to kind of develop the hide of a rhinoceros. But you can't internalize that ... Because if you let that inside, then you can't do the work you're supposed to be doing.

Acting requires emotional vulnerability and openness, so this respondent felt that inuring oneself to the pain of rejection could be damaging if it led one to become emotionally blocked.

This challenge points to another aspect of actors' work identity. At least some actors regard themselves as *artists*. They understand their work as requiring sensitivity, introspection, self-revelation, vulnerability, and creativity. Several of the actors I spoke with felt real ambivalence, if not outright revulsion, toward the business side of acting. They found the demand that they market themselves distasteful or were offended by the crasser side of the business that puts a premium on attractive bodies, for example. Some who pursued acting for the love of the work were dismayed to find that getting work seemed to demand a repertoire of behavior that was foreign and unappealing to them, including intense competitiveness. Disturbed by the sense that doing what they wanted to do might require that they turn into someone they did not want to be, some scaled back their expectations of professional success, choosing to do unpaid work with like-minded others rather than to take on a highly instrumental view of themselves and of other people. An actor who said that "the almost ruthlessness that you need to pursue it in terms of a business really didn't appeal" was now part of a community that worked at a "very off-off-[Broadway] level ... in some cases street theater, thirty-seat-house kind of theater."

In contrast, some actors who had begun their careers with such high-minded aspirations that they had regarded work on soap operas or television commercials as beneath their dignity now looked back with amusement on their more innocent selves. They had learned to accept such high-paying work with pleasure and gratitude when they could get it, if only because it allowed them to continue to pursue the kind of artistic work they preferred.

In their pursuit of acting work, actors frequently face disorienting or painful challenges to important aspects of their identities when they learn that their self-understandings have little relevance when weighed against how agents, casting directors, and other decision makers perceive their type. I spoke with women who were told that they were not pretty enough; with actors of various backgrounds who were told that they were "too ethnic" for many roles; with young actors who were told that they would not be employable for at least another 10 years; and so on.[7] For people who cherish self-conceptions as talented artists capable of playing a broad range of roles, such experiences are deflating and disillusioning. They entirely contradict a professional ideology that values authenticity and artistic uniqueness.

Sacrifices

The actors I spoke with faced challenges not only to their occupational identities, their sense of themselves as artists, and their belief in their individuality. They also found that the tremendous insecurity of their professional lives raised questions about their status as mature, sane adults. While to a large extent these actors accepted the notion that they were sacrificing for their art and some took a certain pleasure in having chosen *la vie boheme*, as time passes the willingness to put up with mistreatment, to work without pay or recognition, and to do without many of the trappings of success or even of adulthood may be stretched thin. Even those who do not regret their choices are likely to be aware that their dedication can seem like self-indulgence, their faith like delusion, and their sacrifice simply like failure.

The sacrifices are of many kinds. A young woman who had recently decided to give up on a career in New York explained some of the costs of pursuing acting as a career:

> You have to be prepared to sacrifice everything else in your life. I mean, you have to be able to go on tour at a moment's notice. And you know, how can you be in a serious relationship if you have to drop that to go away for six months? ... You have to be ready to audition at a moment's notice, so there's a lot of disappointing friends if you're constantly bailing out of things ... I never had any money ... Like going to the movies was a big [decision].

Another actor told me, "You give up any kind of security or safety. You really are taking a leap. And you're betting it all every day. That's a continuous choice." When he spoke of having broken up with his former girlfriend, who hoped for marriage and children, he both acknowledged what he is sacrificing and why he is willing to do so:

> I've given up the majority of what most people have. But then I look at a lot of my friends and what they have, and I don't really miss it. I do ... at certain times, you know. When they just swipe their credit card and just go wherever they want to go ... and buy whatever they want to buy, and their wife and their kids are at home and – I look at that fondly sometimes. But not in spite of who I am. I don't want to give that up.

Although actors generally see themselves as having made a deliberate choice to pursue art rather than security or material comfort, they are not immune to the ordinary understandings that link hard work to success and success to earnings and security. A young Philadelphia woman who has been working quite steadily said:

It's depressing. And it kind of also makes me angry because, you know .... I've been working really hard for six years. And it's a lot of work and it's the kind of work that doesn't end. ... There are a whole set of choices that I've made that have impacted my life in really significant ways .... Finances, relationships, structure of my life and my time – big, big things. And you would figure after that much time, you know, after six years of plugging along pretty well ... that there would be some amount of security ... and it's just not true, and your salary is not going up significantly ... If I think about myself alone for the rest of my life I think (pause) "I could do this, I could make this work." When I think about having a family I wanna scream.

The actor just quoted had had enough success that she was not presently holding down a survival job. The sacrifices and stresses are even more apparent to those who are not having much luck finding acting work and who must support themselves with other jobs. The young woman who gave up the struggle after a couple of years lost heart when she realized that both her financial distress and her self-doubt were likely to be ongoing:

I remember reading *How to be a Successful Actor* and it was talking about long-term careers and saying how, you know, it will never end – the constant scrambling for the next job, trying to find the next thing – will never ever end. And I think that seed in my head was when I started saying, you know, "Oh my God. I don't know that I can live in this state of limbo."

Hence it isn't surprising that aspiring actors frequently hear some version of the advice, "If there's anything else you can do and be happy, do it." One of my respondents, reflecting on her 17 years in the business, put it this way:

I say to people, "... if you don't have to do it, good God, go out and have a normal life ..." I think it's that having to do it, needing to do it – otherwise you wouldn't stay in it. No, it's too hard. There's too much personal sacrifice, you know, too much insecurity. I say to people, "I wait for the day when I wake up and [think], you know what? I don't have to do this any more."

Sustaining Identity

What bolstered identity as an actor, given the many challenges of maintaining that identity? Naturally the thing that supported actors' work identity most effectively was working. This turned out to be easier to do in Philadelphia than in New York, at least among my informants. I had assumed that Philadelphia actors might suffer from the feeling that the only real testing ground for actors is New York. While some Philadelphia actors did aspire to success in New York, many compared their lives favorably with those of their New York friends, primarily because the lower level of competition meant that they spent much more time working and less time searching for work. Not only did they get to exercise and develop their craft and to play a variety of roles, some also felt that they were able to serve the play rather than maneuver to show themselves to best advantage in order to draw the notice of those who could further their careers. However, virtually none of the New York-based actors I spoke with could imagine[8] moving to a smaller market. While not all of them aspired to the kind of fame and prestige that only New York could offer and many spoke of simply wanting to be a working actor, nonetheless they felt that leaving New York was equivalent to giving up on their dream. As one put it, "It's the Apple ... Yeah, this is where it is. You know, this is it. I mean, and [quoting the movie *Sweet Smell of Success*] 'I love this dirty stinking town'."

When paying work was unavailable, actors had to find other means of shoring up their identities as actors. Some had the support of family and friends. Some found work that was related to stage acting and actually provided some income: teaching acting, providing individual coaching to actors or public speakers, doing voice-over work, acting as a "standardized patient" for medical training. Many other activities provided support for the belief that they were indeed part of the theater world, though they produced no income: auditioning whenever possible; participating in unpaid readings and workshops; reading the trade papers; hanging out with theater people; reminding oneself of past successes and of believable predictions of success to fend off suspicions that one is only fooling oneself. One New York actor said:

> Well, I think for me, I don't think being hired or not being hired has anything to do with [whether I say I'm an actor]. Not for me. For me it's just, well, I'm still here. I still go to auditions. I have six auditions this week. So I'm an actor because I go to auditions. Whether I get the job or not doesn't really matter. I mean, of course it matters ... But in a way, it doesn't. Because I am here. I am doing it. I'm pounding the pavement, reading the papers, and my heart's still in it.

Other means of sustaining identity and pursuing work cost money, such as taking classes or individual lessons, joining with friends to self-produce a performance, continuing to send photos and résumés and cover letters to agents and casting directors, and maintaining union membership.

Over time, the balance of dedication to identity as an actor and challenges to it, weighed against the sacrifices and satisfactions of that commitment, causes some people to give up the struggle. Many of the actors I spoke with knew people who had done so. A couple of the people I interviewed described oscillations of optimism about success in the future and despair about ever finding another job, moods which corresponded to their present work status, yet each had managed to hold on to their identity as actors. One simply determined that she would no longer second-guess her career choice:

> I sort of said to the universe, "You know what? I'm not leaving." There was this sort of weight all the time of, "Oh, is that a sign I should quit?" Or "a reasonable person would stop and go to law school," you know, because this isn't working. Then at some point just as an epiphany I sort of said "I'm not leaving," and if it means I'll do showcases for the rest of my life and don't get paid, but I'm working on stuff that matters to me – and that was the big shift, was wanting to choose projects that were important to me and that I could actually have some control over that, or even have something to say, that I could make that meaningful – and I didn't have to quit. And I feel like as soon as that happened like this huge heavy water-soaked cape just came right off my shoulders, so I didn't have to spend all that energy with that ambivalence any more, which can just be so enervating. I can just sort of be in the journey.

Another respondent, who said he relied on therapy to cope with his feelings of rejection and depression when out of work, nonetheless simply ruled out the possibility of choosing some other life:

> Some people have backup plans, and I had decided very early on, before I even went to college, that this was what I was gonna do, it's the only thing I know how to do and it will be my life. Somehow, someway, somewhere [he's referencing a song from *West Side Story*] it's what I'm gonna do. Everyone says, "You should give yourself three years and if you don't make it then quit." No. If you're really passionate about it, it's your love, it's your life, it's what you are put on this earth for, what you believe you're here for is to be a giver of art, to be a gift to people, then that's what I'm gonna do, no matter what. Even if I was, you know, completely depressed and on the verge of quitting, I know I wouldn't, I just couldn't at this point.

This speaker had experienced some important success, including an appearance on Broadway that earned favorable reviews, and he saw no reason to lower his sights. However, many of the actors I spoke with described altering their definitions of success over time. These shifts ranged from achieving fame to working consistently and winning the respect of peers; from ascending levels of prestige to simply being able to quit one's day job; from earning a living by acting to performing regularly enough to hold onto that part of one's identity.

The Longer Term

Actors who enter middle age with no financial security, whether or not they have been artistically successful, often find that they have to reevaluate their decisions when living in permanent poverty becomes less tolerable. Some actors who develop a relatively realistic understanding of the possibilities of supporting themselves through acting try to establish a sideline that will allow them to achieve some financial stability without giving up acting. For example, one of my respondents trained as a massage therapist and another was in the process of launching a small business. Two of the most poignant interviews I conducted were with actors who had endured years of sacrifice, been successful to some extent, but were not sure they would be able to keep up the struggle. One of these actors had had more success at a highly visible level than any of my other respondents; he had played important roles in three Broadway musicals, one of which had earned him a nomination for a major award. Well aware that he did not have many more chances to break through to stardom, he reflected on the ups and downs of his career:

> Now I'm 55, and it's very different from when you're 35 and you sort of feel "I can play any role, and all of that is still ahead of me." I've been in New York for 20 years, you know, I'm still not famous. Practical considerations do have to intervene, and the question is whether or not the right role and the right audience and the world-class career that Trevor Nunn [one of the most prominent directors in the English-speaking theater] predicted is still a possibility.

He went on:

> What I think would make it feel kind of ... you know, tragic for me ... was to say I have this unique combination of talents and it somehow couldn't get recognition. Particularly because I really wanted to utilize those talents to bring some kind of global healing, you know, to be a conduit for that, and not to be able to do that for a planet that sure seems like it needs it.

The second actor was eloquent about his love of acting but spoke with more anger and frustration than sadness about the sacrifices he'd made.

> Basically, I think of acting now as an addiction, like a heroin addict, for example. When a heroin addict is on heroin, you cannot convince him that he's – He's *happy*. Otherwise he wouldn't be taking it. And when he's on heroin, the world is right, and everything's aligned, and he's in the best possible state. But where does it get him in terms of the rest of his life? And that's what acting is for me. The kinds of jobs I've been able to do. I can go out of town, and I can work for eight weeks for a decent amount of money that I can live on for those eight weeks. And I can be high and truly happy, and the world is alive. But where does it get me? Once the job is over? Once I'm

down from the high? The heroin addict, for example, the more heroin he takes, the less able he is to move on with his life, to pay his bills, to not become beholden to the addiction. So it's the same with my acting career. That's the way it was. It was an addiction.

Sticking with the metaphor, he explained, "I want to continue to take heroin, but I also want to be able to pay my friggin' bills and move on with my life and not have to wait tables in between jobs. Because I just can't do it any more." This was the actor who was trying to launch a small business, and he told himself that if he was able to make money with the product he was developing, "Then I swear, I will be happy, just existing in the regional theater world, as long as I don't have to wait tables in between. And then I'll be happy. And that's it. That's all I need."

At another point in the interview, he said that doing any kind of theater (short of community theater) would be enough. He felt that even if was driven out of the profession, his identity as an actor was so deep-seated that nothing could ever shake it. "No matter what happens, I love to do it. That's all. And I may never be in another play, but by now, it does feel like an identity. It's just my identity. It's always been who I am, you know?"

For those actors who saw themselves as a potential conduit for "global healing" or as "a gift to people," never being in another play would be not only a painful abandonment of an extraordinary identity, but also of an obligation to society at large.

CONCLUSION

The foregoing analysis begins to suggest that actors — even those with less exalted views of their calling — feel that their vocation makes them special. They prize their identity as actors, probably to a greater extent than most people's occupational identities matter to them, and they love the work they want to do. But they very often struggle to sustain work identities without actually having the work, especially paid work, to support that self-understanding. They must do considerable identity work to uphold their sense of self and to persuade others to accord them the status they claim. They maintain role distance from paying jobs that would suggest a counter identity. They try to protect themselves from other people's disparagement, incredulity, or ignorance. They immerse themselves in activities and networks that help sustain faith that they are indeed theater artists. And over time, they redefine success in ways that seem more attainable.

Lingo and Tepper (2013, p. 340) argue that "[s]tudying how artists cope with uncertainty and the factors that influence their success should be relevant for understanding ... broader social and economic trends facing today's (and tomorrow's) workforce." What lessons about work and identity can we draw from this study of workers who face a labor market that promises lifelong instability in which they cannot necessarily obtain the kind of work they choose, on which they have based their identity?

It is of course true that workers in an increasing number of occupations face high and apparently rising levels of uncertainty in their jobs, occupations, and the labor market more generally. Changes in the employment relationship have made permanent jobs, secure work, and lifelong careers increasingly unavailable, making it still less likely that identities can be built to last (Kalleberg, 2011; Sennett, 1998). Many contemporary jobs provide little incentive for workers to identify with them. In such cases, workers can be expected to maximize their self-regard by distancing themselves from paid employment, instead embracing identities based in family, leisure, religion, or other non-work endeavors.

But the actors I've discussed do not conform to such a pattern. To them, work identity is highly salient and they struggle against numerous, daunting obstacles to derive and maintain a highly-prized work identity, despite the effort (and pain) they endure. These actors speak about their work as a heroin high, a home, being on top of the world, being free − all of which they view as signs that they were *meant* to be an actor. They do not take on identities as waiters or bartenders or office workers even when they are supporting themselves through such work. Indeed, they seem to invoke symbolic mechanisms that inoculate their selves against any identification with such work.

In this respect, actors do have something in common with other people who have deep investments in their chosen occupational pursuit. Those who consider it a calling, for example, or who have fulfilled an apprenticeship or attained a graduate degree, are also likely to struggle against identity threats to maintain their preferred work identity. Examples are not hard to find, and may in fact become increasingly numerous: Academics whose labor market position compels them to seek out employment as adjuncts; lawyers who, unable to secure permanent employment in their fields, must resort to temping; journalists who must struggle to piece together income on a per word basis; educators who can only find employment as substitute teachers. Professionals in such circumstances, who have invested large portions of their adult lives (and much of their material well-being) can be expected to occupy much the same liminal state in which actors are found. One might therefore expect to find many of them exhibiting much the same forms of identity work as this paper has unearthed.

Still, if the evidence reported above is any guide, actors seem to exhibit a singular attachment to their occupational identities. Indeed, they commonly insist that they have a stable, core self that simply *is* an actor. That is, they tend to adopt an essentialized conception of their own being which seems especially durable, even when confronting material and symbolic challenges of various sorts. The question then becomes why this should be so.

Though my data cannot the answer this question with any degree of certainty, it seems reasonable to speculate that the reason actors' occupational identity is so durable lies in the very nature of their craft, which involves not only training and auditioning, but also, if they are fortunate, intense rehearsals and repeated public performances. Each encounter immerses the performer in an interaction ritual (Collins, 2004) that cannot but make the actor feel connected, engaged, and embedded in the identity they perform. As Durkheim (1965 [1912]) would have it, these events are public rituals that must (if they are successful) generate a sense of collective effervescence that induces intense feelings on the part of those at the center of the ritual performance. Ironically, though actors must induce a sense of suspended disbelief on the part of their audience, the result may well be the opposite on the part of the actors: a sustained attachment to the self which their performances produce. Such enchanting experiences, which in effect consecrate actors' selves, are not to be found in most lines of work. Few of us are rewarded with applause on any consistent basis.

For those whose jobs provide little opportunity to exercise creativity, develop mastery, or experience what they do as expressive of who they *are*, surely it would be better to embrace occupational identity lightly if at all. For their part, actors generally perceive themselves as having chosen to trade off security for joy, or comfort for work that is deeply meaningful to them and that supports a view of themselves as out of the ordinary, as highly individualized, as paradoxically free in a situation over which they have little control. It may even be that actors' willingness to endure despite the meager supports the surrounding society provides for their craft only contributes to the suffering they routinely experience. Like a religious order whose members are willing to endure poverty as a constant and powerful test of their faith, actors may be victims of their own deeply held convictions. But surely this need not be the case. Can a more enlightened cultural policy perhaps address the liminal state in which actors are commonly caught — a state in which identity threats are a daily occurrence; in which heavy sacrifices must be borne, sometimes for decades; and in which one lives with a profound sense of ontological uncertainty? Can efforts to use

the arts as a vehicle for urban development possibly reduce the burdens
that actors routinely face? Are actors' lives more endurable within contexts
that are more hospitable to the arts? Here are questions that future studies
would do well to address.

NOTES

1. In their study of eight types of artists in Australia, Throsby and Zednik (2011,
p. 11) found that actors had the highest levels of non-arts work.
2. Some artists, such as poets, are even less likely than actors to make a living
from their art; unlike poets, actors cannot hope for posthumous recognition
(Craig, 2007).
3. Frenette (2013) describes the prevalence of unpaid internships in the
music industry.
4. Although New York provides some opportunities for work in feature films,
television series, and television commercials, actors who are primarily interested in
making a career in film or television are likely to go to Los Angeles rather than to
New York.
5. East Coast theaters with Equity agreements are required to do so.
6. Lingo and Tepper (2013) note "many artists today spend considerable time in
cities where they attend school."
7. Faulkner (1973) found that orchestral musicians recognize that after the age of
35 they are unlikely to make major career moves. In contrast, it is quite possible for
an actor who has had limited success as a young man to have more success as he
ages (though this is less likely for women).
8. Two of my Philadelphia actors had previously spent some time trying to make
it in New York.

ACKNOWLEDGMENTS

Many thanks to Steve Vallas for invaluable assistance, and thanks also to
Sam Kaplan and Silke Roth for helpful feedback.

REFERENCES

Alvesson, M., & Willmott, H. (2002). Identity regulation as organizational control: Producing
the appropriate individual. *Journal of Management Studies*, 39(5), 619–644.
Anheier, H. K., Gerhards, J., & Romo, F. P. (1995). Forms of capital and social structure in
cultural fields. *American Journal of Sociology*, *100*, 859–903.

Bain, A., & McLean, H. (2013). The artistic precariat. *Cambridge Journal of Regions, Economy and Society, 6*, 93–111.

Barker, J. R. (1993). Tightening the iron cage: Concertive control in self-managing teams. *Administrative Science Quarterly, 38*, 408–437.

Baudrillard, J. (1998 [1970]). *The consumer society: Myths and structures.* London: Sage.

Bauman, Z. (1998). *Work, consumerism, and the new poor.* Buckingham: Open University Press.

Beck, U. (2000). *The brave new world of work.* Cambridge: Polity Press.

Becker, H. S. (1982). *Art worlds.* Berkeley, CA: University of California.

Brown, A. D., & Lewis, M. A. (2011). Identities, discipline and routines. *Organization Studies, 32*(7), 871–895.

Caves, R. E. (2000). *Creative industries: Contracts between art and commerce.* Cambridge, MA: Harvard University Press.

Cohen, R. (2004). *Acting professionally: Raw facts about careers in acting* (6th ed.). New York, NY: McGraw Hill.

Collins, R. (2004). *Interaction ritual chains.* Princeton, NJ: Princeton University Press.

Collinson, D. L. (2003). Identities and insecurities: Selves at work. *Organization, 10*(3), 527–547.

Cornfield, D. B. (2015). *Beyond the beat: Musicians building community in Nashville.* Princeton, NJ: Princeton University Press.

Craig, A. (2007). Practicing poetry: A career without a job. In C. Calhoun & R. Sennett (Eds.), *Practicing culture* (pp. 35–56). London: Routledge.

DiPaola, S. (2015). *2014–2015 Theatrical season report: An analysis of employment, earnings, membership and finance.* Retrieved from ActorsEquity.org. Accessed on March 12, 2016.

DuGay, P. (1996). *Consumption and identity at work.* London: Sage.

Durkheim, E. (1965 [1912]). *The elementary forms of the religious life.* New York, NY: Free Press.

Edwards, R. C. (1979). *Contested terrain: The transformation of the workplace in the twentieth century.* New York, NY: Basic Books.

Faulkner, R. F. (1973). Career concerns and mobility motivations of orchestra musicians. *Sociological Quarterly, 14*, 334–349.

Freidson, E. (1990). Labors of love in theory and practice: A prospectus. In K. Erikson & S. P. Vallas (Eds.), *The nature of work: Sociological perspectives* (pp. 149–161). New Haven, CT: Yale University Press.

Frenette, A. (2013). Making the intern economy: Role and career challenges of the music industry intern. *Work and Occupations, 40*(4), 364–397.

Goffman, E. (1952). On cooling the mark out. *Psychiatry, 15*, 451–463.

Goffman, E. (1959). *The presentation of self in everyday life.* Garden City, NY: Doubleday.

Goffman, E. (1961). Role distance. In *Encounters: Two studies in the sociology of interaction* (pp. 83–152). Garden City, NY: Anchor Books.

Goffman, E. (1963). *Stigma: Notes on the management of spoiled identity.* Englewood Cliffs, NJ: Prentice-Hall.

Gorz, A. (1999). *Reclaiming work: Beyond the wage-based society.* Cambridge: Polity Press.

Hesmondhalgh, D., & Baker, S. (2010). "A very complicated version of freedom": Conditions and experiences of creative labour in three cultural industries. *Poetics, 38*, 4–20.

Hochschild, A. R. (1983). *The managed heart: Commercialization of human feeling.* Berkeley, CA: University of California Press.

Hughes, E. C. (1984 [1951]). Work and self. In *The sociological eye: Selected papers* (pp. 338–347). New Brunswick, NJ: Transaction Books.

Kalleberg, A. L. (2011). *Good jobs, bad jobs: The rise of polarized and precarious employment systems in the United States, 1970s to 2000s.* New York, NY: Russell Sage Foundation.

Kunda, G. (1992). *Engineering culture: Control and commitment in a high-tech corporation.* Philadelphia, PA: Temple University Press.

Lamont, M. (2000). *The dignity of working men: Morality and the boundaries of race, class, and immigration.* New York, NY: Russell Sage Foundation.

Layder, D. (1984). Sources and levels of commitment in actors' careers. *Work and Occupations, 11*(2), 147–162.

Leidner, R. (1993). *Fast food, fast talk: Service work and the routinization of everyday life.* Berkeley, CA: University of California Press.

Leidner, R. (2006). Identity and work. In M. Korczynski, R. Hodson, & P. Edwards (Eds.), *Social theory at work* (pp. 424–463). Oxford: Oxford University Press.

Leidner, R. (2010). Work cultures. In J. R. Hall, L. Grindstaff, & M.-C. Lo (Eds.), *Handbook of cultural sociology* (pp. 419–427). New York, NY: Routledge.

Lingo, E. L., & Tepper, S. J. (2013). Looking back, looking forward: Arts-based careers and creative work. *Work and Occupations, 40*(4), 337–363.

Lloyd, R. (2010). *Neo-Bohemia: Art and commerce in the postindustrial city* (2nd ed.). New York, NY: Routledge.

Margolis, D. R. (1979). *The managers: Corporate life in America.* New York, NY: Morrow.

Matza, D. (1964). *Delinquency and drift.* Berkeley, CA: University of California Press.

Menger, P.-M. (1999). Artistic labor markets and careers. *Annual Review of Sociology, 25*, 541–574.

Menger, P.-M. (2006). Artistic labor markets: Contingent work, excess supply and occupational risk management. In V. A. Ginsburgh & D. Throsby (Eds.), *Handbook of the economics of art and culture* (Vol. 1, pp. 767–811). Amsterdam: Elsevier B.V.

Otis, E. (2012). *Markets and bodies: Women, service work, and the making of inequality in China.* Palo Alto, CA: Stanford University Press.

Padavic, I. (2005). Laboring under uncertainty: Identity renegotiation among contingent workers. *Symbolic Interaction, 28*(1), 111–134.

Pinheiro, D. L., & Dowd, T. J. (2009). All that jazz: The success of jazz musicians in three metropolitan areas. *Poetics, 37*(5–6), 490–506.

Pugh, A. J. (2015). *The tumbleweed society: Working and caring in an age of insecurity.* Oxford: Oxford University Press.

Rogers, J. K. (2000). *Temps: The many faces of the changing workplace.* Ithaca, NY: ILR Press.

Rollins, J. (1985). *Between women: Domestics and their employers.* Philadelphia, PA: Temple University Press.

Schneirov, R. (2003). Contingent faculty: A new social movement takes shape. *WorkingUSA, 6*(4), 38–48.

Sennett, R. (1998). *The corrosion of character: The personal consequences of work in the new capitalism.* New York, NY: W.W. Norton.

Sennett, R., & Cobb, J. (1973). *The hidden injuries of class.* New York, NY: Vintage Books.

Sherman, R. (2007). *Class acts: Service and inequality in luxury hotels.* Berkeley, CA: University of California Press.

Smart, B. (2003). *Economy, culture, and society: A sociological critique of neoliberalism.* Buckingham: Open University Press.

Smith, V. (2001). *Crossing the great divide: Risk and opportunity in the new economy.* Ithaca, NY: ILR Press.

Snow, D. A., & Anderson, L. (1987). Identity work among the homeless: The verbal construction and avowal of personal identities. *American Journal of Sociology, 92*(6), 1336–1371.

Taylor, L., & Williams, K. (1971). The actor and his world. *New Society, 21*(July), 188–190.

Throsby, D., & Zednik, A. (2011). Multiple job-holding and artistic careers: Some empirical evidence. *Cultural Trends, 20*(1), 9–24.

Umney, C., & Kretsos, L. (2014). Creative labour and collective interaction: The working lives of young jazz musicians in London. *Work, Employment and Society, 28*, 571–588.

Umney, C., & Kretsos, L. (2015). 'That's the Experience': Passion, work precarity, and life transitions among London jazz musicians. *Work and Occupations, 42*(3), 313–334.

Weber, M. (1958 [1904–1905]). *The protestant ethic and the spirit of capitalism.* New York, NY: Charles Scribner's Sons.

"I'M A TEACHER, NOT A BABYSITTER": WORKERS' STRATEGIES FOR MANAGING IDENTITY-RELATED DENIALS OF DIGNITY IN THE EARLY CHILDHOOD WORKPLACE

Jennifer L. Nelson and Amanda E. Lewis

ABSTRACT

In this paper we build upon previous research that examines how workers in devalued occupations transform structural conditions that threaten their dignity into resources with which to protect themselves. Through in-depth interviews and fieldwork with early childhood educators (ECE), we examine the work experiences of teachers in four distinct work contexts: daycare centers and within elementary schools, each in either the public or private sector. We find that these different school organizational contexts shape what kinds of identity challenges early childhood teachers experience. Different organizational contexts not only subject teachers to different threats to their work-related identity but also have different potential identity resources embedded within them that teachers

Research in the Sociology of Work, Volume 29, 37–71
ISSN: 0277-2833/doi:10.1108/S0277-283320160000029013

can use on their own behalf. Thus, while all the early childhood educators in our sample struggle with being employed within a devalued occupation, the identity strategies they have developed to protect their self-worth vary across employment contexts. We show that the strategies these interactive service workers use to solve identity-related problems of dignity at work involve the creative conversion of constraints they face at work into resources that help them achieve valued work identities.

Keywords: Work identity; dignity at work; organization and work studies

INTRODUCTION

"The teachers are all Black or foreign. Not many of the students are. Sometimes I feel like [the parents] think – and I don't know if this is about race, or they just know what income we make – it's almost like 'Aww, we know [that you don't make much].' A lot of the teachers will say, 'Oh yeah, my parent took me out to such-and-such restaurant.' And I'm like, 'Okay. I don't need anybody to take me out to a restaurant.' But to me, that's not your job. You're a teacher, and if you want to be respected like a teacher and not a babysitter ... unless you say, 'I'm a teacher. I'm not a babysitter,' it can be like we're the help."
                                     – Rachel, early childhood teacher in a private daycare facility.

How people in particular jobs react to, resolve dilemmas within, and shape the boundaries of their work is an integral part of supporting motivation, meaning, and feelings of self-worth in the subjective experience of a job. As Rachel articulates above, as a teacher of young children she may understand herself as a *teacher*, but is often treated like something else by her "customers." This is a dilemma of identity that is not necessarily unique to Rachel and other early childhood educators but one that workers in stigmatizing or devalued positions face often as they carry out their jobs. Problems of identity at work can take several forms: when workers must follow routines that suppress their selves; when workers must be someone at work that they do not want to be; or when workers must cope with the low public regard for the work they do (Leidner, 1993). This study focuses on the third kind of identity problem, one that Hodson (2001) has described as a denial of dignity at work.

As Hodson (2001) explains, the pursuit of dignity at work conceptually represents an antidote to Marx, Durkheim, and Weber's fears about the damage that work and workplaces can do to people and society. Dignity – defined as a feeling of self-worth or self-respect (Snow & Anderson, 1987) – can mitigate alienation from meaningless work, protect against anomie from dehumanizing work, and transcend rigidities of over-bureaucratized work. All jobs carried out in organizational structures contain challenges and opportunities to restoring one's dignity, though the challenges and opportunities vary by kind and degree (Hodson, 2001; see also Hughes, 1971). Workers navigate challenges to their dignity in order to survive, persist in, and ideally, find ways to enjoy their jobs.

Historically, two broad schools of thought have shaped scholarly approaches to understanding how and how much workers are able to navigate and resolve the identity problems named above. First is research which tends to focus on organizational constraints in working conditions; second is a group of studies that focuses more on workers' agency or behavioral adaptations to identity challenges. The first approach contends that in settings where workers lack control over their working conditions, the inevitable result is low job satisfaction, low motivation, and the experience of alienation (Hackman & Oldham, 1980; Seeman, 1959). This approach focuses on the institutional conditions that generate identity challenges and in most of these formulations, there is little or no latitude for workers to remedy identity problems of stigma and powerlessness. The second approach focuses on worker agency in navigating occupational challenges. This research examines workers' behaviors that actively shape their own identities, often in ways that defend themselves against uncertainty or devaluation at work (Alvesson & Willmott, 2002; Dutton, Debebe, & Wrzesniewski, 2014; Pratt, Rockmann, & Kaufmann, 2006; Rogers, 2000). In the behavior approach, for example, some empirical studies find that workers engage in the creative re-appropriation of environmental constraints into resources, sometimes by engaging in small-scale resistance to control (Burawoy, 1979; Hodson, 1995; Roy, 1959; Scott, 2008).

In this study, we build upon the latter tradition, empirical work that examines workers' strategies to transform structural constraints into resources for recovering or safeguarding their dignity at work. We ask, how do workers employed in a devalued occupation resolve job-related identity problems, and how and why do identity strategies differ between workers in different kinds of settings within a single industry? As we will show below using data from our interviews with and observations of early childhood teachers, regardless of particular context, in an occupation involving care work, there are numerous and regular challenges to workers' sense of worth. Within different contexts, however, the conditions of work vary significantly and lead to different kinds of "identity violations" (Pratt et al., 2006, p. 246) and different possibilities for workers to recover or "achieve" dignity (Cerulo, 1997, p. 391; Chen, 1999, p. 585; Wrzesniewski & Dutton, 2001, p. 185).

BACKGROUND

Below, we outline several bodies of literature that explore the structural challenges of being employed in devalued professions along with how workers respond to the constraints they face. We see both bodies of literature as relevant in our exploration of workers' identity construction, as actors' awareness of both constraints and opportunities in their workplaces is critical to this process (see Boden, 1994, p. 32 for a similar approach). We then review research on how workers strategize to recover their dignity, focusing on identity processes in the workplace. Finally, we provide an overview of the sector we are studying here, early childhood education.

Struggles for Control: Constraints in Interactive Service Work

One major focus for studies that examine structural constraints in the workplace is on questions of control: how much say do workers have over what work they do? While the struggles over control manifest differently across occupations, in Hughes' view (1970 in Hughes & Coser, 1994, p. 70), "if a certain problem turn[s] up in one occupation, it [i]s nearly certain to turn up in them all." Many classical and contemporary social theorists such as Marx have conceptualized the structure of control as a *bilateral* struggle between worker and manager (Alvesson & Willmott, 2002; Kunda, 2006). The bilateral framing captures many important dynamics in the workplace but potentially mischaracterizes the nature of struggles over control in one of the largest and fastest growing sectors in the economy today: interactive service professions (Leidner, 1993; see also Freidson, 2001). Interactive service professions involve a *trilateral* struggle for control where workers contend with challenges not only from managers but also from service-recipients. Early childhood teachers are positioned within an even more complicated *quadrilateral* struggle for control. This complex configuration breeds unique relational tensions, as the teachers must balance the wants, needs, and demands of their fellow (sometimes co-) teachers, managers, parents, and students (e.g., Lareau, 1989; Lewis & Forman, 2002; Uttal, 2002; Wrigley, 1995). Herein teachers must manage the sometimes competing demands of the "recipients" of their service — both parents (indirectly) and students (directly). In both cases, relationships with clients can either be a source of enjoyment or dismay for early childhood educators depending on how much control workers have over those relations (Cohen & Sutton, 1998; Van Ausdale & Feagin, 2001).

Workers' Agency: Behaviors that Transform Constraints into Resources

While, as many scholars have chronicled, workers find themselves enfolded in structural constraints at work, they usually retain some ability to move within them, respond to them, and even use them to create and defend for themselves "spheres of autonomous activity" (Hodson, 1991, p. 61). In fact, worker responses to control are the starting point for any pursuit of dignity at work (Hodson, 2001). For example, Alvesson and Willmott (2002) show that while employment contexts exert regulation over workers' identities, workers respond to these demands quasi-autonomously, by engaging in identity work. In his interview study of manual, clerical, semi-professional, and professional workers, Hodson (1991, p. 47) finds that to protect their identities as autonomous adults, "active workers" engage in a range of behaviors that advance their own agendas (in resistance to competing managerial or coworker agendas). Forms of resistance include gossip, sabotage, withdrawal, foot-dragging, "making out," and brown-nosing. Similar to Hodson, scholars have identified a wide array of large and small ways workers respond to the identity challenges generated by structural constraints they experience in their day-to-day work. By crafting strategies of control, resistance, compliance, or creativity, workers can derive self-efficacy and protect their identities (Gecas & Schwalbe, 1983; see also Gengler, 2012; Wilkins, 2008).

While all workers likely face some identity challenges on the job, recent work has focused specifically on the challenges devalued workers face and on their strategic efforts to reconstitute a valued identity for themselves. For example, in Rogers' (2000) study of temp workers, she finds that these workers enhance their esteem by using strategies such as telling coworkers cover stories about how they are not really a temp, or comparing themselves favorably to other, poorer-quality workers. In addition to distancing themselves from the job or recovering their dignity by comparing themselves to those worse-off, another important strategy workers use is to transform identity challenges within the workplace into resources that help them recover their dignity. For example, in Maroto's (2011) study of people apprenticing to become body piercers and tattoo artists, she found that these workers coped with odious tasks by justifying them as a means to an end: professionalization. In a third strategy, workers ally with whichever constituent of their work (e.g., manager or customer) will allow the worker to leverage their control and enhance their protection (Leidner, 1993).

Identity Processes in the Workplace

Exploring work identities is important as it gives us information about workers' experiences on the job, their satisfaction and turnover, and the employing organization's performance (Ashforth, Spencer, & Kevin, 2008; Elsbach, 2004; Hochschild, 1983; Pratt et al., 2006; Wrzesniewski & Dutton, 2001). These work-related identities can be nested at multiple levels of analysis: occupational, organizational, institutional (Albert & Whetten, 1985; Friedland & Alford, 1991; Glynn, 2008; Selznick, 1957; Walsh & Gordon, 2008). Here we focus on the how individuals construct and navigate their "occupational identity." According to Ashcraft (2007, p. 13), occupational identity is a repertoire of narratives that defines "what counts as legitimate work, what tasks matter more and why, [and] who 'naturally' belongs in particular jobs." Identity construction is the activities (including talk) that people use to create, present, or sustain personal identities (Snow & Anderson, 1987). While identity construction goes on regularly, it can be activated by encountering an identity problem (e.g., a challenge to their dignity, or threats to the value of their work) in the workplace (Stets & Burke, 2000). When this happens, we broadly conceptualize efforts by workers to recover or safeguard dignity at work — when the preceding denial of dignity pertains to an identity-related problem[1] — as *identity strategies* (see Fig. 1).

We aim to shed light on identity-formation processes in the workplace through our investigation of the influence of context-specific factors (such as proximate resources and sources of validation) on identity strategies. Specifically, through a close examination of our respondents' narrations and interpretations of their workplace experiences, we uncover the different challenges teachers face and the different strategies they undertake for managing denials of dignity through identity processes.

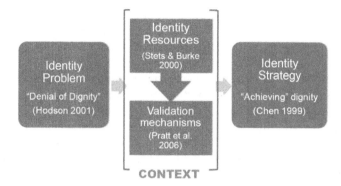

Fig. 1. A Conceptual Framework Relating Identity Problems, Resources, Validation, and Strategies as a Process.

ECE as an Occupation and the Institutional Context of Preschools

The occupation of Early Childhood Education (ECE) makes an ideal subject for the study of identity processes at work because it is an example of extreme contrast to Pratt et al.'s (2006) study of identity among medical residents and Blair-Loy's (2009) study of executive women. Unlike these high-status professions, the low-status of care work involving young children is due both to the kind of work being done but also about who typically is doing the work. Not only do feminized occupations earn less net of skill demands for both men and women, but also for occupations involving nurturance wages are even lower; England, Herbert, Kilbourne, Reid, and Megdal (1994) identify this as sex discrimination in wage setting. The skills themselves are devalued because they are associated with a female's role. But there is a further intersectional wage penalty: in her historical analysis of the shift of care work from private settings to the public sector, Glenn (1992) finds that race-segregation within care occupations leads to differential valuation of care occupations/workers. The pecuniary devaluation of care work by gender (England, 1992; England et al., 1994; Reskin, 1988) is exacerbated by the tracking of women of color into this type of service work (Glenn, 1992). While the shift from domestic work in others' homes to doing similar work in public arenas is beneficial to these workers in many ways (e.g., by finding a social support group in the workplace), the mostly minority female workforce in many care-work sectors still work long hours for low pay and few or no benefits.

In addition to the salience of both gender and race to care work, another characteristic that distinguishes ECE teachers from non-care-work occupations and professions is that the worker's authority in relationship to the service-recipient is not taken for granted (Etzioni, 1969). That is, the service-recipient and even those external to the worker/service-recipient relationship feel justified to question the worker's decisions and skills. Teachers as a semi-professional group are uniquely exposed to public scrutiny and external control of their performance (Lortie, 2002 [1975]). This exposure is potentially more extreme for ECE teachers whose work with young children can be perceived as low-skill no matter what credentials and expertise teachers bring to their work.

A further advantage to studying identity processes among ECE workers pertains to the wide variation of institutional contexts in which they work. This study takes advantage of the expansive preschool/childcare market, in terms of different facilities' cost to parents, accreditation, clientele population, and workplace culture (Davies & Quirke, 2007; Fuller, Loeb, Strath, & Carrol, 2004). At least four general types of facilities exist in this market. Each of these four sectors is included in our sample, and each represents a different kind of workplace, with a greater or lesser degree of conformity to isomorphic pressures, coupling of policy and practice, and formal markers of legitimacy, such as accreditation (e.g., see Davies & Quirke, 2007). First, publicly-subsidized daycare centers with programs such as Head Start provide preschool for children at a reduced cost. Started under federal social-welfare programs of Lyndon B. Johnson's War on Poverty, Head Start still serves low-income families, uses a comprehensive cognitive and social curriculum, and today employs a 50:50 ratio of teachers with Bachelor's degrees and Associate's degrees (Entwistle, Alexander, & Olson, 1997; see also Head Start Act Section 648A, 2007). Second, private daycare centers include local organizations or national chains of childcare providers that are often contracted by corporations as part of employee benefit packages. They provide childcare for long days, longer than a typical school day, some centers being open from 7:30 A.M. to 6:15 P.M. Third, public preschools are usually housed within k-5 elementary schools and are free of charge (though often optional, limited in number, and not guaranteed to all). Fourth, high-end private preschools are costly, have difficult admission standards, and are housed within upscale preK-6, preK-8, or preK-12th grade private schools.[2]

These contexts vary across a number of organizational and experiential dimensions as well. For example, unlike ECE teachers housed in *schools*, pre-primary teachers working in daycare *centers* are often especially marginalized as belonging to para-school, care-work organizations (Kim, 2013). Organizationally, daycare centers and schools operate under different bureaucratic rules. Centers are governed by mandates that tightly regulate their accreditation whereas schools often operate with more flexibility and different rules. "Bright from the Start" is the name of a state-based license that assures that the daycare or dayschool facility meets adequate safety regulations and that its teachers have basic training in childcare. In addition to this base license, organizations can apply for different accreditations. A more selective accreditation, not required but a marker of a higher-status facility, is the National Association for the Education of Young Children (NAEYC). NAEYC is a professional organization that requires the facility and teachers to keep extensive documentation of quality teaching. Schools may seek out NAEYC accreditation or may be accredited by the Southern Association of Colleges and Schools (SACS). SACS accreditation is held only by some public, preK-5 schools and by higher-end, private schools, which generally do not hold NAEYC accreditation. See Table 1 for a listing of schools in each sector and their accreditations.

THE STUDY: METHODS AND DATA

We conducted 27 in-depth, one-on-one, semi-structured interviews of early childhood care workers in the Atlanta metropolitan area. Henceforth, we label this whole group of workers "teachers" for the sake of simplicity but also because all of them identify themselves as either lead, co-, or assistant teachers, rather than as childcare providers. All interviews but one took place in the teacher's classroom or facility, and generally lasted between 45 minutes and 2 hours, with an average length of 66 minutes. Almost all were audio-recorded and transcribed,[3] and twelve were supplemented with fieldwork in the form of one or two informal classroom visits and workplace observations (e.g., of conversations and interactions between coworkers).[4] Twenty-five of the interviews took place over a 12-month period; two additional, targeted interviews took place a year and a half later.

As Tables 1 and 2 show, the sample is stratified and includes teachers of two- to five-year-olds (i.e., both preschool and pre-k teachers) across the four ECE work sectors in the metropolitan Atlanta area. The sample is 93% female, 63% black, 70% have BAs or above, and 67% have ten or more years of experience in ECE. Fifteen informants teach pre-k (i.e., four-year-olds as the average age), while the rest teach the group immediately below that (i.e., two- to three-year-olds). Twenty teachers (74%) have moved centers/schools; of the seven who haven't, three have taught children of other ages within their same center/school.

Teachers were recruited through two primary means. First we accessed social networks to recruit teachers in settings where we had contacts (often because we knew someone who had a child in the setting). We also used snowball sampling to access additional teachers through these initial contacts. Second, we also recruited through in-person visits by the first author to schools where we had no prior connections. In these cases center directors were typically very helpful in informing employees about the study and putting us in touch with potential participants.

The interview protocol asked questions about the preschool program's working conditions (including the teacher's work schedule, daily tasks and duties, access to professional development opportunities) and the teacher's reflections on his/her work (choice of vocation, the hiring process, relationship with colleagues and parents, and work experiences at other facilities). Field notes supplementing the interviews focused on teacher dispositions during the interview, a description of the physical school setting and the spatial set up of the classroom, and in the case of classroom observations, teaching behaviors, such as the nature of teacher-student interaction and conversation, and the interaction of and division of labor between lead and assistant teachers. Thus, almost half of our interviews were ethnographic interviews (Spradley, 1979), which allowed for the interviewer to ask informal follow-up and verification questions based on previous observations of the teacher's practices and interactions with others.

Analysis

Research memos were written throughout the interviewing stage, which documented the initial patterns we noticed emerging from the interviews (Lofland, Snow, Anderson, & Lofland, 2006). For systematic analysis, interviews and field notes were coded in MAXQDA using a progressive, two-stage coding technique. In the first cycle of coding, initial codes were done in a line-by-line fashion, resulting in an elaborate coding scheme that identified several major areas that could have taken this grounded-theoretical project in different directions. The nine main codes and 315 subcodes were used to generate 3,773 coded segments. Major code categories included teacher identity and occupational beliefs; workplace environment; working conditions (including student, parent, and colleague interactions and daily work tasks involving paperwork); curriculum and pedagogy; issues of diversity in the school; work satisfaction/dissatisfaction; and turnover and mobility between schools. For the teacher identity code, we used Sell, Skimmons, and Blewitt (2013) educator/custodian indicators as a starting point, and extended the concept to form two subcodes for the "workplace environment" category: daycare-oriented environment and school-oriented environment. These were initial codes and coding was done by the first author.

In the second cycle of coding (Miles, Huberman, & Saldaña, 2013), codes were focused and consolidated (Charmaz, 1983). The focusing of codes for the purpose of making comparisons was guided by the two categories of teacher identity and working conditions emerging as predominant in the first cycle of codes, which was consistent with the themes emerging in our research memos. We then noticed that identity problems, resources, and validation mechanisms similar to those conceptualized by the identity literature were present in these codes, and set out to examine whether identity problems, resources, and validation mechanisms varied systematically by school context. We selectively "activated" the transcripts in MAXQDA from each of the four school sectors, one set at a time (see Table 1). Identity strategy types emerged as we compared and contrasted components of the identity process across sets (i.e., school contexts). We noticed discernable patterns in how teachers within different contexts narrated the school-specific bureaucratic demands (e.g., paperwork requirements, procedures for getting certified, rules about what to teach) and parent interaction dynamics (e.g., gift-giving, challenging of expertise, requesting special accommodations for their child) they faced. These consolidated theoretical categories capture what are, for these educators, both challenges and resources: Parental Dynamics (good and bad); Bureaucratic Elements (paperwork, credentialing, curriculum regulations); Organizational Identities (faith in/criticism of); and Validation Mechanisms (e.g., professional accomplishments, parent or colleague support).

FINDINGS

Because this study compares the structure of identity processes among teachers of young children across different work contexts, we organize our analysis by organizational type in which our teachers work: public daycares, private daycares, public dayschools, and private dayschools. Of

Table 1. Interviewees' Demographics, Credentials, and Position, by Facility Type.

Teacher (Pseudonym)	School (Pseudonym)	Race	Age	Credentials	Age Group; Lead or Assistant
Public Daycare					
Lauren	Family Community[a]	Black	50s	BA, Elem. Ed	2s/3s lead teacher
Erica	Family Community[a]	Black	30s	BA	pre-k lead teacher
Monica	Strong Oaks[a]	Black	30s	CDA[c]	pre-k assistant
Iris	Strong Oaks[a]	Black	40s	CDA[c], TCC[d]	3s and 4s assistant
Natalie	Little Flower	Black	50s	CDA[c]	2s/pre-k assistant
Renee	Little Flower	Black	30s	BA, Elem. Ed	3s lead teacher
Richard	Bainbrook Place[b]	White	40s	AA, Environmental Science	3s spec ed assistant
Private Daycare					
Rachel	Claiborne School[a]	Black	20s	BA, Marketing	Multi-age co-teacher
Yasmin	Claiborne School[a]	White	50s	BA, Economics	Multi-age lead teacher
Rebecca	Glenwood School	Black	50s	CDA[c]	4s assistant teacher
Bethany	Glenwood School	Black	40s	MA, EC Ed.	4s lead teacher
Sarah	Littleton Preschool	Black	20s	CDA[c]	2s lead teacher
Gabrielle	Littleton Preschool	Black	40s	CDA[c], AA, EC Ed.	pre-k lead teacher
Riley	Downtown Child[a]	Black	20s	BA, EC Ed.	pre-k lead teacher
Nancy	Quality Care	White	50s	MA, Ed.	3–5's sole teacher
Natasha	Rising Stars	Black	30s	TCC[d], EC Ed.	Infants-6s sole teacher
Public Dayschool					
Rita	River Valley Elem.[b]	Black	50s	BA, Elem. Ed.	pre-k lead teacher
Ilene	Crestridge Elementary[a]	White	40s	BA, Psychology	pre-k lead teacher
Allison	River Valley Elem.[b]	Black	40s	MA, Counseling	pre-k assistant

Name	School	Race	Age	Education	Position
Racine	Jonathan Walker Elem.[b]	Latina	40s	BA English, MA Ed.	pre-k lead teacher
Nigelle	Jonathan Walker Elem.[b]	Black	30s	BA and MA, Ed.	pre-k lead teacher
Private Dayschool					
Helen	Yosemite School[b]	White	40s	BA	pre-k lead teacher
Sherell	Yosemite School[b]	Black	40s	BA	pre-k lead teacher
Celine	Yosemite School[b]	White	40s	MA, Special Ed.	3s-4s lead teacher
Patricia	Telluride School[b]	White	50s	BA	pre-k lead teacher
Gary	Telluride School[b]	White	40s	BA	pre-k lead teacher
Cathy	Sierra Ridge School[b]	White	40s	None	2-3s lead teacher

[a] NAEYC accredited schools.
[b] SACS accredited schools.
[c] Child Development Associate Credential.
[d] Technical College Certificate.

course, these categories are not exact, but we use the term "daycare" to refer to facilities where the facility provides childcare for ages infant to pre-k. We use the term "dayschool" to refer to facilities where pre-k and/or preschools are part of preK-5th, preK-6th, preK-8th, or preK-12th grade school. "Public" refers to free or subsidized childcare; "private" refers to facilities requiring tuition.[5]

While we structured our data collection to include early childhood educators across a range of settings, it was during the interviews and data analysis that the objective difference in teachers' work experiences between daycare and school settings became clear. Working in a "school," in proximity to higher grades (K-5, K-6 or K-12), was different than working in a "center," in proximity to infants and/or toddlers. We decided that an organizational level analysis was more fitting than a classroom level of analysis, because even if a teacher structured her/his classroom to look "schoolish," s/he could not escape the organizational norms, expectations, and influence of the facility at large on her/his identity processes. For example, workers' interview responses evidenced that their experiences with parents were influenced by parents' fundamental orientation to the facility as being a "real school" or a para-school "care" organization, not to the teacher's classroom and practices in particular.

In the sections that follow, for each school context, we first explore how teachers describe the identity-related denials of dignity they experience at work. To capture the nature of these denials of dignity in each organizational context we focus on a single teacher as a prototypical representative of teachers in that setting. We also integrate quotes from other informants in similar settings, and we report the frequency with which teachers in that group convey similar experiences. Second, we identify the setting-specific "identity resources" teachers draw on in the dignity-recovery process (Stets & Burke, 2000; see also Alvesson & Willmott, 2002). Thirdly, we examine the pattern of what we call "identity strategies" (efforts by workers to recover or safeguard dignity at work) the teachers deploy within each setting. An overview of identity strategies is summarized in Table 2 below.

Public Daycares

Three public daycare facilities included in our sample, Strong Oaks Child Care, Little Flower Learning Center, and the Family Community Center, share some basic contextual similarities.[6] They each serve an almost exclusively black and Latina/o student and parent population, and are located

Table 2. Identity Resources, Identity Validation, and Identity Strategies, by Context.

	Public Daycare	Private Daycare	Public Dayschool	Private Dayschool
Identity resources				
Parent Interactions	Unappreciative	Dangerous, Patronizing	Helpful, Manageable	Academically demanding
	4/7	6/9	3/5	4/6
Paperwork, rules, and regulations	Heavy	Moderate; Helpful	Heavy	None or few
	5/7	5/9	4/5	4/6
Organizational attributes	Criticism	Faith	Exclusion	Identification
	3/7	8/9	3/5	5/6
Identity validation	Accolades, completed work	Institutional licenses, standards	Parent compliance	Collegial support and trust
	4/7	7/9	4/5	4/6
Identity strategy	Showcasing	Subscribing	Asserting	Broadening
	4/7	6/9	4/5	5/6

in the lowest-income neighborhoods of any of the preschool facility types. Two of the facilities are NAEYC accredited; the third has a Bright from the Start license with a lower-status accreditation. Family Community Center, the center we focus on here, is in a large, new, two-story facility that stands out from its surroundings, which are industrial, littered, and have many abandoned buildings.

Lauren works at the Family Community Center. An African-American woman in her 50s, she spent the majority of her career before ECE as a flight attendant. She graduated from college with a Bachelor's in Early Childhood Education but thereafter choose to go into what she described as "higher-paid" work at an airline. She returned to teaching after her hours and benefits at the airline were reduced. When we arrive in Lauren's classroom one day for our interview, she is sweeping the linoleum floor after the school day is over. Meanwhile, her assistant, a black female in her early twenties, is replacing the cotton coverings that go over the students' naptime cots with fresh ones that have just been laundered. Cleaning is one of Lauren's daily work activities. Her work with toddlers (two- and three-year-olds) means her day is filled with managing bodily fluids (she must facilitate and document four potty breaks a day for each child). In addition to having days filled with cleaning and potty breaks, Lauren also must contend with significant oversight of her classroom and many bureaucratic challenges to her autonomy. As she put it, "Anyone who comes in and sees you're not doing your lesson plan, you'll get in trouble. But sometimes you want to deviate and you can. It seems like someone's coming in almost everyday." Despite these identity challenges, Lauren views herself as a teacher first and foremost and as one of the best teachers in the school. As we illustrate below, her ability to achieve a positive personal identity at work is in large part because of her success in transforming challenges into identity resources.

For example, heavy paperwork requirements are a central part of Lauren's daily work and provide significant challenges as she has little official time on the job set aside to complete this work. However, we found that Lauren strategically uses these requirements as identity resources for recovering her dignity. Lauren goes above and beyond when it comes to fulfilling what she calls her "all consuming" paperwork tasks. She gives more time to filling out paperwork, in fact, than the workday will allow. She types up the documentation on what children do everyday – as part of Head Start and NAEYC requirements – every weekend at home. To illustrate, she waves a fat folder in the air, which she says is 200 pages worth of documentation of child assessments and daily behavior reports, on one of her students. "I am very good at it. I am very organized. I was up for teacher of the year last year," she says. Her skill and commitment to completing required documentation is, for her, evidence of competence. While Lauren was not uncritical of "all the double-dotting and double-crossing," she does not resist it. This sense of competence she achieves from doing paperwork well is not without costs as it requires lots of extra legitimating work. This is consistent with worker behavior theories which posit that employees engaging in job crafting may be creating more work for themselves, even if their choice to execute it that way is voluntarily (Wrzesniewski & Dutton, 2001).

A second denial of dignity Lauren described in her work pertained to her interactions with parents, which she described as devaluing.

> JN: Do you feel that parents value your work? How do you know?
>
> Lauren: No. Some parents verbalize their appreciation, but for me, appreciation is one that's not just about being nice to the teacher. I would appreciate if a parent acknowledges how I am teaching their child, not just taking care of their child. A parent can appreciate that I take care of her child, but not about how I teach her child.

Lauren sees her relationship with parents as problematic, mostly because they view her work exclusively as being about care and supervision, rather than education. Many of the parents are young, and, in Lauren's view, not competent parents themselves. While past research in elementary schools has found that teachers who work with working-class and poor families are often treated as professionals or experts (Lareau, 2000; Lewis & Forman, 2002), Lauren does not enjoy this relative regard; even as parents "appreciate" her, according to her, they fundamentally misunderstand what is valuable about her work. This is an identity problem particular to this context that a majority of teachers in public daycare settings experienced.

Lauren responds to challenging interactions with parents by positioning herself as an expert vis-à-vis unappreciative parents and the organization itself. For example, she sees the Family Community Center as working against itself by having policies that enable parent irresponsibility, such as providing diapers so parents do not have to bring any in, and by having unstructured before- and after-care services. In this way she actually partly forms a work identity that is in opposition to the organizational identity of her employer. She furthers this by contrasting herself with incompetent parents and teachers' assistants (though not her own — she is careful to select and demand to work with an assistant of whom she approves). For example, Lauren contrasts herself from young assistant teachers in her workplace who lack professional behaviors, such as proper dress and diligence.

Instead, she makes herself an example for her coworkers, dispensing professional advice to them; collegial peers serve, at least in part, as an "audience" for her work performance (Wrzesniewski & Dutton, 2001).

The chosen way in which Lauren takes pride in her achievements at
work requires careful attention to documentation to fulfill technical
requirements from multiple agencies (Bright from the Start, Head Start,
and NAEYC). Lauren is focused on doing her instructional work, and
paperwork, correctly. Similar to other daycare teachers, she refers only
rarely to having fun interacting with the children in her classroom. It is in
the paperwork that these teachers verify the quantity and quality of work
they have done. While Lauren expressed great exasperation when she
waved the fat folder of student files around, she was also *showcasing* her
good work. *Showcasing* is the identity strategy she and teachers in her context used to transform the structural conditions in their work, which threaten their dignity, into resources with which to protect themselves. Lauren
recovered a sense of dignity from overwork and low autonomy by taking
pride in a job well done (Hodson, 2001). Four of the seven teachers in our
public daycare sample expressed something similar. These teachers use
paperwork requirements in their work as ritual classifications (DiMaggio,
1987; Meyer & Rowan, 1977) to establish the legitimacy of their work. By
using the strategy of showcasing, Lauren safeguards dignity in her work
through the creative re-appropriation of her structural conditions. She
deflects demeaning treatment from unappreciative parents and meaningless
overwork by engaging in organizational citizenship. The conditions that
create identity problems in her work are transformed into the resources she
uses to restore dignity to her personal identity. In this way, identity processes are structured by the work context.

Private Daycares

Littleton Preschool is tucked inside a middle-class neighborhood, sandwiched between a church and shops and restaurants which many pedestrians frequent. Well-maintained homes line the narrow surrounding
residential streets. Walking up to the door of the preschool, we pass by a
large, colorful flowerbed. The building is secure; we must be buzzed in.
Entering Gabrielle's spacious and sunny classroom, its walls teeming with
handmade posters and framed pictures of students and their families on the
wall, and plenty of toys and books on display and materials organized
throughout the room, we note how different this is from the minimalistic
classrooms in the public daycares.

Gabrielle has been working in ECE for more than 25 years, first working as a "floater" to fill in many classrooms, then with infants for 12 years, and now as a lead teacher in her pre-k classroom. An African-American woman in her 40s, she has an Associate's degree in Early Childhood Education.[7] At Littleton Preschool, her student demographics are approximately 75% White, and 25% Asian, African, and Hispanic. She wears khakis and a polo shirt, a uniform worn by all teachers in the building. At first, she resisted being interviewed and took issue with the lack of a payment incentive and being called a research subject on the consent form, but decided to participate at the last minute because she said, "My daughter is in college, and she might need to do an interview too, so that's why I decided to do it for you." She asked if, after visiting her classroom, we would write her an informal evaluation for her to put in her teacher portfolio. Gabrielle's reaction to our request to be interviewed is indicative of how teachers in private daycares handle identity problems in general: at first self-protecting but ultimately accommodating, using regulations for teacher evaluation in her workplace as leverage in the pursuit of dignity.

Gabrielle's daily work activities are similar to Lauren's, except that she does not do cleaning tasks (e.g., a staff person comes into the classroom and serves the children breakfast and lunch). How Gabrielle does the documentation of student behavior and activities is also different from Lauren's daily behavior logs. Firstly, Gabrielle finishes the documentation during workday hours. Gabrielle spends an hour every morning compiling student portfolios, which includes sorting photos of students from the previous day's activities, notes she and her assistant wrote on students, and filing samples of student work in seven different domains of learning. She has this time organizationally set aside for this purpose, including coverage from a paraprofessional who meanwhile supervises the children outside the classroom and handles check-in and greeting parents.

While teachers in private daycares described their interactions with students as nurturing and fun and their individual interactions with parents as fairly cordial, collectively, parents were a major source of challenges for these teachers. Parents played an ominous role; the specter of getting on parents' bad side always existed. Out on the playground one day during recess while we supervised the students, Gabrielle told us how this year, the students were split across the two pre-k classrooms instead of all in one, and that hers filled up first. Parents had requested to have her, based on her good reputation among other parents and their word-of-mouth to one another. "The parents are close here," she said, "which can be good ... or, it can be dangerous." We asked her to clarify, and she said that a mass of parents can support a teacher, or be a nightmare to the teacher. At this center, the parent's way goes. When parents complain about a teacher, they often skip discussion with the teachers and bring their gripes to the director. Working in a different private daycare, Riley also discussed the challenge of parental limits to teacher power. Parents in her center went to the administrators and asked to have teacher workdays removed from the school calendar, so that parents would not have to make other childcare arrangements. Through these experiences, teachers in private daycare contexts often came to see parents as adversaries.

Gabrielle's "dangerous" comment illuminates both a problem and a resource for teacher identity. The problem is that parents exert managerial-type control over teachers' work. This problem can function as a resource when teachers in these settings develop consensus with one another about defining parents as an out-group. They can then collectively determine appropriate levels of relationship with parents. Gabrielle appears to be a leader in her school (via her tenure and her nickname as "queen") who socializes her coworkers to be cautious of parents. She contributes to coworker relations that encourage benign (in their view) ways to resist parental control. Because active parents who regularly intervene with school administration pose a unique threat to teacher autonomy, dignity, and identity, teachers in the private daycare contexts see organizational standards and on-site certifications as giving them access to a feeling of vocational expertise. As Rachel in the opening quote of this paper says, "I am a teacher." She articulates her occupational membership in order to differentiate herself from a lower group — "not a babysitter." For teachers who moved from first working in a lesser-accredited facility to one with better working conditions, they were also prone to embrace accreditation requirements (such as licenses, certification requirements, and curricula guidelines) as status-boosters rather than view them as constraints. Riley tended to take *an uncritical view* of the accountability systems circumscribing her work; for her, regulations in her work aided her self-image as a competent teacher doing important work, as well as provided job security, lower student ratios, and more interesting work tasks. This posture of faith in the organization's structures (e.g., accreditation rules) and its aligning organizational attributes (e.g., its mission and reputation) was true for eight of the nine teachers in this context.

To recover status losses incurred by their relational work with parents (and less often, students), Gabrielle, Riley, and Rachel (altogether 6 of the 9 teachers in this context) use the identity strategy of *subscribing* to aspects of their organization's structure as evidence of their own personal occupational legitimacy. *Subscribing* is the identity strategy these teachers used to transform the structural conditions in their work, which threaten their dignity, into resources with which to protect themselves. Teachers express buy-in to their school's accreditation (described above) as well as its particular curriculum/pedagogy. Tangibly, these elements refer to documentation procedures (i.e., paperwork), rules, and regulations to which teachers must adhere.

Public Dayschools

Crestridge Elementary is a large elementary school surrounded by soccer fields in a mixed-income, gentrifying neighborhood. It houses three classes each of pre-k through 5th grade, and has a good reputation in the neighborhood and better accountability rankings than the elementary school about a mile away. The pre-k classes, which are filled by lottery, are always full. The demographics of these classrooms are approximately 60% Black and 30% White.

We meet Ilene, a White 34-year-old woman wearing a youthful blue dress with cowboy boots, for the first time in the cafeteria. She is there with her class. When we approach her, she engages us in conversation about the topic of our research, and she invites us to her classroom before we even ask. Ilene, who has a Bachelor's degree in psychology, has been teaching pre-kindergarteners (i.e., three- to five-year-olds) for 12 years. Ilene's daily, academic work tasks are similar to teachers in both sectors of daycare, except that she also keeps grades for each student. She uses the same student portfolio assessment system as Gabrielle, but Ilene submits it electronically and takes her documentation work home with her. Ilene explains the documentation process meticulously, describing student work as *data*. While Ilene does not complain about the heavy paperwork load that comes with the job, she does express frustration with the institutional ways her work is devalued in the school — being less compensated than other teachers, being the only group of teachers in the building who have to clock out or else be written up, and being treated as paraprofessionals. Rita, also a long-time, lead pre-k and kindergarten teacher in a public elementary school, shares a similar annoyance with school regulations that isolate ECE teachers from the rest of the teaching faculty:

> Bright from the Start stuff was a bother. After so long, as a teacher, you really can teach the kids. ... Because according to the regulations, you can do this, not that. Which meant that it had to be operated separate from the rest of the school. This impacted us as teachers too because we felt cut off from the rest of the school, but we wanted to be incorporated.

As an unintended consequence, the regulations relegate early childhood teachers who work in public elementary school settings into a separate and low-status bureaucratic space, an experience shared by three of the five teachers in public school settings. The regulations mark the teachers' work as separate from what is seen as the "real school," which has its own separate regulations for student learning benchmarks. Unlike the helpful, status-boosting role of paperwork, accreditation rules, certification requirements, and curriculum guidelines in daycare contexts, for ECE teachers in public school settings, school regulations negatively separate them from the larger school faculty and present work-related identity challenges, which must be overcome. Even though Ilene uses teaching methods that elementary teachers use, including differentiated instruction and pre- and post-testing to monitor student growth, as well as traditional teaching resources such as her school's subscription to Pearson textbooks for early literacy, her collegial audience of upper-grades teachers do not validate her performance. So, she turns to another resource who can: parents.

Ilene describes her interactions with students in the classroom as "fun," which was representative for teachers in this context as a group. Perhaps unconsciously, teachers' successful affective bonds with students created an advantage for them in their interactions with parents. Teachers spoke of how in earning their students' love, teachers gained the parents' respect. In Ilene's daily work, she interacts with parents heavily, as parents must drop off and pick up their children from her personally, twice daily. About half of the parents are what she describes as over-involved, middle-class stay-at-home-moms, some of them anxious first-time parents; the other half of parents are low-income stay-at-home-moms. Ilene is highly regarded by parents in the community. She derives a sense of occupational competence from the fact that parents request for their children to have her, and when parents of students in other classrooms see the projects she does posted outside her room, they ask, "How come my kid's class isn't doing that?" Parents provide the positive feedback that Ilene esteems, through which her teacher identity is socially validated. While she cannot change the differentness of her specific organizational structures from the rest of the school (i.e., the different rules and regulations applied to her), she can build a teacher identity based on a foundation of parental respect, just as the teachers of higher grade levels in her school can.

Parental respect provides Ilene with leverage to make demands of parents, which will enhance her own professional self-respect and sense of relational control. She describes refusing to fulfill parental requests for traditional care work, which are not part of her daily tasks.

We get that at the beginning of Pre-K. When they get to Pre-K, if you can say to [parents], 'This is your kid's school. Next year, you're going to drop your kid off at the front door, and they're going to walk all the way to the classroom [by themselves]. You don't get a nap schedule. When you get the lunch box back home, whatever food is in there, that's what your child did not eat. Whatever you packed, if it's gone, your child ate it. I'm not going to have a whiteboard to keep track.' I don't want to deal with that.

When roles or tasks don't meet Ilene's standards for respectable and worthwhile work activities, she responds proactively by creating more meaningful, helpful, and dignifying work experiences for herself (Hodson, 2001). She limits caretaking tasks that would make her dissimilar from her k-5 colleagues. By mirroring the design of work that her k-5 colleagues experience, Ilene both engages in organizational citizenship behaviors and safeguards dignity in her work identity. She refocuses some parents' role expectations of care onto her own occupational expectations of autonomy, where *she* determines the terms of her own work. Because she works in the same school building as where her students will attend when they are older, Ilene can defer to her work context as justification for her assertions, making her communications with parents more effective.

Ilene gets a sense of her occupational identity from the act of *asserting* her "*real* teacher" identity with parents, thereby forging more appreciative relationships with parents who have lower class positions than herself, and more egalitarian relationships with parents who share her class status position. These relationship dynamics differ from what daycare teachers experienced with parents. *Asserting* is the identity strategy Ilene and other teachers in her context used to transform the structural conditions in their work, which threaten their dignity — such as varied dynamics with a diverse parent population and being seen as separate by their colleagues who teach upper grades — into resources with which to protect themselves. Four of five teachers in our sample in public schools used this strategy to resolve identity problems they encountered at work.

Private Dayschools

Sierra Ridge School serves two-year-olds through eighth graders and has a student body of about 300. Tuition for half-day preschool and pre-k classes costs approximately $10k/year while full-time K-8 classes at the school cost over $17k/year. It is in a large brick building set near a major city street in a university neighborhood. This school, like all the private day schools in our sample, does not have NAEYC accreditation, but is accredited by

SACS. Student demographics in the classroom we visited at the school were 60% White and 30% Asian.

Cathy is a White woman in her 40s who has been teaching in early childhood for about 10 years. Before that, she worked in the design industry and initially did not intend to return to teaching after she dropped out of college, with a major in Education that she never completed. She got into the field when she had her own children, first volunteering in their preschool program. At Sierra Ridge School, Cathy's daily work entails relatively little paperwork — no fat documentation folders were in sight and anecdotal notes about students are not required. Her daily interactions with parents generally do not include parents approaching her with complaints, as administrators intercept and handle many of parents' concerns. However, teachers in this group are accustomed to competitive, highly educated parents with high academic expectations. Teachers regularly encounter parent demands for providing accelerated learning for their children. For example, a father of one of Cathy's students wanted his preschool-aged child to know fractions; another mother wanted her three-year-old daughter to read. While most settings with professional-class parent clientele must manage high expectations (including some private daycares), the private dayschool teachers we spoke to did not experience those expectations as undercutting or threatening to their authority. As another private dayschool teacher put it, the high levels of parent involvement in her school are not a burden or cause for distrust, but rather a community asset, even for the teachers (Helen). Confident in their position within high-status schools, teachers in this context creatively re-appropriate this potential identity challenge by getting parents on their side.

Rather than resolving parent-driven potential identity violations by distancing themselves from parents or relying on organizational rules, regulations, and documentation to bolster their legitimacy and authority, teachers engage with parents as fellow professionals, on an equal level.

AL: So how would you describe the kinds of parents and families at this school?

Helen: Um, they're very intelligent. They're well-educated. They're um, very engaged and very, um, how can I put this? It's very important for them to do everything they possibly can for their children. ... Um, I think in this population especially, we're respected and really um, become much more than a place to just drop off a child. We've become a part of their lives and vice-versa. ... And you know, I think, pretty much in every case where there is an issue with the parent or the family, once you scratch the surface, you get it. If there's a problem with us and they figure out what we're up to, and we talk through it, they get it and they're all things that can be resolved, because we all want the same thing.

Private dayschool teachers, in instances when they do talk directly to parents about the parents' concerns, "talk through it" with parents. It isn't that private dayschool teachers never experience parents as pushy or as testing their authority. Helen, for example, acknowledges that parents taking issue with teachers' teaching styles is a common frustration teachers experience in their work. But private dayschool teachers mostly easily resolve these potential conflicts by expressing their professional knowledge about developmentally appropriate curriculum and pedagogy (i.e., what is taught and how it is taught, respectively). Directors of private dayschools advise their teachers to promote themselves, to be proactive in parent/teacher relations, and, as full members of their high-status school communities, they are able to do this mostly seamlessly. For Patricia, who teaches in a school like Cathy's, this means engaging in "parent education:"

> I think a lot of the parent education we do is around the value of play that's more child-initiated, that even at home if they set aside just 20 minutes to follow their children's leads — but I think what happens, Amanda, as they're in the classroom and they watch it happening, then it's like, 'oh, so this is what it could be like.' But we put an inordinate amount of time and energy into our initial parent-teacher meeting and we show in lots of different ways the value of play both for the cognitive growth but also for the development of ideas, learning how to describe what it is they're doing, what it is they're feeling, that sort of social emotional growth. That's so important because unless that has been given a solid foundation, then they [i.e., parents] are not really open for the rest.

As Patricia's comment makes clear, parent education requires administrative and collegial support. Trusted administrators and colleagues were part of the re-appropriation process, in that they encouraged it and validated one another. As Sherrell noted, despite her occasional trip to the principal's office when parents in her class have registered a complaint, she has walked away from those meetings with feedback that confirmed that engaging with parents was part of the job. The principal urged her to see the complaint as part of the process rather than as a threat to one's own occupational competence. Sherrell also finds validation from the peer group of teachers she belongs to, noting that she welcomes parent pop-in visits, "because I'm comfortable in myself and my team that we're doing a good job and we have nothing to hide." Thus teachers in private schools not only operate with high levels of institutional legitimacy but also have supervisors and coworkers who back them up. The teachers do not experience the need to defensively assert their authority with parents, or engage in protective limiting in their relationships with parents.

Here we label private dayschool teachers' identity strategy as *broadening*. We adopt Wrzesniewski and Dutton's (2001) terminology here, as it denotes a widening of relational boundaries teachers set around their work. This is similar to Pratt et al.'s (2006) concept of identity enriching, an identity construction process through which professionals gradually come to recognize what their job entails, and embrace it. Through deploying this identity strategy of *broadening*, private dayschool early childhood teachers come to view parents not as a threat to the job but as part of the job. The term *broadening* thus captures how teacher's work identity gets extended beyond the initial service population so that the understanding of the boundaries of one's work gets expanded. In the context of *broadening*, parent behavior that in other contexts often produces a sense of identity-related denials of dignity becomes expected, manageable, and potentially helpful.

Five of the six teachers in our private school sample use an identity strategy of *broadening*. *Broadening* involves teachers more fully identifying with their employing organization and the community it serves, and having a broader social engagement with both their colleagues and with parents than do teachers in the other contexts. These teachers draw on one of the key resources of their organizational contexts, the members of the organization they are embedded in (parents, administrators, and colleagues), to recover from any challenges they face to their occupational dignity. These teachers respond to the wider societal cultural conditions that potentially devalue their work (which a few teachers spoke of) by expanding the limits of their relational boundaries with service-recipients (here, parents), and more fully identifying with the high-status employing organization and its clientele. Also, because these teachers do not face the daily, local challenges other teachers face, and because their work is not characterized by heavy paperwork, accreditation rules, or school regulations (see Table 2), broadening is the only strategy they need. The threats to dignity they encounter are more vague and abstract than those faced by ECE teachers in other contexts.

DISCUSSION

In this paper, we investigate how different school organizational contexts shape what kinds of identity challenges early childhood teachers experience on the job and what kinds of identity strategies they develop to recover their dignity at work. Different organizational contexts not only subject teachers to different threats to their work-related identity but also have different potential identity resources embedded within them that teachers can use on their own behalf. Thus, while all the early childhood educators we interviewed at some level struggle with being employed within a devalued occupation, the identity strategies they develop to protect their self-worth varied across employment contexts. We show that the strategies these interactive service workers use to solve identity-related problems of dignity at work involve the creative conversion of constraints they face at work into resources that help them achieve valued work identities.

Interestingly, while the nature of early childhood educators' interactive service work put them in relation to multiple groups (coworkers, managers, parents, students) on a daily basis, some were much more likely to be a source of identity challenge than others. For example, teachers in our full sample did not very often cite students as sources of either identity problems or dignity protection. Thus, students were not seen by teachers as a source of challenge or as identity resources to safeguard dignity in their work. A vast majority of teachers spoke affectionately of their students (89%), and rarely reported students as a source of stress (22%). On the other hand, overall, teachers did not report very often that students themselves made their work interesting, meaningful, or enjoyable, with the exception of dayschool teachers (64% vs. 25% of daycare teachers). Thus, while teachers routinely stated that they loved their students, this intrinsic reward did not appear to translate into a structural condition that teachers saw as an identity resource for safeguarding their dignity.

Neither did teachers very often cite abusive or incompetent management as a source of devaluation at work. Consistent with Hodson's study of administrative workers and waitresses (1991) and Leidner's study of insurance agents and McDonalds workers (1993), we find that struggles for control at work did not often play out as a direct clash between workers and managers, but as diffuse and symbolic (and sometimes concrete) struggles between workers and service-recipients (here, parents).[8] To manage these challenges, we find that all teachers re-appropriated structural constraints in their working conditions into resources with which to protect themselves from assaults to their dignity. Specifically, teachers in public daycare settings use the strategy of *showcasing*, and those in private daycare settings use the strategy of *subscribing*, leveraging organizational structures such as paperwork, accreditation rules, certification procedures, or curriculum guidelines to restore status lost to them in their interactions with parents. On the other hand, teachers in public and private schools use strategies of *asserting* and *broadening*, respectively, in efforts to restore status lost to them by being excluded from the wider upper-grades teacher communities, or to leverage their authority and inclusion with parent communities, respectively.

We find that across the sample, teachers perceive the bureaucratic structures so rampant in the field of education − that is, paperwork, documentation, accreditation, certification, and curriculum requirements – differently. We think this reveals something interesting about the relationship between workers' race/class match/mismatch with their service-recipients (i.e., both students and parents), and workers' attitudes about clerical aspects of work life. For daycare teachers, paperwork and accreditation-related requirements functioned as tools of resistance, which meant that teachers neither had to withdraw from the organization's rules and management, nor directly challenge the parents. They could salvage pride in their work, by fulfilling paperwork or teacher evaluation requirements (sometimes to a "t") and by satisfying parents' demands without being completely controlled by them. In this way, the teachers remained "model citizens" in their workplaces, even when unappreciative parents, dangerous parents, or overwork (from the quantity of paperwork or numbers of children in their class) contended against a sense of control and dignity in their work. For dayschool teachers, neither school-regulated paperwork nor accreditation- and certification-related requirements assisted in changing their work identity to be more valued; moreover, for the private school teachers, the presence of such requirements was virtually nonexistent. Teachers in school settings appeared to have more leverage with parents because of their shared class and/or race position with parents, possibly making their control strategies less noticeable and more effective than strategies that use a bureaucratic work-around to manage asymmetric status interactions (Gengler, 2012).

In the course of analyzing transcripts by context, we also noticed that there were cases of teachers who did not fit the general identity strategies typical for their context. For exceptions like these, we explored what might account for variation within facilities. Space limitations have prevented us from presenting material on variations in identity strategies within each of the types of schools we have studied but it is important to note that we did indeed find variations. These variations often seemed to stem from a teacher's relative social class background diverging from their clientele's. This status gap led workers to perceive different challenges and employ slightly different variations on the strategies.

Implications for Theory and Future Research

Building upon literature that documents the strategies workers use to resist denials of dignity at work, our data illustrates how even within a single occupation, very different work settings lead to different work-related identity strategies. Future research should explore whether and how identity strategies are kept or changed when workers transition workplaces within an occupation, as well as the role of emotion in the strategies workers use to defend themselves against denials of dignity at work, or estrangement at work (see also Hochschild, 2011).

More generally, our findings can be used to generate hypotheses for expected variation in worker responses to their experiences in other occupations and fields. The structural features underlying the variations in our observations included the presence of a "quadrilateral" model of control. This configuration includes a two-pronged service-recipient: one who makes the decisions about the service (which we will call the "service-decider"), and the other who receives the actual service (the "service-experiencer"). This arrangement produces something akin to a principal-agent problem between the service-decider and the worker, where the worker (agent) has asymmetric information about the service-experiencer and the service-decider (principal) gauges how much to trust the worker and, when necessary, takes steps to limit the worker's power (such as by going over her/his head and complaining to the manager). Such tugs-of-war for control may result, in other occupations as in this one, in the actual receiver of the services not being focal to how the worker builds and protects her/his work identity. When the relational structures underlying one's work are fraught with a principal-agent conflict, then we might expect other structural constraints in the work (such as paperwork or certification regulations, or even service-decider involvement itself) to become assets for workers, which they repurpose for the protection of themselves as valued workers. Based on our findings, conflict is higher where service-deciders and workers have dissimilar status backgrounds. Where the service-decider and the worker have more equivalent statuses (e.g., their social class and/or racial statuses), we expect principal-agent conflict to be lower in this case and for the service-deciders to be a vital resource for workers to reaffirm valued work identities for themselves.

Implications for Policy

One clear lesson from our data is that early childhood educators experience a number of challenges that stem from the general devaluation of their work. The group in our data who experienced the fewest threats to their identity were teachers in high-status private schools who, while they recognized that there is general cultural disdain for teachers of very young children in the culture at large, personally derived relative status protection from their identities (and organizational experience) as teachers within a well-funded and highly regarded school. Unlike public pre-k teachers whose working conditions were better than daycare workers but far worse than the k-5 teachers in their schools (mirroring paraprofessionals), these private dayschool teachers operated as full members within their communities (including pay, benefits, support for the classroom, etc.). These teachers' experiences remind us that while it might be difficult to shift cultural dispositions towards education generally and teaching young children in particular, improving the conditions of work would go far to improving teacher's experiences, reducing their identity challenges on the job, and potentially drawing higher-skilled workers to the profession. Even if we are not concerned about the working conditions of these largely female teaching corps, growing scientific recognition about the importance of educational experiences during early childhood for long-term brain development and educational success should challenge us to think differently about how this work is organized and rewarded. Widespread calls for universal pre-k will likely prove less effective than they might otherwise be if teachers in early childhood classrooms continue to be treated as care-workers rewarded with long hours, low pay, and significant challenges to dignity.

Limitations

As a cross-sectional, exploratory study, this study cannot make claims as to how the process of identity-formation strategies and the ensuing role enactments unfold over time. A longitudinal design may be better suited for this purpose. In addition, causal claims cannot be made as to what types of strategies for building work identities lead to the optimal performance outcomes (in terms of teacher work behaviors or organizational performance). Future research should attempt to strengthen the link between identity and practice by investigating a fuller range of worker narratives and behaviors within a work context with a larger sample and more fieldwork.

CONCLUSION

In conclusion, this is a study about how teachers who encounter challenges to their identity at work recover their dignity. Depending on the nature of the challenge and teachers' social position vis-à-vis their service-recipients, teachers will transform the identity problem they face into resources to resolve the problem. Drawing on interviews with early childhood teachers, we add to ongoing conversations in the occupational identity literature by showing how work identities are constructed within a single, devalued occupation across both high and low-status work environments. By bringing in teachers' perspectives on the organizational strains and supports they encounter in their workplaces, this study underscores that the work context influences identity strategies that Early Childhood Education workers use to build their work identities. We find that workers navigate their work identities by searching for the "open roads" for identity repair or enhancement that are possible within the constraints and available resources of a particular work environment.

One major finding of this paper is that workers can transform constraints into resources, at least as they apply to their identity-related problems. Educators, like other workers, are creative in their efforts to protect their dignity at work. Ideally, however, we might push to reduce potential denials of dignity by valuing and rewarding the work of teachers generally and early childhood educators more highly. Not only is the work that teachers do critical, but also there is a growing body of evidence that when teaching itself is highly regarded, the overall quality of teaching improves along with educational "outputs" – student success (see Sahlberg, 2010 on the "Finnish miracle"). Current political and societal concerns about defining and evaluating teacher quality in schools at all levels could benefit from understanding that developing quality workers may depend on cultivating workplace environments that at minimum protect workers from identity challenges and facilitate development of a strong sense of self-worth on the job.

NOTES

1. In Hodson's (2001) theory of dignity, there are also denials of dignity that are unrelated to identity. For example, mismanagement is one type of denial of dignity, and can include the absence of on-the-job training or poor scheduling skills, which have less direct implications for a worker's identity than managers criticizing an employee publicly. Each type of denial of dignity can take identity-related and identity-unrelated forms.

2. We do not include any license-exempt child care programs in our sample. While the U.S. Department of Human Services estimates that 15% of children receive care in settings legally operating without regulation, in Georgia, only one percent fall into this category (Administration for Children and Families, Office of Child Care, 2013). We did, however, have a couple teachers in our sample who worked in what sounds like unregulated facilities earlier in their early childhood careers. In both cases, the teachers described strenuous, stressful working conditions

and mismanagement (e.g., out-of-ratio classrooms or dishonest communications with parents at the organizational level). From their responses, we predict that teachers from these settings may respond to identity challenges by resisting management and allying with parents, drawing upon parents' resources to meet classroom needs.

3. Interviews were audio-recorded and transcribed, except for three of the interviews, when the teacher declined to be recorded (two teachers) or the recorder failed (one teacher). In these cases copious notes were taken.

4. Although the authors did not conduct interviews and field work together, we use the pronoun "we" throughout this paper for the sake of consistency. All participant names are pseudonyms.

5. Though some of the private dayschools do provide limited financial aid to families.

6. The fourth facility, Bainbrook, is different because only a portion of its programming is non-tuition based, which is less typical of public early childhood settings.

7. We contend that Gabrielle's work experiences are par for the course among private daycare teachers, as Rachel and Riley, teachers with less experience but who have their Bachelor's degrees, expressed mostly similar identity problems, resources and strategies as Gabrielle.

8. An example of a diffuse and symbolic struggle for control can be seen in cases of private daycare teachers who engage in "making out" when they conceal information from parents (Hodson, 1991).

ACKNOWLEDGMENTS

We would like to thank Linda Quirke, Beth Bechky, Richard Rubinson, Steven Vallas, and the anonymous reviewers for their helpful comments on earlier drafts of this paper, and participants' feedback at three conferences where we presented the paper: the Northwestern Ethnography conference (2014); the Sociology of Education Association conference (2015); and the American Sociological Association conference (2015).

REFERENCES

Administration for Children and Families, Office of Child Care. (2013). *FY 2013 preliminary data Table 4: Average monthly percentages of children served in regulated settings vs. settings legally operating without regulation.* Washington, DC: U.S. Department of Health and Human Services. Retrieved from http://www.acf.hhs.gov/programs/occ/resource/fy-2013-ccdf-data-tables-preliminary-table-4. Accessed on November 30, 2015.

Albert, S., & Whetten, D. A. (1985). Organizational identity. *Research in Organizational Behavior, 7,* 263–295. Greenwich, CT: JAI Press.

Alvesson, M., & Willmott, H. (2002). Identity regulation as organizational control: Producing the appropriate individual. *Journal of Management Studies, 39*, 619–644.

Ashcraft, K. L. (2007). Appreciating the 'work' of discourse: Occupational identity and difference as organizing mechanisms in the case of commercial airline pilots. *Discourse & Communication, 1*(1), 9–36.

Ashforth, B. E., Spencer, H. H., & Kevin, G. C. (2008). Identification in organizations: An examination of four fundamental questions. *Journal of Management, 34*(3), 325–374.

Blair-Loy, M. (2009). *Competing devotions: Career and family among women executives.* Cambridge, MA: Harvard University Press.

Boden, D. (1994). *The business of talk: Organizations in action.* Cambridge, UK: Polity Press.

Burawoy, M. (1979). *Manufacturing consent: Changes in the labor process under monopoly capitalism.* Chicago: University of Chicago Press.

Cerulo, K. A. (1997). Identity construction: New issues, new directions. *Annual Review of Sociology, 23*, 385–409.

Charmaz, K. (1983). The grounded theory method: An explication and interpretation. In R. M. Emerson (Ed.), *Contemporary field research: A collection of readings.* Boston, MA: Little, Brown and Co.

Chen, A. S. (1999). Lives at the center of the periphery, lives at the periphery of the center Chinese American Masculinities and bargaining with hegemony. *Gender & Society, 13*(5), 584–607.

Cohen, R. C., & Sutton, R. I. (1998). Clients as a source of enjoyment on the job: How hairstylists shape demeanor and personal disclosures. *Advances in Qualitative Organization Research, 32*, 1–32.

Davies, S., & Quirke, L. (2007). The impact of sector on school organizations: Institutional and market logics. *Sociology of Education, 80*(1), 66–89.

DiMaggio, P. (1987). Classification in art. *American Sociological Review, 52*, 440–455.

Dutton, J., Debebe, G., & Wrzesniewski, A. (2014). Being valued and devalued at work: A social valuing perspective. In *Qualitative organizational research.* Charlotte, NC: Information Age Publishing.

Elsbach, K. D. (2004). Interpreting workplace identities: The role of office decor. *Journal of Organizational Behavior, 25*(1), 99–128.

England, P. (1992). *Comparable worth: Theories and evidence.* New York, NY: Walter de Gruyter.

England, P., Herbert, M. S., Kilbourne, B. S., Reid, L. L., & Megdal, L. M. (1994). The gendered valuation of occupations and skills: Earnings in 1980 census occupations. *Social Forces, 73*(1), 65–100.

Entwistle, D. R., Alexander, K., & Olson, L. (1997). *Children, schools, and inequality.* Boulder, CO: Westview.

Etzioni, A. (1969). *The semi-professions and their organisation.* New York, NY: Free Press.

Freidson, E. (2001). *Professionalism, the third logic: On the practice of knowledge.* Cambridge, UK: University of Chicago Press.

Friedland, R., & Alford, R. R. (1991). Bringing society back in: Symbols, practices and institutional contradictions. In W. W. Powell & P. DiMaggio (Eds.), *The new institutionalism in organizational analysis* (pp. 232–263). Chicago, IL: University of Chicago Press.

Fuller, B., Loeb, S., Strath, A., & Carrol, B. A. (2004). State formation of the child care sector: Family demand and policy action. *Sociology of Education, 77*(4), 337–358.

Gecas, V., & Schwalbe, M. L. (1983). Beyond the looking-glass self: Social structure and efficacy-based self-esteem. *Social Psychology Quarterly, 46*, 77–88.

Gengler, A. M. (2012). Defying (Dis) empowerment in a battered women's shelter: Moral rhetorics, intersectionality, and processes of control and resistance. *Social Problems*, *59*(4), 501–521.

Glenn, E. N. (1992). From servitude to service work: Historical continuities in the racial division of paid reproductive labor. *Signs*, *18*(1), 1–43.

Glynn, M. A. (2008). Beyond constraint: How institutions enable identities. In *The Sage handbook of organizational institutionalism* (pp. 413–430). Los Angeles: Sage.

Hackman, J. R., & Oldham, G. R. (1980). *Work redesign*. Reading, MA: Addison-Wesley.

Head Start Act Section 648A. (2007). Retrieved from http://eclkc.ohs.acf.hhs.gov/hslc/tta-system/pd/fsd/All%20Staff/Sec648AStaff.htm. Accessed on December 18, 2015.

Hochschild, A. (2011). Emotional life on the market frontier. *Annual Review of Sociology*, *37*, 21–33.

Hochschild, A. R. (1983). *The managed heart: The commercialization of feeling*. Berkeley, CA: University of California Press.

Hodson, R. (1991). THE ACTIVE WORKER: Compliance and autonomy at the workplace. *Journal of Contemporary Ethnography*, *20*(1), 47–78.

Hodson, R. (1995). Worker resistance: An underdeveloped concept in the sociology of work. *Economic and Industrial Democracy*, *16*(1), 79–110.

Hodson, R. (2001). *Dignity at work*. Cambridge, MA: Cambridge University Press.

Hughes, E. C. (1971). *The sociological eye: Selected papers*. New Brunswick, NJ: Transaction publishers.

Hughes, E. C., & Coser, L. A. (1994). *On work, race, and the sociological imagination*. Chicago: University of Chicago Press.

Kim, M. (2013). Constructing occupational identities: How female preschool teachers develop professionalism. *Universal Journal of Educational Research*, *1*(4), 309–331.

Kunda, G. (2006). *Engineering culture: Control and commitment in a high-tech corporation*. Philadelphia, PA: Temple University Press.

Lareau, A. (1989). Family-school relationships: A view from the classroom. *Educational Policy*, *3*(3), 245–259.

Lareau, A. (2000). *Home advantage*. Lanham, MD: Rowman and Littlefield.

Leidner, R. (1993). *Fast food, fast talk: Service work and the routinization of everyday life*. Berkeley, CA: University of California Press.

Lewis, A. E., & Forman, T. A. (2002). Contestation or collaboration? A comparative study of home–school relations. *Anthropology & Education Quarterly*, *33*(1), 60–89.

Lofland, J., Snow, D., Anderson, L., & Lofland, L. H. (2006). *Analyzing social settings*. Belmont, CA: Wadsworth Publishing Company.

Lortie, D. (2002 [1975]). *Schoolteacher: A sociological study*. Chicago, IL: University of Chicago Press.

Maroto, M. L. (2011). Professionalizing body art: A marginalized occupational group's use of informal and formal strategies of control. *Work and Occupations*, *38*(1), 101–138.

Meyer, J. W., & Rowan, B. (1977). Institutionalized organizations: Formal structure as myth and ceremony. *American Journal of Sociology*, *83*, 340–363.

Miles, M. B., Huberman, A. M., & Saldaña, J. (2013). *Qualitative data analysis: A methods sourcebook*. Los Angeles, CA: SAGE Publications. Incorporated.

Pratt, M. G., Rockmann, K. W., & Kaufmann, J. B. (2006). Constructing professional identity: The role of work and identity learning cycles in the customization of identity among medical residents. *Academy of Management Journal*, *49*(2), 235–262.

Reskin, B. F. (1988). Bringing the men back in: Sex differentiation and the devaluation of women's work. *Gender & Society*, *2*(1), 58–81.

Rogers, J. K. (2000). *Temps: The many faces of the changing workplace*. Cornell University Press.

Roy, D. (1959). 'Banana Time': Job satisfaction and informal interaction. *Human Organization*, *18*(4), 158–168.

Sahlberg, P. (2010). The secret to Finland's success: Educating teachers. *Stanford Center for Opportunity Policy in Education Research Brief*. September 2010. Retrieved from https://edpolicy.stanford.edu/sites/default/files/publications/secret-finland's-success-educating-teachers.pdf. Accessed on March 14, 2016.

Scott, J. C. (2008). *Weapons of the weak: Everyday forms of peasant resistance*. New Haven, CT: Yale University Press.

Seeman, M. (1959). On the meaning of alienation. *American Sociological Review*, *24*, 783–791.

Sell, K., Skimmons, R., & Blewitt, P. (2013). Teachers' characteristics and low income preschoolers' elaborative word knowledge. Annual meetings of the Eastern Psychological Association, New York, NY.

Selznick, P. (1957). *Leadership in administration*. New York, NY: Harper and Row.

Snow, D. A., & Anderson, L. (1987). Identity work among the homeless: The verbal construction and avowal of personal identities. *American Journal of Sociology*, *92*(6), 1336–1371.

Spradley, J. (1979). *The ethnographic interview*. Belmont, CA: Wadsworth.

Stets, J. E., & Burke, P. J. (2000). Identity theory and social identity theory. *Social Psychology Quarterly*, 224–237.

Uttal, L. (2002). *Making care work: Employed mothers in the new childcare market*. New Brunswick, NJ: Rutgers University Press.

Van Ausdale, D., & Feagin, J. R. (2001). *The First R: How children learn race and racism*. Lanham, MD: Rowman & Littlefield Publishers.

Walsh, K., & Gordan, J. R. (2008). Creating an individual work identity. *Human Resource Management Review*, *18*(1), 46–61.

Wilkins, A. C. (2008). *Wannabes, goths, and Christians: The boundaries of sex, style, and status*. Chicago: University of Chicago Press.

Wrigley, J. (1995). *Other people's children*. AZ: Basic Books.

Wrzesniewski, A., & Dutton, J. E. (2001). Crafting a job: Revisioning employees as active crafters of their work. *Academy of Management Review*, *26*(2), 179–201.

PART II
AUTHORITY AND CONTROL
AT WORK

JOB AUTHORITY AND STRATIFICATION BELIEFS

George Wilson and Vincent J. Roscigno

ABSTRACT

Sociological research on work and job authority, while most often high-lighting the material implications of workplace status, has largely over-looked the implications of experiential aspects of work for broader orientations toward the social world including, most poignantly, stratifi-cation beliefs. Building on classic and contemporary statements regard-ing the centrality of workplace experiences, and utilizing data from the 2012 General Social Survey, we analyze job authority specifically and its consequences for general beliefs surrounding inequality. Results, which account for a variety of other status attributes and material benefits of employment, demonstrate how authority tasks, especially in concert with authority tenure, shape traditionally conservative ideological stances, specifically: (1) restrictive support for socioeconomic redistributive pol-icy, and; (2) perceptions of the functional necessity of socioeconomic inequality. These patterns are robust in the face of controls, though tend to be stronger among Whites and private sector workers compared to African American and public sector workers. Our findings inform inequality scholarship by highlighting the significance of workplace experiences for stratification worldviews and arguably support for redis-tributive policy. They also extend the sociology of work literature by

Research in the Sociology of Work, Volume 29, 75–97
Copyright © 2016 by Emerald Group Publishing Limited
All rights of reproduction in any form reserved
ISSN: 0277-2833/doi:10.1108/S0277-283320160000029014

relating how workplace experiences are carried into the broader social world.

Keywords: Authority; stratification; ideology; workplace

Empirical research over the past few decades has produced a relatively stable consensus about job authority and its relation to status, identity and class position in advanced post-industrial societies (Dahrendorf, 1959; Wright, 1985). Undertaking authority tasks – that is, exercising supervision over the status, rewards and task assignments of others as well as developing and implementing business and personnel policies (Smith, 2003; Wilson, 1997) – is, in fact, positively related to personal/family outcomes through income acquisition, wealth possession and the inter-generational transmission of status (Conley, 1999; Smith, 2002; Wilson, 1997). Additionally, having and exercising job authority has implications for the opportunity trajectories of others (i.e., by dictating whom to hire, fire, promote) (McGuire, 2000; Smith, 2003, 1997; Wilson, 1997) and for the directions and futures of firms (Dahrendorf, 1959; Halaby & Weakliem, 1993).

There may be additional and no less profound implications of workplace authority, however – implications that have yet to be adequately theorized or empirically explored. Foremost among these, we suggest below, are potential consequences for interpretations of inequality in general and what those interpretations mean for action in the broader political realm. Specifically, we are referring to general stratification beliefs, how they may be shaped heavily (if not forged) within the context of employment, and with genuine consequences for interpretations surrounding the distribution of opportunity and inequality.

Research over the last few decades (Hochschild, 1995; McCall, 2013) has been informative in the aforementioned regards, albeit with some conceptual variation in attention to, for instance, distributive justice (Della-Fave, 1998; Kluegel & Smith, 1986), causal attributions for socioeconomic fate (Hochschild, 1995; Hunt, 1996) and support for socioeconomic redistributive policies (Bobo & Kluegel, 1993; Wilson, 2001). Such interpretations of inequality have "real world" consequences, impacting support for social policies not limited to reforms aimed at limiting the size and scope of government (McCall, 2013), government entitlement programs including welfare (Edsall & Edsall, 1991; Lee, Jones, & Lewis, 1990) and the structure of the U.S. tax code (Edsall & Edsall, 1991). But from where do such interpretations derive? Might experiences of hierarchy and authority within the context of employment especially play a role? Such questions point to a "critical" shortcoming in the understanding of stratification beliefs, as alluded to by a growing number of studies in sociology and psychology (Shelton & Wilson, 2012); namely, that underlying foundations and causal underpinnings to stratification beliefs have been narrow in scope, seldom theorized, and rarely analyzed in systematic fashion (DiTomaso & Parks-Yancy, 2014; Hunt, 2014).

Daily experiences within core institutional domains, most notably workplace, have been suggested as arguably important (Dallinger, 2010; Hunt, 2014; Shelton & Wilson, 2012). To be sure, material rewards, self-interest and their relation to workplace authority are part of the answer (see for instance Bobo & Kluegel, 1993; Form & Huber, 1973; Gilens, 1999; Steele, 2015). Yet, following classic work in the field, such as Kohn's (1969) insights on "social structure and personality" as well as Ridgeway's (2000, 2001) attention to status reproduction and interaction, there is ample reason to suspect that the impact of authority encounters on stratification beliefs runs deeper and may be tied to experiential aspects of work.

This article builds on classic and contemporary statements on the centrality of work and workplace experiences to identity and worldviews, and analyzes the link between job authority and stratification beliefs. We draw from the 2012 General Social Survey (GSS) to examine how job authority tasks shapes adherence to two crucial tenets of beliefs about the inequality system, namely: (1) levels of support for income redistribution policy and (2) perceptions of the functional necessity of socioeconomic inequality. We also consider authority tenure and its interplay with authority tasks. Such foci, and specifically our grounding within the key institutional, hierarchical, and interactive domain of work, reflect an important extension of inequality scholarship − scholarship that has merely scratched the surface when it comes to the institutional and interactional foundations undergirding beliefs. Equally pertinent are the implications for the sociology of work literature − literature that has been especially insightful in highlighting the material consequences of workplace status, yet somewhat shortsighted when it comes to recognizing the significance of workplace interactions, social relations, and experiences for more general worldviews and orientations.

WORKPLACE EXPERIENCES AND
STRATIFICATION BELIEFS

The possible connection between workplace experiences and stratification beliefs, particularly in relation to the question of job authority, is informed by a rich tradition of theorizing stretching back to the classics. We highlight such work below, as well as three distinct and non-mutually exclusive streams of empirical research that has begun to pinpoint the very processes by which hierarchical workplace relations and particularly authority may be meaningful.

Marx's (1965) dictum that "as man labors so he is," expressed in *The German Ideology* (1965), constitutes the historical materialist emphasis about the centrality of work for worldviews and inequality orientations. Specifically, class-based laboring in the sphere of production encompasses "fundamental aspects of self," according to Marx, and extends to sentiments that justify privileged position (Giddens, 1970). Weber (1968) similarly maintains that work and the hierarchical experiences it often entails are crucial for meaning-making and a source of orientation for politically laden, position-based norms. Finally, Durkheim (1984, p. 106), in the *Division of Labor in Society*, maintains that "occupational groupings" in highly differentiated societies are characterized by distinct mechanisms of socialization that "provide orientations toward the political world," such that "groups who are most well-off encounter others in a fashion from which derives the development of a privileged sense of selves and general attitudes that reinforce it."

Alongside such foundational statements, several other well-known discussions of workplace inequality explicitly or implicitly tie job authority to the development of ideological orientations toward the world that, presumably, extend to the more specific realm of stratification beliefs. Mills, for instance, in *White Collar* (1951) maintains that managerial positions are conducive to the creation of a distinctive "ethos of White collarism that encompasses unique worldviews." Tilly similarly maintains in *Durable Inequality* (1998) that a "fundamental and intractable source of value dissensus" is created by the categorical distinction "managers versus workers."[1] Such theoretical speculation, to be sure, offers an important sociological base for thinking about workplace hierarchical authority in relation to generalized beliefs. Three related but more specific streams of research — research on job conditions, hierarchical interactions, and managerial tasks — offer further leverage and insight on when it comes to plausible and non-mutually exclusive mechanisms undergirding such relations.

Stratification Beliefs as a Consequence of Job Conditions

Subsumed under the "social structure and personality" school (Kohn, 1969, 1983; Lorence & Mortimer, 1985), several streams of work offer some support for Marx's contention that "man makes himself" through the manner in which he labors. Most notable here is the important work of Kohn (1969), who takes seriously how and why job conditions might structure "conceptions of self in society." His analyses of the socializing role of performing job tasks – tasks that are non-routinized, substantively complex and that require high levels of "intellective functioning" with the development of self-directed (versus conforming) orientations toward the world generally – provide an important launch point for taking job conditions seriously. As Kohn himself (1969, p. 31) concludes in his classic work, *Class and Conformity* (1969), attitudinal outcomes extend to the development of sociopolitical orientations:

> Among those laboring in white collar work ... The most reasonable hypothesis is that in industrialized society, where work is central to people's lives, what people do in their work directly affects their values, their conceptions of self, and their orientation to the world around them—"I do therefore I am." Hence, work at this class level leaves a fundamental imprint on value orientations ... that we speculate may well extend to general sociopolitical beliefs as Marx long ago asserted.

Stratification Beliefs through Hierarchical Interactions

A second approach, found within several strands of the work and inequality literature, including "status generalization" (Berger, Bert, & Zeldich, 1972; Pugh & Wahrmann, 1983; Ridgeway, 2000, 2006; Ridgeway & Correll, 2006) and "social identity" theory (Stryker & Burke, 2000; Tajfel & Turner, 1979; Turner & Oates, 1986), assumes an interactionist perspective and highlights the potential spillover of hierarchical workplace encounters. Status generalization theory points to the fact that hierarchical regimes in the workplace are reproduced through interpersonal relations among those occupying divergent positions. Attributions regarding the self and others are seen as emanating from such interactions – interactions wherein a privileged occupational position constitutes a hierarchically-based "master status" (Berger et al., 1972). To the extent that authority and power infuses workplace relations, and is fortified through repeated and prolonged interactions, attributions and the internalizing of relative competence and status will result. As Ridgeway (2001) implies, this can include sociopolitical attitudes, particularly among those who experience ongoing interactions within the context of privileged occupational positions.

Social identity theory, in a somewhat similar vein, has suggested that individuals are intrinsically motivated to achieve "positive distinctiveness" (Tajfel & Turner, 1979) and strive for a "positive self-concept." Significantly, categorical distinctions in the workplace, most notably "management versus worker," contribute to behaviorally favoring the in-group as well as identifying and internalizing its values. This may, of course, extend to values in the broader sociopolitical realm, especially when such values have the effect of legitimizing one's own self-concept.

Stratification Beliefs as a Function of Managerial Tasks

Dahrendorf's (1959) analysis of the class structure of advanced capitalist societies is perhaps the most explicit when it comes to the dynamics of authority attainment. Acknowledging the fundamental divorce between ownership and management in advanced capitalist societies, he posits that class position can traced to one's placement in the authority structure. Indeed, the distribution of authority within firms is increasingly meaningful in the contemporary era, and constitutes "imperatively coordinated associations."

The distinction between those wielding authority and those who do not is the basis underlying the core dichotomy between the "command class" and "obey class." Members of the command class perform managerial functions – that is, ensuring profitability as well as controlling and sanctioning subordinates – in the interest of ownership and, according to Dahrendorf, thus identify with owners as a direct function of the amount of authority exercised and the length of time authority is exercised over the work career. This identification "entails the most fundamental aspects of social and political beliefs," resulting in the adoption of inequality interpretations that resemble the owners whose firms they manage.

Empirical Support and Expectations: Authority and Beliefs

Classic theoretical statements as well as more specific attention to the experiential pathways through which workplace hierarchy may matter, discussed thus far, offer important foundational leverage for the few empirical studies (Corbeta & Pasuele, 2013; Hodson, 2001; Kitschfelt & Rehm, 2014; Lee, 2007; Leicht & Fennell, 2001) that most directly focus on job authority and stratification beliefs. Based on their distillation of studies, Kitschfelt and Rehm (2014, p. 1675) suggest that:

> There is a connection between occupational experiences among those directing others and sociopolitical attitudes that appear to be one of generalization and transposition from one important sphere of life—work—to others, and especially from private experiences ... People apply the kinds of reasoning, heuristics and problem-solving techniques they learn and use at work in all realms of life.

The three potential pathways through which authority experiences may matter − that is, work conditions, hierarchical interactions and managerial functions − are represented in these empirical studies. Moreover, the pathways are not mutually exclusive and, in fact, can operate simultaneously through interactions and experiences that are both "vertical" and "horizontal" in character (Kitschfelt & Rehm, 2014; Roscigno, Lopez, & Hodson, 2009).

Hodson (2001), in his analyses of a nationally representative sub-sample of managers, finds that: (1) ensuring efficient firm operations at the organizational level, and; (2) incentivizing and inducing performance at the individual level in conjunction with organizational forces, including historically-based "inertia and cultural conservatism" of firms, are associated with "deeply-entrenched" firm level suspicion of labor that is generalized to the broader American labor market. Similarly, Lee (2007), in a sample of managers and executives, finds that the task of sanctioning and directing subordinates constitutes "a role through which identification with the political values of elites are internalized and accepted." Finally, Kitschfelt and Rehm's (2014) analyses of a sample of managers and executives from the European Social Survey reveal that "ensuring and communicating" with owners that financial ends are being met and sanctioning employees to induce productivity and better performance are highly associated with low levels of support for income redistribution policy and the belief that opportunities for economic advancement are abundant.

The importance of work conditions and the hierarchical nature of authority-related interactions to stratification beliefs emerge, perhaps most explicitly, from studies by Kitschfelt and Rehm (2014) and Corbeta and Pasquele (2013). These studies combine foci consistent with status expectations theory and social identity theory as well as the class-based labor approach by Kohn, described earlier. The core emphases include: ambiguity in problem resolution; whether sanctioning of employees is unilateral of negotiated; the extent to which status boundaries with subordinates are clear-cut; complexity of problem solving in performing job tasks; and the amount of authority tasks performed and length of time over the work career performing them.

To be sure, the research we are describing focuses on the first four of these tasks. Corbeta and Pasquele (2013), for instance, find in their cross-national analyses of managers that the greater the status differences between managers and those they sanction as well as the more that sanctioning is unilaterally imposed with no negotiation or input from the sanctioned, the more likely managers are to express skepticism about the propriety of redistributing rewards in the workplace and income in the broader society. Similarly, Kitschfelt and Rehm's (2014) analyses of a sample of managers and executives from the European Social Survey reach several noteworthy conclusions regarding the horizontal dimension: more ambiguity as well as complexity in resolving problems with subordinates, especially when advanced analytic skills must be invoked, are highly correlated with increased support for income redistribution policy and the view that there are structural barriers to economic advancement. Notably, however, such studies have paid less systematic attention to the fifth dimension, noted above and the core focus of our analyses below — namely, amount of authority tasks and authority tasks in conjunction with tenure.

Classical theoretical statements and contemporary perspectives, which have been more explicit regarding why the experiential nature of work and authority should be of relevance to inequality orientations, offer a strong foundation for our expectations. Most explicitly, we expect that the enactment of authority tasks at work will shape stratification beliefs in a generally conservative manner and net of strictly material rewards of the position. Specifically:

> The amount of authority tasks undertaken in the workplace will be positively related to the development of traditionally "conservative" views about the workings of the stratification system, namely, adhering to: (1) restrictive support for socioeconomic redistributive policy, and; (2) perceptions regarding the functional necessity of socioeconomic inequality. Such an influence will be especially pronounced when one holds lengthier authority tenure.

Although we do not empirically specify causal pathways in our modeling, our earlier overview of prior literature makes clear that the experiential processes underlying this relationship (i.e., work conditions, hierarchical interactions, and authority tasks) are non-mutually exclusive and very likely operate simultaneously.

We caveat our core prediction with recognition that the association we are describing very likely varies by context and group. Some analyses, for instance, have found that factors outside of the "intrinsic" (Vallas, 1987) nature of work, such as regionally-based political traditions (e.g., class consciousness and the perceived propriety of labor unionism), exert significant effects on attitudes (Kimeldorf, 1985; Low-Beer, 1978; Vallas, 1987). In this regard, we test for regional effects and interactions specifically with authority tasks. As the reader will see, an interaction between the South as a region and authority tasks in relation to redistributive policy proves to be significant and conservatizing in character.

Second, there is good reason to expect that the relation between authority tasks and inequality orientations may vary by both the race of respondents and whether they are employed in the private versus public sector. In the first regard, sociological research over recent decades has documented quite clearly that, at all occupational levels, perceptions of historical and contemporary discrimination lead African Americans compared to whites to adopt a "liberal caste" view of the American stratification system. Recognition of a relatively closed opportunity structure (Kluegel & Smith, 1986) and extra-individual sources of inequality in general (e.g., ongoing discrimination) will hold clear-cut implications for race differences in interpretations socioeconomic inequality (Hunt, 1997; Kluegel & Smith, 1986) among those in positions of authority.

There is also now a well-documented, historically-based and "deeply-ingrained business culture" (Kamarck, 2007) within private sector employment characterized, for instance, by more hierarchically-based relations and managerial "financial bottom line" pressures. It is plausible that within such a context, the link between the experiential realities of authority and inequality orientations will be more pronounced. Specifically, and drawing from what we know regarding sector and race, we expect that:

> The effects of workplace authority on stratification beliefs will be more pronounced and decidedly more conservative for whites relative to African Americans, and for those working in the private compared to the public sector.

DATA AND METHODS

Our analyses draw on the 2012 General Social Survey (GSS) to examine the impact of authority experiences on stratification-related beliefs. The GSS is a full probability sample of English speaking adults living in households in the United States (for a full description of the GSS see Davis, Smith, & Marsden, 2007). Individuals between the ages of 20 and 62 who worked full-time when interviewed were included in the sample. This amounts to 2,721 individuals, 55% men and 45% women. The appendix contains descriptive information for the GSS sample.

We use multiple imputation with a "chained equations" (Graham, 2009) approach and a fully conditional specification of predicted equations to handle missing data. This method accounts for statistical uncertainty in single imputations and replaces missing values with predictions based on associations observed in the sample in generating imputed data sets (Rubin, 1987). To impute, we specifically use the MICE program in R 2.9 (Royston, 2005) and, ultimately, combine the empirical results across the imputed data samples. This helps account for variation within and between imputed data sets to arrive at unbiased standard errors of the coefficient estimates (Rubin, 1987). In supplementary analyses, we used a listwise deletion procedure which generated findings largely consistent with those reported below.[2]

Dependent Variables

Two well-documented tenets of American stratification ideology — support for socioeconomic redistribution policy and perceptions of the functional necessity of inequality — constitute our key outcomes of interest.

Support for Redistributive Policy
This dimension of stratification beliefs is measured with one item and is worded as follows:

> In general, some people feel that the government in Washington should see to it that every person has a good job and a good standard of living. Others think the government should just let each person get ahead on their own. Where would you place yourself on this scale?

Respondents placed themselves on a 7-point scale with "Government See to Job and Good Standard of Living" coded 7 and defining one end of the scale, and "Government Let Each Person Get Ahead" defining the opposite end and is coded as 1.

Functional Necessity of Inequality
This dimension of stratification attitudes or interpretation is an additive index composed of two questions. The first surround whether "Large differences in Income are necessary for America's prosperity." Respondents placed themselves on a 4-point scale with "differences are necessary in

America" coded 4, and "large differences are not necessary for America" coded 1 (defining the opposite end of the scale). The second component centers on the view that "Inequality does not benefit the rich and powerful," coded as 4 versus the more critical stance that "inequality benefits the rich and powerful" (coded 1 on the scale). A principle components factor analysis was performed for these two items and several other GSS items that address attitudes about inequality, and the two loaded on the same dimension. The scale also revealed strong reliability with an alpha of .7.

Independent Variables

Amount of Authority Tasks

We constructed a single ordinal variable "task level" that captures the amount of supervisory job tasks performed. We draw specifically from two questions: (1) "In your job, do you supervise anyone who is directly responsible to you?" and (2) "How often do you sanction workers or interact with them to resolve problems or improve productivity/services?" Those who exercise authority and sanction/interact with subordinates "more than several times a day" are coded 3; those who exercise authority and sanction/interact with subordinates "several times a day" are coded 2; and those who exercise authority and sanction/interact with subordinates "approximately once a day or less" are coded 1. Those who do not exercise job authority serve as the referent for this indicator.

Authority Tenure

Authority tenure refers to the amount of time, measured in months, that respondents have been performing authority tasks. We suspect that that authority tasks will matter more for those with significant authority tenure and, thus, test of the impact of tenure and its interaction with the amount of authority tasks performed. Authority tenure is coded as a continuous variable and is based on how long respondents have had tenure on present job.[3]

Other Independent Variables

Ideology

To ensure we are capturing the impact of authority rather than broader political orientation, we include alongside our authority measures an indicator of political party affiliation (2 = Democrat, 1 = Independent, 0 = Republican).

Workplace and Human Capital Characteristics

Several workplace-specific and human capital variables are included in the statistical model to bolster confidence that the authority effects we observe are related to tasks and experiences of authority rather than background attributes, overall satisfaction with work, or context. First, job satisfaction is measured by the questions, "On the whole, how satisfied are you with the work you do — would you say you are very satisfied, moderately satisfied, a little satisfied, or very dissatisfied?" with successive levels of satisfaction receiving higher scores in the coding scheme. Second, we include a central indicator of human capital characteristic, namely education, coded in years. Third, and consistent with one of our earlier predictions regarding context, we include and indicator of sector (1 = private, 0 = public), and explore interactions between this and authority tasks in our modeling.

Material Rewards in the Workplace

Since ideological orientation may very well be partly a function of the tangible rewards of the job and job position, we felt it essential to include an indicator of income. This indicator is measured as annual personal income (in broad categories of between five and ten thousand dollars) and is subject to a natural logarithmic transformation. Further, we include an indicator of job benefits, drawing on two questions: "does our employer provide you with a retirement plan?" and, "does your employer provide you with medical benefits?" Those who received both were coded as 2, those who received either were coded as 1 and those who received neither were coded as 0. These two indicators are crucial, in our view, for disentangling the potential impact of the material benefits of a job from the experiential dimensions of authority.

Sociodemographic Indicators

The effects of age (years), race (1 = White, 0 = African American), gender (1 = women, 0 = men), region of work (1 = South, 0 = others), and marital status (1 = married, 0 = not married) are included in the statistical model. Race will be, according to our earlier predications, more central to the patterning of stratification beliefs and may be conditionally related to the impact of authority experiences.

ANALYTIC STRATEGY AND RESULTS

Given the nature of our dependent variables, we make use of ordered logit regression. Ordered logit is appropriate when a dependent variable is measured by three or more discrete categories that can be rank-ordered, yet the distance between ranks is arbitrary. Because there are no truly standardized regression coefficients in logistic regression, we utilize odd ratios by computing the exponent (i.e. antilog) of each beta parameter. The metric regression coefficients in ordered logit denote the log odds of being in a particular category of the dependent variable relative to the reference.

We begin (Table 1) by analyzing at an aggregate and descriptive level the relation between authority tasks and our two indicators of stratification beliefs. Our main analyses, reported in Table 2 and which uses ordered logit modeling, assesses each of the two tenets of stratification beliefs separately, beginning with a model reporting the main effects of all independent variables. We then run these models, but with interaction terms between authority tasks and tenure as well as race and sector of employment. These models help specify: (1) the extent to which authority tasks shape inequality beliefs uniquely depending of levels of authority tenure, (2) whether authority matters differentially depending specifically on race and sector, as specified previously, and (3) the extent to which authority experiences matter above and beyond material returns to the position and other human capital and sociodemographic attributes.

Authority Tasks and Stratification Beliefs

Table 1 reports results from an ANOVA procedure that assesses how the primary independent variable of interest, the number of authority tasks performed, impacts stratification beliefs. This affords an initial glimpse of our relations of interest across hierarchical levels of authority tasks (i.e., sanctioning and interacting with subordinates) in accordance with its coding in the GSS (i.e., ranging from none to "more than several times a day").

Findings clearly denote a strong relationship, and with both outcomes. Increases in authority tasks seem to induce classically conservative beliefs, with differences at all task levels being statistically significant. Indeed, and when it comes to support for redistributive policy, those who perform authority tasks "more than several times a day" express significantly lower support (2.45) than those who do not perform authority tasks (5.82). Those

Table 1.   ANOVA for Adherence to Tenets of Stratification Beliefs By
Authority Task Level.

	Redistributive Policy	Functional Necessity of Inequality
Authority task level		
Greater than several times a day	2.45[a,b,c]	6.52[a,b,c]
Several times a day	3.65[d,e]	5.74[d,e]
Once a day or less	4.77[f]	4.11[f]
No Authority	5.82	3.01

Differences relative to referent:
[a]From several times a day $p < .01$.
[b]From once a day of less $p < .001$.
[c]From no authority $p < .001$.
[d]From once a day or less $p < .05$.
[e]From no authority $p < .01$.
[f]From no authority $p < .05$.

performing moderate levels of authority tasks, "several times a day" (3.65)
or "once a day or less" (4.77) fall in the middle, as one might expect, and
display intermediate support for redistributive policy. Such findings highlight a nearly linear relationship: more authority tasks appear to result in
significantly more conservative interpretations of inequality and the desire
for redistribution.

Our results pertaining to the "the functional necessity of inequality" are
largely parallel. Those with the highest levels of authority task are most
aligned with the belief that inequality is functionally necessary (a difference
of 3.5 points compared to those who do not perform authority tasks).
Those with intermediate levels of authority performance again fall in
between. But do such effects vary by authority tenure, as well as race and
sector, as speculated about earlier? And, do these patterns — patterns that
imply a deep impact of the experiential nature of work on broader views
regarding inequality — remain even when controlling for background attributes and the more material returns to employment? Such questions are
tackled systematically within our multivariate analyses.

*The Impact of Authority Task by Tenure and Context, and in the
Face of Controls*
Table 2 reports our multivariate analyses. Notably, findings are largely
consistent with expectations and in several regards. First, the higher the
intensity of authority tasks, the more conservative the respondents

Table 2. Ordered Logit Regressions for Determinants of Adherence to Stratification Beliefs.

| | Redistributive Policy Support | | | | Functional Necessity of Inequality | | | |
| | Model 1 | | Model 2 | | Model 1 | | Model 2 | |
	(Coeff.)	(Odds ratio)	(b)	(Odds ratio)	(b)	(Odds ratio)	(b)	(Odds ratio)
Authority								
Task Level	−.21**	.80	−.18**	.81	.23**	1.25	.22**	1.23
Tenure	−.19**	.81	−.16**	.83	.21**	1.22	.20	1.21
Material rewards								
Income	−.08*	.92	−.07	.93	.09*	1.09	.08*	1.08
Benefits	−.03	.97	−.02	.98	.13	1.13	.07	1.07
Ideology								
Democrat	.14*	1.14	.13*	1.13	−.07	.93	−.06	.94
Workpl/H.C.								
Satisfaction	−.15**	.85	−.14**	.86	.16**	1.16	.13*	1.13
Education	.03	1.03	.03	1.03	.18*	1.18	.15*	1.15
Private sector	−.16*	.84	−.15*	.85	.18*	1.18	.16*	1.16
Sociodemographic								
Age	−.01	.99	−.01	.99	.01	1.01	.01	1.01
Race (1 = White)	−.13	.87	−.12*	.88	.16*	1.16	.15	1.15
Gender (1 = Female)	−.01	.99	−.01	99	.02	1.02	.02	1.02
South	−.01	.99	−.01	.99	.03	1.03	.02	1.02
Married	−.02	.98	.01	.99	.04	1.04	.03	1.03
Interactions								
Authority task * Authority tenure			−.14**	.86			.16**	1.16
Authority task * South			−03*	.97			.02	1.02
Authority task * Race			−.22**	.87			−.23**	.86
Authority Task * Private sector			−.20**	.79			−.21**	.81
Constant	−3.23		−3.14		−3.06		−3.02	
Log Likelihood	−240.61**		−247.63**		−242.11**		−245.61**	
Model X^2 change			116.73*				117.73*	

****$p < .001$, **$p < .01$, *$p < .05$.

inequality orientations are for both outcomes and, importantly, net of all statistical controls including income. Second, these effects vary by and are most pronounced among those with the greatest, authority tenure. Finally, and consistent with our conditional expectations regarding race and sector of employment, the conservatizing impact of authority is especially pronounced among whites more so than African Americans, among those working in private compared to public sector employment, and for those residing in the South (though only relative to redistributive policy).

Model 1 suggests that unit increases authority tasks decreases by 20% the odds of supporting socioeconomic redistributive policy. Further, a unit increase in the authority tenure decreases the odds by 19% of supporting socioeconomic redistributive policy. Model 2, which introduces an interaction between authority tasks and tenure, is statistically significant and negative ($p < .01$), suggesting a compounding and conservative effect overall. Indeed across successive categories of authority tenure, task level reduces support for socioeconomic redistributive policy. Interactions between authority tasks and race and sector of employment are also statistically significant. The conservatizing impact of authority tasks on support for socioeconomic redistributive policy is more profound among Whites ($p < .01$) and those working in the private sector ($p < .05$).

Findings surrounding the perceived functional necessity of inequality are, by and large, parallel. Model 1 indicates that increases in authority tasks exacerbate the odds (by 25%) of seeing inequality as necessary. Authority tenure exerts its own independent conservatizing impact, yet more central to our expectations is its statistically significant interaction with authority tasks − an interaction that both lends itself to the most conservative orientation (i.e., wherein inequality is seen as quite necessary) and that is significant under the .01 level. Finally, the link between performing authority tasks and perceptions of the functional necessity of inequality is stronger among Whites than African Americans ($p < .01$) and those in the private relative to the public sector ($p < .01$).

Attributing Causation to Authority Experiences
Additional findings bolster our contention that the relations our analyses have uncovered, and indeed the impact of authority experiences on stratification beliefs, are far from spurious. Specifically, we ran a two-stage least squares regression for all multivariate analyses to assess possible reciprocal effects between authority and the two dimensions of stratification beliefs modeled above. Results from these analyses did capture some reciprocity (i.e., orientations shaping authority attainment and thus an ideological-based

selectivity factor operating). However, the magnitude of these effects was actually quite minor compared to the causal direction both specified in our theoretical discussion and implied by our modeling.

We also note that job satisfaction in our modeling is a statistically significant predictor of conservative stratification beliefs. The statistical significance of satisfaction, defined as an constituting an "investment in, and commitment to, one's job" (Kalleberg, 1977) is an additional indicator that work experiences, generally – and, in our case, the exercise of authority – are not spurious when it comes to shaping broader orientations to the world and to inequality more specifically.

CONCLUSION

Sociological research has, to date, largely overlooked broader attitudinal outcomes – such as adherence to stratification beliefs – that may very well be forged within the context of workplace experiences, including those surrounding hierarchy and authority. Utilizing data from the 2012 General Social Survey, our analyses revealed that this form of workplace experience, both in terms of the number of authority tasks performed and duration of time spent performing them across the work career, plays an important part in the structuring of stratification beliefs. Indeed, increases in the number of authority tasks one performs at their job and especially its joint interplay with authority tenure are positively associated with: (1) restrictive support for redistributive policy and (2) perceptions of the functional necessity of socioeconomic inequality. Such effects are strong and notably hold even when controlling for workplace material rewards and general satisfaction levels.

Such results contribute to several important stratification literatures in sociology. First, and relative to the "work and personality" (Kohn, 1969, 1983) tradition, our findings extend the range of both workplace experiences that trigger attitudes and the attitudes that are triggered. It indeed appears from our findings that aspects of laboring that are attitude-relevant in the workplace extend beyond, for instance, the extent to which work is routinized or is substantively complex. The character of supervisory tasks, especially supervisory responsibility over subordinates and the determining of sanctions, status, rewards and task assignments, matters as well and appears to have consequences for ideological orientation. Moreover, such experiences of authority on the job are relevant above and beyond associated and job-specific material rewards. Such findings compliment, to be sure, broader work on global factors (i.e., media exposure) impacting inequality and political orientations, but point to the workplace and inter-actions and experiences within as a possibly central institutional experien-tial context – a context warranting much more attention.

Our findings also hold implications for important work surrounding class position in advanced post-industrial societies as well that regarding hierarchy and contemporary changes in the labor process. In the first regard, our analyses extend on prior conceptions of authority and class (Dahrendorf, 1959; Wright, 1985) by recognizing how it is meaningful for material returns, to be sure, but also class reproduction in the ideological sense. In the second vein, and when it comes to the transformation of work, recent scholarship (Crowley, Tope, Chamberlain, & Hodson, 2010; Kalleberg, 2009) has denoted a reorganization of employment such that delayering is now commonplace as is the downward pressure and shift in authority responsibilities. To the degree that this is the case and we were to we treat our findings seriously, one might plausibly expect a politically con-servatizing impact of workplace changes even in the face of increasing material inequality and precariousness.

Qualifications to our core findings emerged, relative to context, and thus deserve more elaboration. Most notably, strength of association between author tasks and interpretations of inequality clearly varies by race and sec-tor of employment. The unique legacy of discrimination experienced by African Americans seems to induce a relatively liberal posture when it comes to stratification beliefs – an effect that tends to mute the potentially conservatizing impact of authority for African Americans and that intensi-fies the effects we find for Whites. Similarly, the relatively hierarchically structured and pronounced business culture forged in the private sector induces more conservative orientations when it comes to stratification beliefs, and this is only bolstered for those in positions of authority.

Despite such caveats, we must underscore the importance of our core findings regarding experiences of authority and stratification beliefs espe-cially in the face of our modeling and inclusion of potentially countervail-ing arguments surrounding, for instance, material rewards and benefits. The experiential aspects of work-specific authority are clearly meaningful to broader worldviews and inequality-specific orientations. The experience of work, as sociologists have long theorized and documented, constitutes an important "meaning system" (Hodson, 2001) such that, through his labor, "man makes himself." Our findings suggest that this meaning system extends to sociopolitical orientations such that – and building on, most importantly, Marx and more recently, Kohn – one can also conclude that laboring plays a pivotal role in the making of one's political beliefs.

This article, of course, reflects merely an initial attempt to explore the interrelation of workplace authority experiences and stratification beliefs. The robust nature of our findings underlies our basis for advocating for additional research on this specific topic and the more general relevance of workplace experiences to orientations outside of employment. We believe that first-hand examinations of workplaces – examinations that could arguably unpack how specific authority tasks operate – would be especially useful for elaborating on which tasks may be especially consequential and how such experiences act to socialize incumbents ideologically. Analyses of additional stratification beliefs (e.g., views on distributive justice and perceptions of the extent to which the opportunity structure is viewed as open) in relation to workplace hierarchy, position and tasks will likewise produce a more comprehensive rendering of the role, importance of, and interconnection of work to social life more generally. We very much look forward to such work.

NOTES

1. There are other sociological literatures we can draw from to establish the basic associations between the exercise of authority tasks and the formation of stratification beliefs. For example, studies addressing "bureaucratic control" in the sociology of work literature (e.g. Edwards, 1979; Blauner, 1964) discusses how the creation of hierarchy in workplace status and positions – particularly among those with high status/position – cognitively establishes "rigid and formal bounds" (Edwards, 1979) related to attitudes about treatment of subordinates and general belief sets.

2. Bivariate correlations and collinearity diagnostics indicate there is no multicollinearity among the independent variables in the models. In addition, the Weisberg-Cook test of the assumption of variance across predicted values for the dependent variable was performed and findings indicate there is little heteroscedasticity in the statistical model.

3. We recognize that this is not a perfect measure of how long respondents have exercised the kind and amount of authority they presently exercise as they may change with incumbency in the same job. For example, as employers' confidence in an employee grows we can well imagine they would be asked to undertake additional authority tasks. Nevertheless, the GSS does not allow us to assess longitudinally the authority that respondents exercise.

ACKNOWLEDGMENTS

The authors are grateful to Steven Vallas, Editor, and three anonymous reviewers of *Research in the Sociology of Work* for their thorough and thoughtful suggestions on an earlier version of this piece. We dedicate this article to Melvin Kohn as well as Bill Form and Joan Huber, each of whom's important and early research on work, inequality and ideology planted the seeds underlying the questions raised here.

REFERENCES

Berger, J., Bert, C., & Zeldich, M. (1972). Status characteristics and social interaction. *American Sociological Review*, *36*, 241–255.

Blauner, R. (1964). *Alienation and freedom*. Chicago, IL: University of Chicago Press.

Bobo, L., & Kluegel, J. (1993). Opposition to race-targeting: Self-interest, stratification ideology or racial attitudes? *American Sociological Review*, *58*, 443–464.

Conley, D. (1999). *Being black but living in the red*. Berkeley, CA: University of California Press.

Corbeta, P., & Pasquele, C. (2013). Job precariousness and political orientations. *European Society and Politics*, *18*, 333–354.

Crowley, M., Tope, D., Chamberlain, L., & Hodson, R. (2010). Neo-Taylorism at work: Occupational change in the post-fordist Era. *Social Problems*, *57*, 421–447.

Dahrendorf, R. (1959). *Class and class conflict in industrial society*. Palo Alto, CA: Stanford University Press.

Dallinger, U. (2010). Public support for redistribution: What explains cross-national differences? *Journal of European Social Policy*, *20*, 333–349.

Davis, J., Smith, T., & Marsden, P. (2007). *The general social survey*. Ithaca, NY: The Roper Center.

Della-Fave, R. (1998). Ritual and legitimation of inequality. *Sociological Perspectives*, *34*, 21–38.

DiTomaso, N., & Parks-Yancy (2014). The social psychology of inequality at work: Individual, group and organizational dimensions. In J. McCleod (Eds.), *Handbook of social psychology of inequality* (pp. 437–451). New York, NY: Springer.

Durkheim, E. (1984). *The division of labor in society*. New York, NY: Macmillan.

Edsall, T., & Edsall, M. (1991). *Chain reaction: The impact of race, rights and taxes on American politics*. New York, NY: W. W. Norton.

Edwards, R. (1979). *Contested terrain: The transformation of the workplace in the 20th century*. New York, NY: Basic Books.

Form, W., & Huber, J. (1973). *Income and ideology: An analysis of the American political formula*. New York, NY: Free Press.

Giddens, A. (1970). *Capitalism and modern social theory*. Cambridge: Cambridge University Press.

Gilens, M. (1999). *Why Americans hate welfare: Race, media and the politics of antipoverty policy*. Chicago, IL: UC Press.

Graham, J. (2009). Missing data analysis: Making it work in the real world. *American Annual Review of Psychology*, *35*, 241–260.

Halaby, C., & Weakliem, D. (1993). Ownership and authority in the earnings function: Non-nested test of alternative specifications. *American Sociological Review*, *59*, 5–21.

Hochschild, J. (1995). *Facing up to the American dream*. Princeton, NJ: Princeton University Press.

Hodson, R. (2001). *Dignity at work*. New York, NY: Cambridge University Press.

Hunt, M. (2014). Ideologies. In J. McCeod, E. Lawler, & M. Schwalbe (Eds.), *Handbook of the social psychology of inequality* (pp. 325–352). New York, NY: Springer.

Kalleberg, A. (1977). Work values and job rewards—A theory of job satisfaction. *American Sociological Review, 42*, 124–143.

Kalleberg, A. (2009). *Good jobs, bad jobs*. New York, NY: Russell Sage.

Kamarck, E. (2007). *The end of government ... As we know it*. Boulder, CO: Lynne Reiner.

Kimeldorf, M. (1985). Working class culture, occupational recruitment and union politics. *Social Forces, 64*, 359–376.

Kitschfelt, H., & Rehm, P. (2014). Occupations as a site of political preference formation. *Comparative Political Studies, 47*, 1670–1706.

Kluegel, J., & Smith, E. (1986). *Beliefs about inequality*. New York, NY: Aldine du Gruyter.

Kohn, M. (1969). *Class and conformity: A study in values*. Chicago, IL: University of Chicago Press.

Kohn, M. (1983). *Work and personality*. New York, NY: Ablex.

Lee, B., Jones, S., & Lewis, D. (1990). Public beliefs about the causes of homelessness. *Social Forces, 69*, 253–265.

Lee, C.-S. (2007). Why do some employees support welfare states more than others? *Social Science Research, 36*, 688–718.

Leicht, K., & Fennell, M. (2001). *Professional work: A sociological approach*. New York, NY: Wiley-Blackwell.

Lorence, J., & Mortimer, J. (1985). Job involvement through the life-course. *American Sociological Review, 50*, 56–578.

Low-Beer, J. (1978). *Protest and participation: The new working class in Italy*. New York, NY: Cambridge.

Marx, K. (1965). *The German ideology*. London: Plenum.

McCall, L. (2013). *The undeserving rich: American beliefs about inequality, opportunity and redistribution*. New York, NY: Cambridge University Press.

Pugh, M., & Wahrmann, R. (1983). Neutralizing sexism in mixed sex groups. *American Journal of Sociology, 88*, 746–762.

Ridgeway, C. (2000). Social differences and social connection. *Sociological Perspectives, 43*, 1–11.

Ridgeway, C. (2001). Gender, status, and leadership. *Journal of Social issues, 57*, 637–655.

Ridgeway, C. (2006). Expectation state theory and emotion. In J. Stets & J. Turner (Eds.), *Handbook of sociology of emotions* (pp. 346–367). New York, NY: Springer.

Ridgeway, C., & Correll (2006). Consensus and creation of status beliefs. *Social Forces, 85*, 431–454.

Roscigno, V., Lopez, S., & Hodson, R. (2009). Workplace incivilities: The role of interest conflicts, social closure. *Work, Employment and Society, 23*, 747–773.

Royston, D. (2005). Multiple imputation of missing values. *The Stata Journal, 5*, 1–14.

Rubin, D. (1987). *Multiple imputation for non-responses in surveys*. New York, NY: Wiley.

Shelton, J., & Wilson, G. (2012). Race, class and the basis of group alignment: Support for redistributive policy among privileged blacks. *Sociological Perspectives, 52*, 385–408.

Smith, R. (1997). Race, income and authority: A cross-temporal analysis of black and white men, 1972–1994. *Social Problems, 44*, 701–719.

Smith, R. (2002). Race and gender authority in the workplace. *Annual Review of Sociology, 28*, 509–552.

Smith, R. (2003). Race, gender and authority in the workplace: Theory and research. *Annual Review of Sociology, 28*, 509–542.

Steele, L. (2015). Income inequality, equal opportunity and attitudes toward redistribution. *Social Science Quarterly, 96*, 444–464.

Stryker, S., & Burke, P. (2000). The past present and future of an identity theory. *Social Psychology Quarterly, 63*, 284–297.

Tajfel, J., & Turner, J. (1979). The social identity theory of intergroup behavior. In S. Worschel & A. William (Eds.), *The social psychology of intergroup relations*. Monterey, CA: Brooks/Cole.

Turner, J., & Oates, P. (1986). The significance of the social identity concept for social psychology with references to individualism, interactionalism and social influence. *British Journal of Social Psychology, 25*, 237–252.

Vallas, S. (1987). The labor process as a source of class consciousness: A critical examination. *Sociological Forum, 2*, 237–255.

Weber, M. (1968). *Economy and society*. New York, NY: Vantage Press.

Wilson, G. (1997). Pathways to power: Racial differences in the determinants of job authority. *Social Problems, 38*, 48–64.

Wilson, G. (2001). Support for redistributive policies among the African American middle class: Race and class effects. *Research in Social Stratification and Mobility, 18*, 97–115.

Wright, E. O. (1985). *Classes*. London: Verso.

APPENDIX

Table A1. Characteristics of GSS Sample.

	X	Std. Dev.
Dependent variables		
Policy support	4.2	1.1
Functional necessity of inequality	5.6	1 4
Independent variables		
Authority		
Task level	1.9	.4
Tenure	42.4	5.6
Ideology		
Democrat	54%	
Workplace and human capital		
Satisfaction	2.2	.6
Education	11.9	2.1
Private Sector	79%	
Material rewards		
Income	$50,206	
Benefits	2.1	.5
Sociodemographic		
Age	37.7	5.3
Race (1 = White)	72.3%	
Gender (1 = Female)	46%	
Married	68.6%	
Non-South	87.4%	

MATCHING UP: PRODUCING PROXIMAL SERVICE IN A LOS ANGELES RESTAURANT

Eli Wilson

ABSTRACT

In high-end interactive service work settings, asymmetries between workers and customers are typically reflected in the service interaction. Workers must carefully control their emotional and aesthetic displays towards customers by relying on protocol provided by management. Customers, in turn, need not reciprocate such acts. By contrast, this paper theorizes service interactions that, paradoxically, aim to narrow the social distance between those on either side of the counter. Drawing on ethnographic data from a higher-end Los Angeles restaurant, I introduce the concept of proximal service as performed relationships in which server and served engage in peer-like interactions in a commercial setting. I show how management structures this drama through hiring, training, and shopfloor policies, all of which encourage select workers to approach customers using informal, flexible, and peer-like performances. I close by discussing how a branded experience of service amongst equals relates to symbolic exclusion and social inequality, and suggest that proximal service may be on the rise within

Research in the Sociology of Work, Volume 29, 99–124
ISSN: 0277-2833/doi:10.1108/S0277-283320160000029015

upscale, urban service establishments seeking to offer a more "authentic" consumption experience.

Keywords: Proximal service; interactive service work; restaurants; emotional labor; Los Angeles; peer culture

INTRODUCTION

Just as the growth of interactive service work today parallels an increasingly unequal U.S. society, and the relationship between those on either side of the service counter is thought to embody these socioeconomic divides. In upscale restaurants, retail stores, and hotels, interactive service workers engage in status-producing exchanges with (and for) affluent customers by outwardly displaying some combination of deference, professionalism, and respect behavior (Bearman, 2005; Finkelstein, 1989; Hochschild, 1983; Macdonald & Sirianni, 1996; Sherman, 2005). The performative toolkit these workers draw on – the smiles of airline stewardesses, the pleasant greetings of hotel receptionists, the attentive postures of doormen – is thought to be carefully calibrated a-priori by management (Hochschild, 1983), and personalized as a form of luxury product (Pettinger, 2004; Sherman, 2007, p. 6).

An emerging body of literature now examines the skills that interactive service workers use in producing their immaterial labor. Stemming from Hochschild's (1983) seminal work *The Managed Heart*, scholars recognize the various kinds of emotional and "aesthetic" labor (Nickson, Warhurst, Witz, & Cullen, 2001; Warhurst and Nickson, 2007) that service workers perform towards customers. These workers must "look good and sound right" for the job, drawing as much on their bodily appearances and embodied characteristics as they do controlled displays towards customers. Yet while recent scholarship on aesthetic and emotional labor has moved us towards conceptualizing a "new social construction of skill" in service work (Warhurst, Tilly, & Gatta, 2016), the *relational dynamic* between workers and customers in the service encounter remains undertheorized. In this sense, "the customer is king" may still be the most common philosophy regarding the service encounter, but assuming such hierarchical relations necessarily play out in micro-interaction neglects variation in how the relationship between the two may be symbolically recast. Drawing from ethnographic data within a higher-end Los Angeles restaurant, this study builds from a paradoxical finding: instead of *reinforcing* the status superiority of affluent patrons, many service interactions in this upscale environment aim to *minimize* the social distance between workers and customers. I refer to this style of service interaction as *proximal service*, defined as performed relationships of social closeness between server and served in a commercial setting.

In practice, proximal service is not necessarily new. Many who patronize service establishments, particularly those in working-class neighborhoods or explicitly casual in theme (cafes, dive bars), do so in part to purchase the feeling of family and intimacy that service workers provide (Erickson, 2009). One may also choose to patronize to the same hair salon time and time again because of a developed relationship with its workers (Gutek, Cherry, Bhappu, Schneider, & Woolf, 2000), or hang out at a particular establishment because friends or family member works there (see Besen, 2006). In such instances, one would expect some service formalities to be dropped in favor of conveying social familiarity in the relationship (Gutek et al., 2000).

There is also evidence that middle-class consumers today appear less interested in formal and/or formulaic consumption experiences of all kinds compared to half a century ago. More people, particularly those in the "creative class" (Florida, 2004), are reaching past big-brand beers for eclectic microbrews, just as they are opting for more "real" traveling experiences (Larson & Urry, 2011), indie movie selections (Ortner, 2013) and authentic dining options (Warde & Martens, 2000). To such consumers, the overt distinctions of class, culture, and exclusivity of traditional luxury service is likely to appear old-fashioned or even uncomfortably patronizing. By contrast, a socially proximate style of elite service appears to offer a refreshing alternative: the opportunity to consume peer-like social space within the market.

Following a review of literature on interactive service work, I begin by detailing how proximal service is assembled in a luxury service environment. Who is allowed to perform proximal service and what are the requisite "skills" needed to do so? I then show how workers and customers do proximal service on the shopfloor, mutually imbuing the service sequence with exchanges of social and symbolic closeness.

PRODUCING INTERACTIVE SERVICE WORK

Scholars understand that in interactive service work, one's dress, smile, emotions and speech are part of the labor process itself (MacDonald & Sirianni, 1996). Each is almost always structured a-priori by management, in different degrees and different forms. Some service establishments rely on Taylorist management techniques to sculpt efficient, blandly pleasant, and highly standardized service transactions (Ritzer, 2000). McDonald's remains the exemplar of such a corporate strategy that seeks to rationalize the service labor process, deskill the skills needed for employment, and routinize the service encounter (Leidner, 1993). More upmarket and luxury-oriented service establishments seek to compete based in part on greater customization of the client experience. This can be designed to evoke client prestige (Yano, 2011), such that guests are made to enjoy the feeling of "limitless entitlement to the workers' individualizing attention and effort" (Sherman, 2007, p. 6).

In both cases, structuring the customer service relationship begins with hiring and training a certain kind of worker. Management must first select what kind of individuals they want interacting with customers. Based on the particularities of the workplace, this frequently involves hiring those who "look good" and "sound right" for the company brand (Williams & Connell, 2010). These individuals must also be able to perform emotional labor, done chiefly by interacting with customers using the right emotional tones (Hochschild, 1983). Aside from basic skill prerequisites, interactive service workers may be selected based on gender (Hochschild, 1983; Spradley & Mann, 1975), race/ethnicity (see Yano, 2011), class (Wright, 2005), body type (Warhurst and Nickson, 2007), and/or "soft skills" (Moss & Tilly, 2001). Quite often, it is an intersection of multiple of these embodied characteristics that managers use to fill out a customer service staff (see Warhurst et al., 2016).

Once equipped with a suitable staff, management continues to fine-tune the "service theater" offered (Sherman, 2007) by regularizing the frontstage appearance and behavior of employees. Staff may be required to wear standardized uniforms and rely on rehearsed scripts to respond to a number of service situations. McDonald's, still the exemplar of mass-produced service, expends considerable resources to training store managers who are then expected to disseminate the corporate message to customer-facing employees (Leidner, 1993). By contrast, many other kinds of interactive service workers perform emotional and aesthetic labor with customers in ways that management cannot fully anticipate (and attempt to control). Particularly true in settings where customer interactions do not take place at a fixed and easily monitored point — such as in restaurant table service (see Crang, 1994), door-to-door insurance sales (Hochschild, 1983) and city tours (Wynn, 2010) — interactive service workers often possess some degree to which they can customize relations with clients. Here these workers must function as skilled emotional managers (Bolton & Boyd, 2003), juggling a flexible repertoire of strategies for dealing with a range of customer interactions. Not all of these strategies are consistent with managerial expectations. For example, Mann (2004) notes that with each service encounter, workers *choose* whether to display approved dispositions (e.g., alert postures, smiles), or deviant ones (fatigue, disinterest). In this sense, workers may subtly resistance disagreeable service protocols by mocking them behind the scenes or performing them ironically (see Leidner, 1993). Therefore, despite hiring workers who look good and are *trained* right, customer service can still be produced in ways inconsistent with organizational expectations (Lopez, 2010).

Yet the aims of management need not be thrown out of alignment when service workers improvise from scripted lines, or otherwise make the service interaction their own. For example, Pettinger (2004) notes that service in high-end, "aspirational lifestyle brand" retail stores tends to be more personalized and performed by workers who call themselves "consultants." The variability of service workers' conduct can itself also be an attraction to customers. For example, Erickson (2009) argues that at a casual neighborhood restaurant in the Midwest, the sociability of the staff is one of the restaurant's primary draws. As she writes, "managers allow servers the freedom to determine their work performance; customers enthusiastically support, if not insist, that servers go beyond the basics of the service exchange" (*ibid.*, pp. 59–60).

Customers, then, play a key role in shaping the style of service offered at a given service establishment. The perceived tastes of customers can shape not only management's hiring criteria for customer-facing workers, but also how service is subsequently structured. The relationship between customer demand and service at themed restaurant chains like Hooter's is clear enough (the brand unashamedly offers sexualized service to a primarily male clientele). Yet a similar logic also operates at suburban retail chain stores such as that studied by Williams and Connell (2010): management hires fashionable young adults as frontline workers, then adorns them in store-brand clothing in an attempt to cater to a young, middle-class consumer base. In this sense, patrons may find it more appealing to encounter workers who themselves appear to possess similar cultural capital and lifestyle choices to their own (see Wright, 2005). For example, Lloyd (2010) notes that the bars and nightclubs in "neo-bohemian" urban districts often hire tattooed-artists and aspiring entertainers in order to match the "gritty," artsy neighborhood vibe (chapter 4).

Customers also have an active role in shaping the service dynamic they wish to have, since they themselves are participants in the interpersonal drama. As symbolic interaction, the service encounter frames certain roles for workers and customers. Each participant must respond to one another by reading cues of "face" and "line" (Goffman, 1967), maintaining one's own image as well as that of the interactant throughout the course of the interaction (Goffman, 1974). Within the service exchange, customers – as opposed to servers – largely choose whether to invite dialogue and friendly banter with service workers or assert a strictly functional relationship with them (Bolton & Houlihan, 2005). For example, as Bearman (2005) shows, doormen in New York City must learn to respond to their affluent tenants' desire to feel distinct by providing service with a personal, yet not "overly" invasive tone (e.g., learning a tenant's favorite chocolate but not commenting on rumors of marital trouble). In restaurants, Mars and Nicod (1984) show that diners dictate the boundaries of their relationship with servers by choosing either to include them in table conversation ("boundary-open"), or exclude them from private conversation ("boundary-closed").[1] In "boundary-open" instances, customers invite their server to actively participate in their table conversations and possibly other aspects of their dining experience.

Prior scholarship thus tends to conceptualize service interactions as mere reflections of the unequal relationship between service workers and customers. This is thought to be particularly true in luxury service settings, where customers are treated to "limitless entitlement to the worker's individualizing attention and effort" (Sherman, 2007, p. 6). While privately workers may contest and reframe these relations (Mars & Nicod, 1984; Sherman, 2005), outwardly, they are thought to remain straightjacketed by asymmetrical service conventions performed using frontstage displays of deference, courtesy, and professionalism (Goffman, 1959; Sherman, 2007). Emotional labor is done *by* workers and *for* customers (not the other way around), just as the aesthetic labor must be to the tastes of customers. Neither showcases how the symbolic relationship between workers and customers itself may vary in service micro-interactions. Taking a relational approach towards analyzing the service encounter, I turn now to describe how *proximal service* is both assembled by managers and enacted through tableside service interactions.

METHODS

The data used in this study draws from fourteen months of field research conducted between 2012 and 2013 within Match Restaurant ("Match"). Working as a waiter, I documented my experiences in the field starting from the hiring process and through employee training, daily work shifts, company parties, formal meetings, and informal outings. All data was recorded in typed field notes immediately following the day's activities. The data presented in excerpts throughout this paper remain as true as possible to the conversations and situations I experienced during this time.

Since this study takes the production of proximal service as its focal point, primary data was drawn from observations of interactions between waiters, customers, and to a lesser extent, managers within the workplace. In order to flesh out themes of this study, I also supplemented my ethnographic data with a set of ten semi-structured, in-depth interviews with Match servers. I selected interviewees based non-random search criteria, and attempted to gain as diverse perspectives as possible. For instance, most of these interviewees represented prominent server types present within the restaurant while I was there, including: a young server new to waiting tables, a veteran waitress of ten years, a part-time server who also worked outside the restaurant industry, an aspiring actress working shifts around her auditions, and a college student at a nearby university. I conducted these interviews in settings near the restaurant that where agreeable to the subjects such as bars, restaurants and parks, and each interview varied in length from forty-five minutes to two hours. Record of these conversations was kept with a combination of written and voice-recording devices, and transcribed to electronic file following the interview. All informants were aware of my research intentions, and are referred to in this article using pseudonyms.

MATCH RESTAURANT

Match is a mid-sized, "casual-upscale" dining spot located in western Los Angeles. It has been open for six years, and employs approximately 45 front of the house workers (servers, bartenders, hostesses, etc.), 30 back of the house workers (line cooks, prep cooks, dishwashers, etc.), and a management team that includes a general manager, marketing director, executive chef, and a handful of shift managers. Match is nestled on a small business strip within two miles of the beach next to swank hotels, offices and nightlife venues and only a stone's throw away from the affluent neighborhoods of Santa Monica and Brentwood. Like other contemporary service establishments that prescribe to a kind of dressed-down luxury aesthetic, Match has done away with white-linen tablecloths and similar embellishments of exclusivity in favor of more casual décor. That said, considerable resources and designer-touches have been spent on the restaurant's main public areas. The main dining room features high ceilings with tasteful mood lighting, red leather booths around the perimeter, stained cherry wood tables, and beach-themed accents. A beautiful wrap-around patio is also located next to the dining room, spilling out onto a major commercial street.

Match Restaurant's menu follows many food and drink trends of the moment, and at a relatively high price point. Neither makes it uncommon for the area. A typical lunch entrée runs between $14 and $21 and focuses on health-conscious offerings such as lightly dressed salads and sandwiches with grilled organic meats. Dinner entrees range between $18 and $30 and are slightly more substantial: wild salmon with seasonal vegetables ($24), brick-roasted chicken with garlic mashed potatoes ($22), and *carne-asada* fajitas ($25). A dinner for two at the restaurant can run nearly $100 (after tip), easily surpassing this with the addition of alcohol.

Amongst the staff, most front of the house workers at Match are employed part-time, and are scheduled three to four shifts per week. Like in other U.S. restaurants, the majority of these workers earn minimum hourly wage ($9 in California in 2012), and garner most of their earnings from tips. Here the high check averages and consistent business at Match are to the waitstaff's economic advantage: because most customers base their tip around the total bill and adjust up or down slightly for service (see Azar, 2007), by default, servers and bartenders at Match enjoy higher tips per table than their counterparts in lower-priced restaurants. Most Match servers expect to make between $100 and $175 in tips per shift (which my own experience confirmed), though day-to-day fluctuations can be substantial. Over a six-hour shift at Match, servers typically net over $25 in tips plus base wage, putting their earnings slightly higher than industry averages (Haley-Lock & Ewert, 2011). As a result, while no Match server told me they were getting rich from waiting tables, most expressed that their earnings allowed them to live "comfortably" (I discuss worker characteristics in more detail later).

Match Restaurant's clientele draws primarily from local residents with a smattering of tourists visiting the nearby attractions of Santa Monica and Venice Beach. According to recent Census data, the average household income in the neighborhoods surrounding Match was upwards of $70,000, with the majority of the population college-educated and non-Hispanic White (United States Census Bureau, 2012). Whether in couples or in larger groups, the typical diners to the restaurant are white men and women in their 20s and 30s – or as one Match manager put it, "yuppies" and "hipsters." These diners consistently pack the house most days of the week, allowing the restaurant to remain not only a successful and profitable restaurant but also a fixture in the neighborhood's dining scene.

The social ambiance in Match's dining room remains one of its most salient and prized attributes. The constant hum of conversation, laughter, and clanking silverware fill the air. Diners readily enjoy people watching during their meals, gazing upon a crowd of trendy-dressed, physically attractive, (primarily) white patrons of both sexes. As a venue for a particular brand of shabby-chic luxury consumption and social exclusivity, Match is similar to many other upscale "bohemian" retail and service establishments found in post-industrial cities and gentrifying neighborhoods across the country (Deener, 2012; Lloyd, 2010; Zukin, 1995). This is reflected in Match's online reviews, which feature comments such as, "[Match] is a very trendy spot for brunch on the weekends. It is also my friends' go to brunch spot whenever they are recovering from a night of partying," or, "[Match] is a perfect casual/trendy place to grab dinner + drinks with friends." Another review concludes, "Match is a dimly lit restaurant, the artwork and music are amazing, and the general mood is casual but hip."

Management helps facilitates the hip dining room vibe through generous practices towards restaurant "guests." Floor managers frequently stroll from table to table joking and shaking hands with diners, and, on occasion, "comping" (giving away) food and drink. While Match's *formal* policy on comping states three occasions to which discounts may be applied (for immediate family, for off-the-clock employees, and for guests celebrating a special occasion), in *practice*, "free stuff" (McClain & Mears, 2012) is given out at the restaurant much more liberally. For example, regular diners at the restaurant may on occasion find their appetizers or desserts mysteriously taken off the final bill by managers. Front of the house workers also may issue de facto comps: operating more stealthily, they may drop off drinks to friends free of charge who come in to dine. Bestowed upon the "right" kind of guests, comping helps solidify the dining room as a space for social and symbolic inner-membership as well as exclusivity (I return to this later).

ASSEMBLING PROXIMAL SERVICE

Management at Match Restaurant shapes a socially proximate style of service in several important ways. Most fundamentally, those hired on as servers and bartenders (and to some extent hostesses) are screened for a particular array of embodied characteristics that in turn allow them to resemble the age, race, and class-cultural characteristics of the restaurant's primary clientele. As a result of selective hiring, front of the house workers at Match not only adhere to a narrow range of physical types, their image blurs distinctions with those who most commonly dine at the restaurant.

The waitstaff at Match contrasts typical public and scholarly depictions of restaurant workers in the United States as disproportionately working-class, female, and/or of immigrant background (see Cobble, 1991; Ehrenreich, 2001; Paules, 1991). By comparison, Match's corps of servers maintains characteristics more likely to resemble the restaurant's primary clientele: young, white, and educated. For example, amongst the 38 total servers at Match, the overwhelmingly majority are white or mixed-white, with only two African Americans and two Latino immigrants on staff. In contrast with gendered stereotypes about service work, women only slightly outnumber men (20 to 18). Moreover − and perhaps most remarkably given the low skill requirements for waiting tables − all but two servers hold university degrees or are actively enrolled in school to receive one.[2]

The social homogeneity of those working as servers at Match and their collective resemblance to the restaurant's primary clientele also extends to age. If the typical Match patron is in their 20s or 30s, the age range of Match's servers splits the difference: nearly all servers at the restaurant are between 22- and 29-years old, with the median age being 25 (only one server, a Mexican immigrant named Carlos, was over the age of 35). Though not all servers fit the age, race, and educational typecasting perfectly, most have at least a few of the traits. For example, amongst the four non-white servers − a Jamaican woman, an African American woman, and two Latino men − all but one is college-educated.

The tendency towards social similarity amongst the staff is not lost on servers themselves. A 27 year-old white waitress named Mel remarked:

> It's like whenever they want to hire someone new, they look for the same person. The new staff ends up looking just like the people that leave! I mean look at the last group [of hirees], all the girls are pretty similar, and it's been that way forever. (7/23/12 field note)

Moore and Leroy, two male servers in their late twenties, echo similar sentiment on the hired waitstaff at Match:

> EW (author): What do you think management looks for when they are hiring servers?
>
> Moore: To me, I think it boils down to image. Like, a lot of the people that work at our restaurant are attractive white people, like they are out of a casting call. They are trying to hire a certain kind of image.

Leroy: It's crazy 'cuz it comes back to race, they are trying to hire a certain type of person to represent the company. They are not going to hire, I'm sorry to say, Armando [Hispanic] to be a server. Or, like, Charlie's roommate [Charlie's roommate is noticeably overweight]. (Interview, 11/25/12).

As Warhurst and Nickson (2009, p. 389) note, companies desire employees who either have a particular "look," or are good looking — or both. Mel, Moore and Leroy all agree that servers hired at Match consistently exhibit class and gender-coded ideals for beauty. Many of the female waitresses at Match have a traditionally feminine physique (slender, clear skin, long hair, etc.), while male waiters reflect Western ideals for masculinity — most are around six feet tall, physically fit, and white. As Leroy alludes to above, those who do not fit this aesthetic typecast are unlikely to get "cast" as a server at Match.

Hired servers at the restaurant must also be able to demonstrate certain forms of cultural knowledge and embodied dispositions befitting of the restaurant's brand of service. This screening process is first woven into hiring. After submitting a resume for the server position in person, one may then be invited back for two rounds of interviews with different hiring managers. Should both interviews go well (either manager's rejection terminates the process), management will green light the new "personality" (their word for applicant) for orientation and training. The exact criterion for selecting new hires remains purposely loose. This allows the hiring process to be dictated by a manager's gut feeling instead of any formal set of requirements or credentials (Moss & Tilly, 2001; Rivera, 2012). This screening mechanism clearly disadvantages those who not only cannot display the right bodily aesthetic for a place like Match, but also those who struggle to produce the right "soft skills" (Moss & Tilly, 2001) for socially proximate service.

The hiring interview for server applicants at Match further showcases selectivity based on socio-cultural membership. When I interviewed for the position, I was asked to respond to questions like, "name three beer styles and describe how they taste," "what does good service means to you?" and, "describe your favorite restaurant experience. What made it special?" In each case, the manager would let me speak at length on the topic, interjecting only to encourage me to "say more." While I may have been allowed the opportunity to interview based on the fact that my physical characteristics roughly fit the target criteria, I was left pondering the difficulties of securing the job should I would have stuttered when describing the characteristics of a *Saison*, or not being able to wax poetic about the excellent service I had received years ago when dining at a fancy French restaurant in Beverly Hills.

Match is not unusual in relying on thinly cloaked questions to screen interactive service work applicants for cultural capital (see Wright, 2005). Other restaurants use even more rigorous gatekeeping strategies to weed out applicants that do not possess both industry experience and cultured tastes. For example, when I was applying to other upscale Los Angeles restaurants in the spring of 2012, I was subjected to numerous on the spot quizzes by hiring managers demanding that I "name as many California wine regions as you can," "describe Bearnaise sauce," and act out how I would interact with a VIP guest. As is the case with Match's hiring procedure, those who make it past such pop quizzes of class distinction (in the Bourdieuian sense) must demonstrate skills not listed on any resume.

Hiring selectivity for the waitstaff at Match also incorporates an institutional logic prioritizing those with leisure and lifestyle tastes perceived to be similar to those of Match's patrons. The ideal, convenient enough to measure, is one's propensity to dine at places like Match when *off the clock*, or engage in any number of other leisure activities associated with middle- and upper-class tastes. As a result, while at work servers frequently gossip over current fashion, discuss going out to eat at pricey new restaurants, debate the merits of faddish dieting and exercise regimes, and eagerly plan international travel. On more than one occasion, I would arrive for my shift only to hear that a fellow server "just left for Europe," or was taking the day off to attend a rooftop party, live concert, or impromptu date. Juxtaposed with their professional career interests (outside the restaurant industry), many Match servers view their time waiting tables as an enjoyable but temporary engagement. Yet while these individuals' apparent nonchalance towards restaurant labor might blacklist them as unreliable employees in other types of establishments, at Match it has arguably the *opposite* effect. Hiring servers with an upper-class outlook is consistent with management's goal of maintaining a server corps that possesses the right *habitus* (Bourdieu, 1984). By contrast, an applicant seeking a *full-time* career as a server at Match would, on these grounds, likely be considered a poor fit for the job.

The orientation and training process are another way in which management unofficially screens new hires for class-privileged traits. Spanning a total of seven days, hirees are told to clear their schedule to accommodate the training sessions, which range from four to eight hours each day and involve small written homework assignments and educational seminars on wine, beer, food, and service. Without the prospect of making tips, new hires must be financially able to weather between one and two weeks of making minimum hourly wage (currently $9 an hour in California as of

2013). This effectively ensures those financially unable to do so either must look elsewhere or apply for a different job within the restaurant; bussing tables or working kitchen prep both offer shorter training periods. Thus, management effectively "sets the table" for proximal service not only by hiring individuals who are in a specific time in their lives, but have the economic resources to essentially work for free for an extended period of time (see Frenette, 2013).

Obviously, not all aspects of Match's service style can simply be hired for. During the training process, server-hires are given guidelines for demeanor and self-presentation when with customers. However, the guidelines for "proper" behavior when with guests often involve considerable flexibility, customization and autonomy. This contrasts the routine and monotony of many other interactive service jobs (Leidner, 1993). As Match's trainer noted during my orientation, service at Match means, "practicing a certain brand of friendliness":

> Sarah (trainer) acts out what a timid server looks like, as she tip toes with an aghast expression on her face towards our trainee table (six of us). We laugh as her eyes dart back and forth, shoulders hunched, trying to stutter out a word. She then snaps out of the skit, bellowing "*be* confident! For god's sake, they know they are at a restaurant, and the server is there to do a job. They expect to be interrupted at some point!" She follows this with: "A lot of service is *confidence*. When you have to interrupt a table in conversation, do so boldly and with purpose. When you are walking by a table on a busy shift, slow down and appear *calm*. Customers take a lot of cues off the waitstaff, so if you appear out of control, that is how they will perceive the service." (3/22/12 field notes)

Unlike explicitly themed service featured at places like Hooters (sexually suggestive service), Dick's Last Resort (surly service), or Bubba Gump's (movie-themed service), Match provides few required scripts, acts, or routines for how to interact with diners. The "training" of Match's variety of proximal service is in this sense a far less conspicuously engineered product that can be stamped on. As a guideline, Match trainers suggest servers exhibit a confident, calm, and affable style of service as opposed to too deferential or business-like. As Sarah reiterated, we should not be so rushed so as to feel uncomfortable if a customer wants to chat. In effect, servers are encouraged to appear *cool* in multiple senses of the word, embodying leisure rather than serious labor.

On the service shopfloor, Match's official appearance guideline for front of the house workers also contrasts norms found in many other service workplaces. In the latter setting, workers may be required to dress uniformly, stripped of virtually all personalization save for a small nametag.

Such dress codes mark workers as workers, and emphasize the boundaries between service workers and customers. Match's dress code for servers provides them with substantial leeway in what may be worn to work so long as it displays "good personal hygiene," and features "no large logos, advertising or slogans." Tops (blouses for women and collared shirts for men) must be at least partly white, though color patterns such as plaid or stripes are encouraged. Match's dress code plays up servers' sense of personal style and fashion, and sets the tone for their interaction with guests. Floor managers exaggerate this with loose monitoring of server attire:

> The manager on duty, Kyle, gathers the servers together for a pre-shift meeting at 8am and says, "as you know, our dress code is to dress trendy with the primary color being white." The servers look at each other and smirk. Crystal rolls her eyes and says jokingly, "am I trendy enough for you today?" She points to her striped, loosely hanging black-and-white t-shirt.

> Kyle pauses to look at her, then, with a shrug, says, "sure?" He resumes reading off his meeting notes. (11/4/12 field notes)

Servers are encouraged to thread the line between fashion and function with their attire, and face only minor sanctions for dress code violations. As a result, servers assert extensive fashion vanities on the job. For example, female servers will often come to work wearing a combination of jewelry, scarves, hats and jackets, all of which are virtually unregulated by the dress code. Match's dress code facilitates more conspicuous attention drawn to servers' personal fashion choices and sexualized labor in the workplace (Warhurst and Nickson, 2007). This helps to frame a dining room environment where fashion-savvy workers are "on display" (Crang, 1994) amidst the hip, monied patrons who come to the restaurant to consume the whole experience. The displayed similarities (aesthetic, social, and cultural) between service workers and service recipients in the dining room also produce a dramatic effect. On multiple occasions, I witnessed restaurant diners who, unable to rely on conspicuous visual cues to differentiate staff from patron, would inquire *do you work here?* to a series of people before finally arriving at someone who could direct them towards the restroom.

Other policies at the restaurant also help facilitate proximal service. Flexible scheduling and liberal time-off procedures allow servers the ability to "have more going on" in their lives than just work. The relative ease with which schedules can be switched and shifts can be covered mean that employees are not locked into a rigorous schedule of labor. While some choose to use this spare time to work second jobs or attend school, others embrace privileged leisure activities. For example, in order to attend a popular three-day music concert in Southern California on only a few day's notice, Chris, a male server in his mid-twenties, got coworkers to cover his three weekend shifts during that time. Upon informing a manager of the shift switches, the manager's only comment was, "have a blast!" Chris proceeded to talk excitedly about attending the festival anytime he worked the rest of the week, and with anyone who would listen — servers or customers alike. In this way, Match servers face little resistance from management for switching shifts (so long as it is done to protocol); for the restaurant, it is just another way to attract a certain kind of employee in a particular life phase to job in the dining room.

DOING PROXIMAL SERVICE IN SERVICE INTERACTIONS

At Match, proximal service plays out most directly at the dining table and within service interactions that symbolically emphasize shared social space while deemphasizing service role hierarchies. Match servers do proximal service throughout the course of the meal and in specific ways, using informal speech styles, extending peer-like gestures, and demonstrating similar tastes with diners. Customers, in turn, participate in this interpersonal drama (Goffman, 1967) by acknowledging, responding to, and collaborating on such acts, and often extending some of their own. While roles in the service relationship do not change, a proximal style of service minimizes the symbolic and social distance between the two.

Proximal service can be initiated when a server greets a new group of diners. Servers frequently lead with informal and/or personalizing statements towards diners. For example, while pouring water into each customer's glass, female servers may remark on the cute top that a female patron is wearing, followed by *is that from around here?* A male server might point out a sports team's logo on a diner's shirt, and give a personal anecdote about living in that city years back. Or tell a joke. Leroy (male, 26-year-old server) says of his opening routine, "I like to make them [diners] laugh right off the bat. It just gets them in a good mood and starts the meal off right, you know?"

Servers at Match often follow an informal greeting towards customers with a more conversational style of service that infuses the service sequence with personal elements:

> Jerry approaches a five-top (three men and two women, all white) who appear in their early thirties. "What's up you guys, how's it going?" he says. They respond, looking up

at him and smiling. He begins to go around the table clockwise, pouring water in their glasses.

"How are you, man?" one of the male diners asks.

"I'm great, just great," Jerry says, "so, looks like y'all are heading to the beach?" They nod along, smiling. "Awesome ... well, I'll be there, like, *right* after I'm outta here myself!" Everyone laughs.

"So ... what're we eating today?" Jerry says (Field notes, 3/27/12).

Jerry frames himself as a socially proximate individual to the customers throughout this service interaction. After receiving a positive and symmetrical response to his casual opening (the male diner says, *how are you, man?*), Jerry asserts peer-like status by stepping outside of traditional service boundaries to infer about the diners' private activities outside the restaurant (*looks like you all are heading to the beach?*), and alludes to his similar post-work agenda using generational slang (*I'll be there, like, right after I'm outta here myself*). This type of exchange at the front end of the dining service encounter sets the tone for proximal service throughout the remainder of the meal.

While Jerry and Leroy verbally cue socially proximate interactions, other workers draw on company resources to help them accomplish the same. For example, Match servers take advantage of the restaurant's liberal policies on discounting and comps (described earlier) as tools to help them establish rapport with diners. For example, when Charlie (white, 27 year-old waiter) identifies someone he has waited on before sitting in his section, he will sometimes use both official and unofficial comps within his service routine. First, he approaches the diners like old friends, calling out, "it's so nice to see you both!" placing a glass of orange juice or coffee on the table without ringing it up. Later, he punctuates his performed familiarity with a statement like, "oh, and when you finish eating, you *gotta* try my favorite cookie we make here. Its on me!" Charlie will then ask for manager approval to discount the cookie off the final bill by claiming the diners were celebrating a birthday or other special occasion.

During the middle of meal service, management may also initiate discounting and comping practices that in turn assist servers in performing proximal service. An example of this occurred on a Thursday afternoon when I was waiting on a white couple in their late twenties. From my field notes:

The couple has just finished their meal, and I walk back to the server station to process their bill. Scott [manager], who is standing nearby, tells me to show him the couple's check. He wordlessly comps their two alcoholic drinks and takes 50% off the rest of the bill. "She works down the street," he says, and walks away. Surprised at Scott's generosity, I drop the bill off to the couple and smile, "hey, it was great having you two! [pause] Oh, and we got a nice surprise for you here."

The woman replies, "Oh how cool! Is Scott working today?" I nod. She says, "he comes in a couple times a week to the pizza place I work at up the street. I'm always there. You should come in some time! What is your name? I'm Brittany."

I shake hands with her and her boyfriend and introduce myself. I add, addressing the woman, "I'll be sure to come see you there!" (Field Notes, 1/15/13)

Because of management's actions, Match servers gain context to enter into a more personalized service exchange with the customer. By remaining outside the service interaction (as Scott does in the above example), managers also allow frontline service workers to take ownership of the gesture (e.g., its on *me*; *we* got a nice surprise for you).

To be sure, Match servers do not approach every new group of diners using the cues of proximal service such as breezy opening statements or comped food and drink. The two contexts in which servers often opt for a more deferential service posture are when facing customers who are clearly older and formally dressed, or following some serious error of service such as forgetting to order a customer's meal or overcharging a credit card. Here *customers* may choose to reframe hierarchical service relations to be more socially proximate. The following occurred on a busy Sunday brunch shift:

Two female customers who appear in their late thirties have been sitting for almost ten minutes without anyone greeting them or taking their order. Charlie, who has been busy attending to other tables, hustles over, then stiffly says, "good afternoon ladies, I'm *so* sorry for leaving you here, how are you all doing today? [quickly turning to one guest] May I get you with something to drink, ma'am?"

The women smile at him with slightly amused expressions. One girl waves her hand in the air and leans in towards Charlie, "don't worry at all, we understand. We come here all the time – Sundays are always crazy. So yeah, take your time."

Charlie looks up and smiles, "oh, well, ... you're awesome then!" Everyone laugh. (1/19/13 field note)

Drawing from interactional cues initiated by customers that signal informality (*don't worry at all* ...), servers are able to quickly re-adjust their approach to proximal service (evident in Charlie's response, *you're awesome then!*). Similarly, customers can also trigger a more socially close interaction by offering up personal information that alludes to a shared identity, present or past. This is particularly relevant in the case of customers who are clearly older or status-superior than Match workers. For example, a middle-aged diner may make reference to a past career as a waitress, or point out a mutual leisure interest, such as a TV show. By intentionally interacting with workers in ways that transcend service-dictated roles, customers too, help sculpt a proximal service dynamic in the dining room.

The inverse is also true. Proximal service risks disruption when either servers or customers violate its principles by reverting to more asymmetrical service norms. For example:

> A new table in my section is a four top of men in their mid-twenties. I begin by addressing them as "you guys," to which there is good rapport, with responses like, "hey what's up?" and "howzit going, man." One man asks me if I watched the Dodgers game on television last night; I reply no. I take their order, and the mood is light. During their meal, I check up on them frequently. When clearing one of their plates, I absent-mindedly say, "are you all set with that, *sir*?" He stares at me with his brow slightly furrowed, then nods. As I clear the plate and start to move away, I hear him lean in and not-so-quietly tell the other men, "did you hear he called me 'sir?'" They chuckle and shake their heads as I walk away. (11/17/12 field notes)

In this situation, the proximal service we had established using informal language and peer references was breached by my use of an inconsistent marker of formality. "Sir" suggested our social distance and bright role distinctions as server and customer. Following their social sanction of my utterance (*did you hear he called me 'sir'*), my subsequent interactions with the group not only evinced a good degree of embarrassment (Goffman, 1956), it garnered me a poor tip.

Disruptions of proximal service are the exception to the rule. More commonly, socially proximate exchanges are maintained throughout the duration of the meal. This can result in collaborative and participatory exchanges between servers and diners in the restaurant. Consider an impromptu event at the restaurant that Match servers still refer to as "hat day":

> A male, thirty-something diner gave Leroy two brightly colored, 80's-style trucker hats, the same kind he himself was wearing. Leroy returned to the server area and gave one hat to Charlie. The two of them promptly put the hats on and approached the table where the diner was sitting. They wore their hats playfully, adjusting them backwards and sideways, returning to strike poses with the gifting table. Surrounding diners began to laugh too, and the hats became a running joke every time either Leroy or Charlie would walk by. This occurred throughout the shift, well after the table left. I asked Charlie and Leroy about the hats afterwards. "Its cool, huh?" Charlie said, "all the tables get a kick out of it. Its fun, plus I get good tips."

Leroy added, "yeah, its pretty rad, dude. The guy gave me his business card, told me to hit him up sometime. Apparently he makes these [pointing to his hat]!" (9/3/12 field note)

For Leroy and Charlie, the hats initially indicated their social rapport with the gifting customer. They soon came to stand for more than that, helping each server perform proximal service with subsequent groups of diners.

Customers also occasionally suggest games to be played that invite the server to participate as a willing collaborator. These games can overlay new symbolic boundaries of inclusion onto the service relationship. One such game is known as "credit card Roullette," which nearly all servers at Match are familiar with. In its simplest form, each diner hands over a credit card to the server, who then randomly charges one card and hands back the rest. Servers often take it upon themselves to add panache to the game, such as by setting multiple check presenters down on the table and making customers guess which one has the charged card. In this sense, while the customer must initiate such a game, the server often decides how it proceeds – to the amusement of all involved. These acts transform a simple service sequence (payment) into a collaborative ritual performed between diners and servers.

Certain rituals surrounding tipping on both the part of servers and customers can stand as a capstone to a socially proximate relationship. In order to convey themselves as social and economic peers, Match servers must not appear too needy or dependent on customers' tips. As a result many servers do not even motion to collect the paid bill (and their tip) until after the diner has left the establishment. Leroy (described earlier), for example, likes to casually chat with diners about their plans for the rest of the day as they finish their meal. Leaving the check on the table, Leroy walks with the diners towards the exit, often shaking their hands and smiling like a host seeing invited guests out.

Tipping poses several running contradictions for performed social proximity. Though tips constitute the majority of servers' earnings (see Haley-Lock & Ewert, 2011; Paules, 1991),[3] servers at Match must publicly act like they do not matter (can one demand a high tip after "hanging out" with a friend/diner?). Both Leroy and his customers above therefore play out a proximal service encounter in ways that belie the extent to which the check contents have unequal significance for both parties. Yet customers too, must approach tipping in a way that does not violate the principles of proximal service. A tip too big or too small risks emphasizing the asymmetries of the service relationship, and the social distance between server and served (Bearman, 2005, chapter 6). Match servers overwhelmingly see a "good" tip of around 20% (particularly if rounded up) to solidify their proximal service interaction with diners ("he was a good guy!"), whereas an uncharacteristically high or low tip risks violating the performance of social closeness.[4] This is reflected in servers' own tipping practices when dining out in which tipping generously is a symbolic extension of treating industry peers with respect, humanity, and reciprocity.

Service-based interactions at the table also frequently spill over into close friendships and romances at the restaurant. In this sense, proximal service not only sets the stage for performances of shared social space but also enduring social relations that transcend the dining room. This is evident in the many social ties between those working and those playing at the restaurant: friends, lovers, and family of workers socialize amongst the staff and occasionally hang out long after their meal has concluded so workers can accompany them to nearby bars, restaurants, and movie theaters.

Of course, the formation of intimate relationships between servers and customers is hardly unique to Match Restaurant or under proximal service conditions. Yet I suggest two reasons that a service model built around the drama of social proximity is more likely to encourage intimate exchanges between servers and customers. First, intimacy between servers and customers (initiated by either) is entirely consistent with the aims of portraying social closeness across the service encounter. Second, the hiring selectivity of workers yields many socio-cultural similarities between workers and customers at the restaurant, increasing the likelihood that real ties between the two may form.[5] As case in point, many servers (both men and women) claim they have gone on dates with Match patrons, and it is not uncommon to see restaurant regulars at employee-hosted parties after work.

Match's socially and sexually charged dining floor thus doubles as a veritable meeting ground for patrons and service workers alike. Charlie (the waiter described earlier) commented to me that on given day at work, "you never know whom you might meet or where a relationship with a customer might take you." Male and female workers frequently engage in flirtatious tableside exchanges with customers as well as indirect observation of them. These activities can be embedded within the flow of service:

> Erin and Andy (waitresses, late twenties) are excitedly talking near the central server station in the middle of the restaurant. Neither appears to have tables that need their assistance at the moment. They discuss male diners that they think are "hot" and "cute" in the restaurant right now. Andy smiles and cautions a glance in the direction of an unassuming group of men sitting near the street-facing window. She quickly

whispers to Erin. "Back at it ladies?" I say with a smile. "So which guy you got your eye on now, huh?"

They giggle. "How do you always catch us in the act??" Erin replies, "I know [the male servers] do it too, don't lie. So we get to have some fun too." (9/3/12 field notes)

Charlie, Jerry and Moore are discussing attractive girls dining at Match today. "Dude, look at the girl at table 30, bombshell!" Moore says.

"Charlie, I think you're gonna love that chick sitting outside, table 124, just your type!" Jerry says.

"OK, I'm on it! I'll let you know what I think. Gimme a coffee pot." Charlie grabs a coffee pot and heads outside. He walks straight up to table 124 and makes a joke directed towards the aforementioned female diner. She laughs. He then offers her coffee with a smile. Jerry and Moore laugh, noting that Charlie has completely passed by many other tables with empty coffee mugs to accomplish his singular goal. (3/9/13 field notes)

The relatively lax rules for service at Match allow servers like Charlie, Erin and Andy to simultaneously engage in their own social agendas while "working the floor." These objectives need not contradict one another: Charlie (selectively) refills coffee in order to talk to a cute girl, while Erin and Andy monitor their tables just as they monitor for potential romantic partners.

DISCUSSION AND CONCLUSION

As a strategic and stylized form of customer service, proximal service aims to narrow the symbolic distance between service-worker and service-recipient in commercial settings. In contrast to more hierarchical styles of service that require the use of heavily scripted lines or deferential postures, proximal service encourages servers and customers to interact in ways that evoke their shared social space. Drawing from the case of an upscale restaurant in Los Angeles, I have shown how management sets the stage for proximal service through a carefully curated hiring and training process that favors middle-upper class tastes, culture, and embodied dispositions (Hochschild, 1983; Warhurst & Nickson, 2009; Rivera, 2012). Armed with the right staff, management loosely oversees the service shopfloor, allowing these select workers to engage in highly flexible and peer-like interactions with the restaurant's affluent diners. Interactive service workers often flirt boldly and chat casually with customers, all while displaying personal style that resembles that of customers. These characteristic service interactions constitute a core part of Match's service brand.

To be sure, not *all* service exchanges at Match Restaurant evoke social closeness between servers and customers. As mentioned earlier, a number of servers opt for a more formal style of service when interacting with diners that are clearly age- or status-superiors, or upon committing a service faux-pas. Customers can and do occasionally reject the cues of proximal service, choosing to reassert their symbolic power over the waitstaff by inducing more hierarchical interactions. (By my estimate, those most likely to refuse to engage in socially proximate service are often foreign tourists or wealthy seniors, both of whom often arrive at Match with different codified expectations for the service encounter.) Yet these customers are in the decided minority at Match, due in part to a self-selecting process: those who do not enjoy the experience do not return.

Proximal service builds most directly on the concepts of aesthetic labor and emotional labor, incorporating both in its dynamic. In comparison to aesthetic labor, proximal service is more *interactive* and *performative* than purely a "look" or sound. Match servers must indeed possess embodied characteristics (indicative of aesthetic labor), but it is in the qualities of the service relations that results that the concept describes. Like proximal service, emotional labor theorizes a kind of labor and skill that is done through service-based relations. Yet the concept largely assumes inequality in the relationship between interactive service workers and customers (the latter are due courtesies that need not be reciprocated). Under this frame, unscripted informality expressed in service relations is typically cast as resistance, either to management or customers (Leidner, 1993). Proximal service offers a service typology to describe the *intentional* production of peer-like exchanges within commercial service establishments.

Understanding proximal service is important for two primary reasons. First, service establishments offering this style of service appear to be on the rise, particularly in affluent, urban centers of youth consumption. A growing number of service establishments — artisanal coffee shops, craft beer gastropubs, and "casual-upscale" restaurants — appear to be staffed by shabby-chic hipsters and filled with patrons who look similar (see also Zukin, 1995). The "vibe" of proximal service also likely resonates with growing consumer demand for more personalized products and authentic consumption experiences (Warde, Martens, & Olsen, 1999). It fits with recent trends that abandon hierarchical formality and move towards "flatter" relations (Warde & Martens, 2000). In this sense, for affluent consumers, proximal service may feel appealingly less like a transaction with a member of the "emotional proletariat" (MacDonald & Sirianni, 1996, p. 3) and more like an interaction with a social and cultural peer.

Second, it is important to consider how a service model based on performing social *equality* acts as a mechanism of *inequality* and social closure. In orchestrating an exclusive, club-like service atmosphere, management necessarily excludes those who do not embody the "right" traits (race, class, age, gender, as well as bodily capital) to convincingly engage customers as socio-cultural peers.[6] While the logic of proximal service most typically involves hiring privileged white workers to interact in socially close ways with privileged white customers, these characteristics for inclusion/exclusion will vary based on the establishment and its target patrons. One could conceivably imagine how such a proximal service model in an affluent African American neighborhood in Atlanta or a wealthy Chinese "ethnoburb" (see Zhou, Tseng, & Kim, 2008) in Los Angeles would involve a different set of criteria.

In sum, situated within social geographies of relative youth, whiteness, and affluence, the production of proximal service at Match Restaurant points to ways in which peer-like service relations may be becoming a prominent variety of customer service. Within these settings, the characteristic experience of informality evokes a club-like atmosphere of inner circle membership encompassing those serving, as well as those served.

NOTES

1. The authors note that boundary-closed relationships with restaurant servers are more common. Under these conditions, "the waiter is someone who is present, but whom others treat as if he is not there" (*ibid.*, p. 101).

2. A smaller fraction of Match servers also possess post-bachelor education, or professional certification. For example, in the spring of 2013, one female server was enrolled in a Master's program for journalism, while another was in her second year of a Masters of Social Work program. A third, a 26-year-old man, had just completed a certificate for specialized film production.

3. Despite their own relatively privileged backgrounds, many of the young adults working at Match live independently and shoulder the majority of their daily expenses using earnings from the restaurant.

4. It could be said that the meaning of a tip is inherently ambiguous. Yet as Sutton (2007, p. 198) notes, "while some [restaurant] customers no doubt use tip calculators to calculate an exact 15% addition to their bill, most do not, and indeed use the tip to say something about themselves, *about their server, and about the relationship between the two*" (italics mine).

5. Social scientists have long noted that as far as social networks and intimate partnerships go, "birds of a feather flock together" (McPherson, Smith-Lovin, & Cook, 2001; see also Lazarfeld & Merton, 1954).

6. Other individuals who do not fit the profile for proximal service work in a privileged, white setting often do labor within the same service establishments but are concentrated in non-interactive roles. For example, many immigrant Latinos work within restaurant kitchens (see Waldinger & Lichter, 2003; Restaurant Opportunities Centers United, 2014).

ACKNOWLEDGMENTS

I wish to thank Ashley Mears, the editor of the RSW Journal, and three anonymous reviewers for their insightful comments on previous drafts of this paper. I also thank Ruben Hernandez-Leon, Jack Katz, Rachel Sherman, Chris Tilly, Christine Yano, and members of the UCLA Ethnography Working Group for their assistance with this paper at various stages. All remaining errors are my own.

REFERENCES

Azar, O. (2007). The social norm of tipping: A review. *Journal of Applied Social Psychology*, *37*(2), 380–402.

Bearman, P. (2005). *Doormen*. Chicago, IL: University of Chicago Press.

Besen, Y. (2006). Exploitation or fun? The lived experience of teenage employment in suburban America. *Journal of Contemporary Ethnography*, *35*(3), 319–340.

Bolton, S., & Boyd, C. (2003). Trolley dolly or skilled emotion manager? Moving on from Hochschild's managed heart. *Work Employment Society*, *17*, 289–308.

Bolton, S., & Houlihan, M. (2005). The (mis)representation of customer service. *Work, Employment, and Society*, *19*(4), 685–703.

Bourdieu, P. (1984). *Distinction: A social critique of the judgment of taste*. Cambridge, MA: Harvard University Press.

Cobble, D. (1991). *Dishing it out: Waitresses and their unions in the twentieth century*. Chicago, IL: University of Illinois Press.

Crang, P. (1994). It's showtime: On the workplace geographies of display in a restaurant in Southeast England. *Environment and Planning D: Society and Space*, *12*, 675–704.

Deener, A. (2012). *Venice: A contested bohemia in Los Angeles*. Chicago, IL: University of Chicago Press.

Ehrenreich, B. (2001). *Nickel and dimed: On (not) getting by in America*. New York, NY: Henry Holt and Company.

Erickson, K. (2009). *The hungry cowboy: Service and community in a neighborhood restaurant*. Jackson, MS: University of Mississippi Press.

Finkelstein, J. (1989). *Dining out: A sociology of modern manners*. New York, NY: New York University Press.

Florida, R. (2004). *Rise of the creative class*. New York, NY: Basic Books.

Frenette, A. (2013). Making the intern economy: Role and career challenges of the music industry intern. *Work and Occupations, 40*(4), 364–397.

Ginsberg, D. (2001). *Waiting: The true confessions of a waitress.* New York, NY: Harper Perennial.

Goffman, E. (1956). Embarrassment and social organization. *American Journal of Sociology, 62*(3), 264–271.

Goffman, E. (1959). *The presentation of self in everyday life.* New York, NY: Anchor.

Goffman, E. (1967). On face-work: An analysis of ritual elements in social interaction. *Reflections, 4*(3), 7–13.

Goffman, E. (1974). *Frame analysis: An essay on the organization of experience.* Cambridge, MA: Harvard University Press.

Gutek, B., Cherry, B., Bhappu, A., Schneider, S., & Woolf, L. (2000). Features of service relationships and encounters. *Work and Occupations, 27*(3), 319–351.

Haley-Lock, A., & Ewert, S. (2011). Waiting for the minimum: US state wage laws, firm strategy, and chain-restaurant job quality. *Journal of Industrial Research, 53*, 31–48.

Hochschild, A. (1983). *The managed heart.* Los Angeles, CA: University of California Press.

Larson, J., & Urry, J. (2011). Gazing and performing. *Environment and Planning D: Society and Space, 29*, 1110–1125.

Lazarfeld, P., & Merton, R. (1954). Friendship as a social process. In M. Berger, T. Abel, & C. H. Page (Eds.), *Freedom and control in modern society* (pp. 118–166). Princeton, NJ: Van Nostrand.

Leidner, R. (1993). *Fast food fast talk: Service work and the routinization of everyday life.* Berkeley, CA: University of California Press.

Lloyd, R. (2010). *Neo-bohemia: Art and commerce in the postindustrial city* (2nd ed.). New York, NY: Routledge.

Lopez, S. (2010). Workers, managers, and customers: Triangles of power in work communities. *Work and Occupations, 37*(3), 251–271.

Macdonald, C., & Sirianni, C. (Eds.). (1996). *Working in the service society.* Philadelphia, PA: Temple University Press.

Mann, S. (2004). 'People-work': Emotion management, stress and coping. *British Journal of Guidance & Counseling, 32*(2), 205–221.

Mars, G., & Nicod, M. (1984). *The world of waiters.* London: George Allen & Unwin.

McClain, N., & Mears, A. (2012). Free to those who can afford it: The everyday affordance of privilege. *Poetics, 40*, 133–149.

McPherson, M., Smith-Lovin, L., & Cook, J. (2001). Birds of a feather: Homophily in social networks. *Annual Review of Sociology, 27*, 415–444.

Moss, P., & Tilly, C. (2001). *Stories employers tell: Race, skill, and hiring in America.* New York, NY: Russell Sage Foundation.

Nickson, D., Warhurst, C., Witz, A., & Cullen, A. M. (2001). The importance of being aesthetic: Work, employment and service organization. In A. Sturdy et al. (Eds.), *Customer service.* Basingstoke: Palgrave.

Ortner, S. (2013). *Not Hollywood: Independent film at the twilight of the American dream.* Durham, NC: Duke University Press.

Paules, G. F. (1991). *Dishing it out: Power and resistance among waitresses in a New Jersey restaurant.* Philadelphia, PA: Temple University Press.

Pettinger, L. (2004). Brand culture and branded workers: Service work and aesthetic labour in fashion retail. *Consumption, Market and Culture, 7*(2), 165–184.

Restaurant Opportunities Centers United. (2014). *The great service divide: Occupational segre-gation and inequality in the US restaurant industry.* Technical report. Restaurant Opportunities Center of New York, New York.

Ritzer, G. (2000). *The McDonaldization of society: New century edition.* Thousand Oaks, CA: Pine Forge Press.

Rivera, L. (2012). Hiring as cultural matching: The case of elite professional service firms. *American Sociological Review, 77*(6), 999–1022.

Sherman, R. (2005). Producing the superior self: Strategic comparison and symbolic bound-aries among luxury hotel workers. *Ethnography, 6,* 131–158.

Sherman, R. (2007). *Class acts; Service and inequality in luxury hotels.* Berkeley, CA: University of California Press.

Spradley, J. P., & Mann, B. (1975). *The cocktail waitress: Woman's work in a man's world.* New York, NY: Wiley.

Sutton, D. (2007). Tipping: An anthropological meditation. In D. Beriss & D. Sutton (Eds.), *The restaurants book: Ethnographies of where we eat* (pp. 191–204). New York, NY: Berg.

United States Census Bureau. (2012). Retrieved from http://quickfacts.census.gov/qfd/index.html

Waldinger, R., & Lichter, M. (2003). *How the other half works.* Berkeley, CA: University of California Press.

Warde, A., & Martens, L. (2000). *Eating out.* New York, NY: Cambridge University Press.

Warde, A., Martens, L., & Olsen, W. (1999). Consumption and the problem of variety: Cultural omnivorousness, social distinction and dining out. *Sociology, 33*(1), 105–127.

Warhurst, C., & Nickson, D. (2007). Employee experience of aesthetic labour in retail and hospitality. *Work, Employment & Society, 21*(1), 103–120.

Warhurst, C., & Nickson, D. (2009). 'Who's got the look?' Emotional, aesthetic and sexualized labor in interactive services. *Gender, Work and Organization, 16*(3), 385–404.

Warhurst, C., Tilly, C., & Gatta, M. (2016). A new social construction of 'skill'. In C. Warhurst, K. Mayhew, D. Finegold, & J. Buchanan (Eds.), *Oxford handbook of skills and training.* Oxford: Oxford University Press.

Williams, C., & Connell, C. (2010). 'Looking good and sounding right': Aesthetic labor and social inequality in the retail industry. *Work and Occupations, 37*(3), 349–377.

Wright, D. (2005). Commodifying respectability: Distinctions at work in the bookshop. *Journal of Consumer Culture, 5*(3), 295–314.

Wynn, J. (2010). City tour guides: Urban alchemists at work. *City and Community, 9,* 145–164.

Yano, C. (2011). *Airborne dreams: "Nisei" stewardesses and pan American world airways.* Durham, NC: Duke University Press.

Zhou, M., Tseng, Y., & Kim, R. (2008). Rethinking residential assimilation: The case of a Chinese ethnoburb in the San Gabriel Valley, California. *Amerasia, 34*(3), 53–83.

Zukin, S. (1995). *The culture of cities.* Oxford: Blackwell.

CONTROL FROM ON HIGH: CLOUD-COMPUTING, SKILL, AND ACUTE FRUSTRATION AMONG ANALYTICS WORKERS IN THE DIGITAL PUBLISHING INDUSTRY

Michael L. Siciliano

ABSTRACT

This chapter addresses research on worker skill, technology, and control over the labor process by focusing on routine immaterial labor or knowledge work. Based on participant observation conducted among analytics workers at a digital publishing network, I find that analytics workers appear paradoxically autonomous and empowered by management while being bound by ever-evolving, calculative cloud-based information and communication technologies (ICTs). Workers appear free to "be creative," while ever-evolving ICTs exert unpredictable control over work. Based on this finding, I argue that sociology's tendency to take organizational boundaries and technological stability for granted hampers analyses of contemporary forms of work. Thus, sociologists of work must extend outward — beyond communities of practice, labor markets, and the state — to include the ever-evolving, infrastructural, socio-technical

Research in the Sociology of Work, Volume 29, 125–153
ISSN: 0277-2833/doi:10.1108/S0277-283320160000029020

networks in which work and organizations are embedded. Additionally, research on the experience of immaterial labor suggests that ICTs afford pleasurably immersive experiences that bind workers to organizations and their fields. Complicating this emerging body of research, I find workers acutely frustrated *by these unpredictable, ever-evolving, cloud-based ICTs.*

Keywords: Skill; labor process theory; information and communication technologies; immaterial labor; creative industries; cognitive capitalism

INTRODUCTION

Audiences around the world turn on their computers, opening web-browsers. They visit YouTube, a popular blog, or another advertising-supported website. As they immerse themselves in digital media content, a few advertisements graze their eyes. Preempting their desired consumption, advertisements display messages from global brands about consumer products. A variety of technological systems count and store information about the audiences' experiences. In cities such as New York, London, San Francisco, and Los Angeles, workers analyze this information in order to sell audiences' attention to advertisers. Through this work process, audience attention to advertising becomes a saleable commodity. In this chapter, I focus on this immaterial production process.

More specifically, I focus on the affective and structural relationships between workers and calculative cloud-based information and communication technologies (ICTs) that facilitate this immaterial production process. At a digital publishing network I call Obsession,[1] workers use calculative cloud-based ICTs (i.e., web-traffic monitors, advertising servers, and advertising exchanges) to collect and construct information about Obsession's audiences. Within Obsession's advertising operations department (AdOps), these workers monitor audience behavior, produce immaterial inventory of "impressions" − a type of "audience commodity" (Smythe, 1977; see also Scholz, 2013) − and generate sales reports. Monitoring and reporting this information determines the size of Obsession's inventory of "impressions" or saleable views of advertisements.

I use the term calculative, cloud-based ICTs when referring to applications and computing systems that perform calculative procedures. My data and analysis focus on cloud systems that count and calculate measures of audience attention. Information from these cloud systems allows Obsession to sell audience attention to advertisers – claiming that online audiences spend 287,000,000 minutes per month reading these blogs and viewing advertisements. Like all cloud systems, these systems are accessed by way of internet connections to servers owned and controlled by companies located offsite and outside of the organization.

In the United States, information, knowledge, or creative industries tend to be the most valuable in terms of corporate profits and worker remuneration.[2] Termed "symbolic analysts" (Reich, 1991), "immaterial labor" (Hardt & Negri, 2001), "self-programming" knowledge workers (Castells, 2010), or the "creative class" (Florida, 2002), these workers produce and circulate immaterial commodities and experience goods (i.e., music, film, performance). Over the past several decades, work in these fields has grown as a research topic. Many studies focus on the "boundaryless" (Arthur & Rousseau, 2001; Tolbert, 2001) or networked careers of freelance professionals (Anderson-Gough, Grey, & Robson, 2006; Barley & Kunda, 2011; Damarin, 2006; Osnowitz, 2006) or expressive, media industry occupations (Hesmondhalgh & Baker, 2011; Lingo & O'Mahony, 2010; Mears, 2011). In these industries, highly uncertain labor markets, ever-evolving technologies, and, in the case of media, radically uncertain demand (Salganik, Dodds, & Watts, 2006) compel immaterial laborers to engage in constant skill development, social capital accumulation, and reputational maintenance. Blurring the boundaries between work and non-work due to constant social-network development inside and outside organizations, these processes form a normative type of control over work (Osnowitz, 2006).

While studies of networked or boundaryless workers advance sociological knowledge regarding expressive and professionalized immaterial labor, less can be said about workers that remain within an organization performing routine, non-professional work. I address this gap by examining a *routine*, immaterial labor process. Lacking control over the abstractions through which they work (Abbott, 1988), analytics workers perform non-professional, routine data analysis. The routine work described in this chapter requires less codified skillsets and occurs within a particular organization under standard employment conditions (i.e., full-time with benefits). This situation suggests that constant networking and skill-development *outside* the workplace appear less salient. Based on these omissions, I ask how, if at all, full-time, routine, immaterial workers *within* an organization experience constant changes in skill found in previous studies of immaterial labor?

Relatedly, research suggests that technology serves as a key source of control over immaterial labor. Embedded within dense socio-technical networks, workers experience technology as a serious constraint or source of control (Damarin, 2013). Relatedly, an abundance of research suggests that workers in "creative" or knowledge industries tend to experience high levels of immersive, "flow" states wherein worker and task experientially "merge" (Amabile, Barsade, Mueller, & Straw, 2005; Quinn, 2005; see also Csikszentmihalyi, 1990). These moments tend to be associated with technology (Cetina & Bruegger, 2000; Kaiser, Müller-Seitz, Lopes, & e Cunha, 2007). In these cases, technology exerts control over work by structuring how workers approach problems (Rennstam, 2012) and work's sensual or "aesthetic" dimension (Siciliano, 2016). Illustrating how ICTs provide pathways to meaningful social action that reinforce positive workplace affects, this emerging body of research provides few contemporary examples of everyday frustrations found in earlier studies of workplace ICTs (Adler, 1988; Baker, 1991; Gasser, 1986). From here I ask how and when cloud-based, calculative systems elicit positive and negative affects in the context of routine, immaterial labor under the condition of relatively standard employment?

In addressing these questions, I extend research on workers' skill and workplace control by illustrating how calculative cloud-based ICTs structure and limit the exercise of skill, thus controlling the "content of work" (Simpson, 1985). In accord with theories of flexibilization (see, e.g., Harvey, 1989; Sennett, 2000), I find that managers demand a skilled, inventive or "creative" workforce, however Obsession's workers lack control over the calculative processes that structure the information that they analyze. As such, cloud-based, calculative ICTs control work by exerting "power...at the level of the labor process" (Heydebrand, 1989, p. 326) and thus function as a form of technical control. Paradoxically, management allows workers to "be creative" while said creativity appears bounded by cloud-based systems. Complicating recent research on immersive technological experiences at work, I illustrate how technology offers both immersive, pleasurable experiences and what I call *acute frustrations*. Both experiences emerge from interactions between workers and cloud-based, calculative ICTs.

In what follows, I discuss worker skill and workplace control with regard to technology and recent studies of immersion and workplace ICTs. I then provide background information regarding digital, advertising-supported media organizations, and discuss method before describing processes by which analytics workers produce audience commodities — quantified, saleable aspects of audience attention. I conclude by discussing my findings' theoretical implications.

SKILL, TECHNOLOGY, AND CONTROL

Notoriously difficult to measure and often subject to differing, disputed definitions (Attewell, 1990; Vallas, 1990), worker skill may be defined broadly as learned competencies or earned certifications of competencies necessary or perceived to be necessary for particular work tasks and processes. Control over the use of skill represents a crucial source of power over the labor process. In labor process theory, autonomous planning and execution of work's procedures and processes tends to be deemed skilled (see, e.g., Braverman, 1974; see also, Attewell, 1990). The opposite — deskilling — tends to be linked to the implementation of new, labor saving technologies and managerial techniques that diminish workers' power and autonomy while securing low labor costs. Initially theorized by Braverman as an inherent tendency of capitalism, deskilling consistently appears unevenly distributed (Attewell, 1987) and undoubtedly mediated by local workplace cultures, variations in worker power (Choi, Leiter, & Tomaskovic-Devey, 2008), and the contingent effects of organizational technologies (Barley, 1986).

Recent economic shifts toward logics of "flexible accumulation" (Harvey, 1989) and "flexible specialization" (Piore & Sabel, 1984) suggest a prevalence of upskilling and reintegration of planning and execution of tasks (Vallas, 1999). Here, implementation of new technologies tends to be associated with upskilling and concurrent increases in labor market polarization that favors workers with skills demanded by said technologies (Gallie, 1991). As such, deploying skill at work appears largely contingent upon industry, occupation, workplace culture, managerial strategies, worker resistance, and, most important here, technical relations at work.

These variables may mediate managerial control over skill, but including these variables does not significantly alter who or what attempts to exert control. In all cases, technologies that deskill, reskill, or upskill tend to serve management's interests. Considered as studies of fixed technologies that remain, once implemented, within organizational boundaries, these findings tell us rather little with regard to a variety of contemporary workplace technologies that find their use inside an organization but over which the organization does not maintain control (e.g., calculative, cloud-based ICTs).

For immaterial labor, skill development and reskilling appear as constant features of work (Deuze, 2007; Huws, 2014; Kotamraju, 2002). In post-bureaucratic organizations wherein knowledge work tends to take place, management occupies a diminished role (Sewell, 2005), and control over work (and thus over skill deployment) stems from the labor market

(Adler, 2001), professionalism (Abbott, 1988), the demands of networking (Anderson-Gough et al., 2006), and the constraints imposed by socio-technical networks (Damarin, 2013).

In knowledge or creative industries, socio-technical networks include technologies outside the control of organizations. This includes media distribution platforms (e.g., YouTube, iTunes, Vimeo) and "cyberinfrastructures" (Winter, Berente, Howison, & Butler, 2014) such as research infrastructures (e.g., supercomputers, computing and hardware standards) and the calculative, cloud-based ICTs described later. These cyberinfrastructures embed "societal and field-level" interests rather than those of management (Winter et al., 2014, p. 252). This suggests that constraint or control over skill stems, in part, from infrastructure's owners and thus a need to extend analyses beyond the aforementioned sources of control over skill.

Focusing on socio-technical networks, Cetina and Bruegger term these technologies "global microstructures" (2002) insofar as many micro-level interactions occur through or in relation to similar, if not identical, ICT interfaces (Huws, 2014). Building on Cetina and Bruegger's concept, Damarin (2013) likens these technological microstructures to Becker's concept of conventions (1984) and argues that technology serves as a major form of control upon otherwise autonomous employees by limiting the range of possibilities afforded to workers. Conventions tend to remain relatively stable, acting as a reference that facilitates coordination (Becker, 1984), yet many cloud-based infrastructures operate with proprietary algorithms that can change instantaneously and without notice (Gillespie, 2014). This suggests that while technology may constrain the use of skill, the relations of production along with the temporal relations between technology, organization, and worker appear fundamentally different.

PLEASURABLY IMMERSIVE TECHNOLOGIES

Relatedly, interactions between workers and contemporary ICTs affectively "attach" or bind employees to their objects of labor (Cetina & Bruegger, 2000). These technologies afford pleasurably immersive "flow" experiences (Cetina & Bruegger, 2000; see also Csikszentmihalyi, 1990) that elicit a "passion" for knowledge (Kaiser et al., 2007). In the case of software programmers, Chun calls this combination of pleasurable immersion and technologically-mediated social action "causal pleasure" (2005, pp. 38–39) or positive affects associated with the ability to cause changes within a screen environment. In media and entertainment, these pleasurably immersive experiences tend to be associated with creative acts that appear intimately dependent upon ICTs such as audio recording or video editing (Hesmondhalgh & Baker, 2011).

Recently, interactions such as these have been theorized as forms of control. Solving the contemporary labor process problem of the "indeterminacy of knowledge" (Sewell, 2005), these constitute forms of "object control" that both guide decision-making (Rennstam, 2012) and enroll workers into organizational projects by modulating workers' sensual experiences (Siciliano, 2016). This dovetails with speculative theorization of immaterial labor under "cognitive capitalism" (see, e.g., Boutang, 2011; Fuchs, 2011; Lazzarato, 2014; Marazzi, 2011) wherein workers' *desire* to learn how to work through complex ICT systems (Boutang, 2011) and organizations depend upon workers' flexible capacities for the creative deployment of embodied, virtuoso-like cognitive skill in a variety of tasks (Virno, 2004). Thus, workers and organizations require technology in order to, respectively, deploy and appropriate skills. Using a cybernetic master/slave metaphor, Lazzarato (2014) calls this "machinic enslavement." Similar to empirical research, cognitive capitalist theory suggests that rather than exerting power by forbiddance, contemporary technical control exerts power through affordances (Zammuto, Griffith, Majchrzak, Dougherty, & Faraj, 2007) or loosely structured pathways to action. This suggests that ICTs afford workers the possibilities of deploying skill and enacting some personal or organizational goal (i.e., to make a transaction, to make a decision, to render a judgment) while experiencing immersive subjective states.

In what follows, I address the questions raised above by focusing on an immaterial production process: the fabrication of impressions, a type of audience commodity. I show how workers autonomously plan and execute analytic procedures and tasks and thus how management depends upon workers' virtuoso-like skills. This autonomy, however, does not extend to the planning and execution of calculation and thus workers appear controlled, partially, by ever-evolving, calculative, cloud-based ICTs — a form of cyberinfrastructure. Much like factory machines in the 19th and early 20th centuries, or even earlier ICTs, cloud-based, calculative technologies appear to employees as blackboxes. Unlike a lathe or a local mainframe, however, cloud ICTs remain outside the control of management and few if any employees understand or control the inner-workings of cloud-based, calculative technologies. Workers exercise control over analytic

interpretation and data reorganization while cloud-owners control and frequently change calculative procedures and data structure. Before presenting
ethnographic data, I provide background on advertising-supported media
industries followed by descriptions of case features and methodology.

BACKGROUND ON ADVERTISING-SUPPORTED MEDIA AND THE SALE OF AUDIENCES

Like traditional advertising-supported media (e.g., broadcast television,
radio, and newspapers), advertising-supported digital media organizations
earn revenue by selling audiences' attention to advertisers. These media
organizations produce two products: media content for consumers and an
"audience commodity" or audience attention for advertisers (Smythe, 1977;
see also Ettema & Whitney, 1994). In television, radio, and digital media,
the sale of the latter pays for content production. The term audience commodity refers to media audiences as they come to be constituted by and
sold by media industries. The fabrication of audience commodities depends
heavily upon measurement systems — forms of sensemaking that structure
organizational fields and decision-making (Anand & Peterson, 2000).

Digital media firms depend upon measurements of audiences' media
consumption in order to constitute audiences as a saleable commodity.
While broadcast TV and radio continue to rely upon entrenched media rating systems such as Nielsen or Arbitron (Napoli, 2003, 2011; see also
Buzzard, 1990; Gitlin, 1983), digital media relies upon more fine-grained
measurement systems in order to sell exact measures of audiences.
Following a larger pattern of rationalized quantification within media
industries (Napoli, 2008), digital media organizations rely upon cloud-
based, calculative ICTs rather than time-use diaries and other forms of
self-reported data used by TV and radio. Calculative, often cloud-based,
systems measure visits to websites ("pagevisits" and "pageviews"), clicking
links ("click-thrus," "click-thru rates," or CTR), time spent on websites,
and time spent viewing videos (minutes-watched). Notably, one of the largest providers of these cloud-based ICTs (Google) also depends, primarily,
upon advertising revenue (Hern, 2016) and thus has a clear vested interest
in controlling and maintaining infrastructures that produce information
about digital audiences.

In industry terms, these measurements constitute saleable "inventory" of
audience behaviors (e.g., clicking advertisements, "sharing" or "liking"

content on social media). Firms such as Obsession sell discrete amounts of audience activities to advertisers as types of audience commodities. These audience commodities include impressions (viewing advertisements), click-thrus (clicking advertisements), and conversions (click-thrus that generate an online sale). In this chapter, I focus on impressions. The term impression refers to the number of advertisements loaded or "served" when a media consumer views media content. For example, one visit to a website (pagevisit) may include viewing multiple portions of said site (pageviews). With each pageview, media audiences may be "served" a number of advertisements. On each page, the advertisements that impress themselves upon audience eyeballs count as impressions. Viewing three pages, each with three advertisements counts as nine impressions sold to advertisers.

In order to generate an inventory of impressions, Obsession and similar organizations rely upon cloud-based, calculative systems that provide estimates of future impressions based on past web-traffic. As such, the counting of impressions and estimates of future impression inventory constitute important, core aspects of revenue generation. Sales brochures from Obsession and similar companies highlight average audience size and estimates of audience activities along with demographic and socio-economic characteristics. Along with the active trafficking or uploading of advertisements to websites, analytics workers at Obsession provide reports of inventory to the sales team, executive staff, and editorial team. Before describing their work, I provide further details about Obsession and discuss my methodology.

CASE FEATURES AND METHODOLOGY

This study draws from 15 months of multi-sited, participant observation at two digital media organizations and 30 interviews with executives, managers, and employees. In this chapter, I focus on five months of fieldwork conducted in 2013 within the advertising operations (AdOps) department of Obsession, a digital publishing network. Obsession publishes numerous blogs and employs 31 full-time staff members in Obsession's main office where I conducted fieldwork. In this office, people perform managerial, editorial, administrative, sales, data-analytic, and executive functions. Obsession's media content production occurs in the United States and around the globe in a network of freelance writers, video production teams, and web designers.

Here, I focus on AdOps's analytic workers that "traffic" or upload and integrate advertisements into Obsession's blogs while also analyzing web-traffic data in order to ensure that the company "makes good" on product sales (impressions). Obsession's mostly female AdOps employees ranged in age from 22 to 38 and work under standard employment conditions (i.e., full-time and salaried with benefits). All were college educated, though only one AdOps worker held a degree in marketing and advertising. Most AdOps employees held liberal arts degrees in varying disciplines such as political science, English literature, media studies, and poetry. Salaries in AdOps ranged from $35,000 to $60,000 with mostly male department managers earning the highest in that range. Turnover appeared quite high with only one team member having been there longer than three years. Highlighting the precariousness of their "standard" employment, the entire department was laid off just prior to the end of my fieldwork.

White-collar with a relatively flat hierarchy and an open-office floorplan, Obsession resembled an ideal-typical "no-collar" workplace (Ross, 2004). Culturally, no-collar workplaces appear similar to white-collar technology industry workplaces (Kunda, 1992) that display the broader trend of increased participatory demands upon workers (see Boltanski & Chiapello, 2005) and a blurring of the boundaries between personal life and work. As such, this work environment serves as a theoretically purposive case that allows for the extension of theories outlined above. Rather than expressive, unmoored workers, analytics workers serve as an organizationally-bound case of the creative industries' "humdrum" work (Caves, 2000) or routine, immaterial labor (Hardt & Negri, 2001).

Following the extended-case method (Burawoy, 1998), I entered the field in order to extend theory through an examination of this particular case. Working two to three days a week, I wrote fieldnotes after each five-to eight-hour shift and coded fieldnotes using theoretical categories as well as inductively generated codes. Based on previous research in these areas, I expected to find a flexible, upskilled workforce. As I show later, fieldwork met this expectation, however, a portion of workplace experience exceeded extant theory. This excess serves as an anomaly to be explained.

As an unpaid intern and overt researcher, I regularly performed or supported many of the tasks described in this chapter. Though this granted me insight into organizational life at Obsession, my low status as an intern and the prevalence of non-disclosure agreements (NDAs) seemed to cause difficulty in obtaining interviews at Obsession. Most frequently, employees cited their lack of time, stated that they simply "did not want to be interviewed," or did not respond to multiple interview requests. Despite official permission from the organization, employees expressed concern that an interview might violate the NDAs required by many media and technology firms. As such, my analysis draws primarily from participant observation and lunchtime conversations. I supplement observational data with interviews from managers and employees at other digital media firms. I now turn to my data to describe how AdOps employees perform analytics work wherein they process information in order to describe, analyze, and ultimately sell the attention of digital media audiences to global advertisers. Technologically dense, their work requires the use of several, cloud-based, calculative systems. I begin by describing interactions between employees and these systems.

ASSEMBLING AN AUDIENCE COMMODITY

Obsession's analytics employees engage in technically complex, routine, repetitive work that requires creative interpretation of information. Inside AdOps, analytics workers' main tasks include uploading advertisements to servers, devising new sizes and placements of advertising, tracking the performance of these advertisements over time, and providing reports to other departments regarding estimated audience size and advertising revenue. Calculating website traffic and audience size feature prominently in the majority of these tasks. In what follows, I describe the process by which analytics workers produce estimates of future impressions. After completion of these processes, AdOps workers "release" impressions to sales staff for sale to advertisers.

In order to illustrate how worker skill and autonomy depend upon technical systems, I begin by describing workers' typical interactions with these systems. A typical worker's computer screen includes an email application, an instant-messaging application, and as many as five windows of a browser, each with multiple "tabs" or layered sub-windows. These web-browsers display interfaces of multiple, cloud-based applications. At Obsession, analytics employees tended to work within a single screen and thus encountered a series of half-visible, overlaid windows that depicted charts, graphs, and tables along with messages from co-workers.

This layered work area contained three globally ubiquitous technologies within contemporary ad-supported media organizations: web-traffic monitors (monitors), advertisement servers (Ad-servers), and advertising exchange servers (Ad-exchanges). Monitors calculate the size of blog audience and time spent by audiences on blogs. Ad-servers place digital advertisements into websites ("serving," "firing," or "trafficking"). Servers calculate the number of times that an advertisement has been "fired" at or "served" to particular audience segments ("targets"), allowing Obsession to sell finely segmented impressions. For a typical advertising campaign, Obsession might sell 100,000 impressions of affluent male blog-readers aged 25–29 to a company such as Levi's jeans. This earns roughly $1800–$3500 based upon cost-per-thousand or "cost-per-mille" (CPM) ranging from $18 to $35. Ad-exchanges algorithmically calculate prices and sell impressions in real-time – often without human supervision – and these prices fluctuate from minute to minute.

In order to ensure that these technologies sell space to advertisers and display advertisements to intended audiences, employees frequently ran reports ("ad-hoc reporting"). Employees first logged into a combination of monitors, servers, and exchanges in order to perform this common task. Logged in, analytic workers generated reports by selecting from a menu of variables within the monitors, ad-servers, and ad-exchanges. Typically, employees requested information from all three types of application to gather data related to unsold impression inventory, projections of future impression inventory, realized profit, and projections of future revenue. These systems ostensibly provide redundant information, however, reports often failed to provide what should have been, according to employees, identical data. Far from providing clear, unmediated information, the data often required translation that I describe later.

User-interfaces for servers and exchanges display a series of toggle boxes for selecting variables, a time period selection box, and a "submit query" button. Upon submitting a query, employees waited for cloud-based software to generate a report. Rather than instantaneous access to information, there exists a significant, temporal gap between query and response. This gap may be as short as several seconds or as long as several hours. Often these time-delayed reports revealed discrepancies that did not become apparent until after this temporal lag. Much of the work that I performed and observed at Obsession consisted of attempts to translate incorrect information or to develop workarounds. This included labor-intensive workarounds whereby employees gathered and recombined information from each system in order to translate the data into actionable information.

This can be seen in a meeting that began with a manager explaining how a cloud-based web-traffic monitor "regularly reports inaccurately." It is worth noting that Obsession pays tens-of-thousands of dollars per month for use of this application. After determining that Obsession's other cloud-based systems could not provide information promised by the monitor, the manager instructed workers to "figure out how to make this work and figure out why reporting is way off." Interestingly, he asked if there was a way to know how "wrong" the system was. The AdOps workers told him that there was not and the manager agreed. As he said, "Yeah, there's no way." Impression inventory does not exist outside of the measurement system. Obsession's products (impressions) lack the "objectivity" associated with physical, commonplace, or "closed-box" commodities (Cetina & Bruegger, 2000, p. 149) such as a car or steel. Impressions, as immaterial commodities, appear as "objects of knowledge" that exist as "processes and predictions rather than definitive things" (Cetina & Bruegger, 2000, p. 149). Impression inventory is not a fixed object, but a flow of information condensed into a measurement by calculative systems (monitors, ad-exchanges, and ad-servers).

As the meeting continued, an employee displayed reports from these cloud systems on a large flatscreen display. The goal of generating these numbers was to provide information to executive staff. Executives required reports of impressions by site, advertisement type, audience operating system (i.e., Windows or OSX), and audience location. The monitors, ad-servers, and ad-exchanges gave conflicting numbers and everyone groaned. Employees decided to combine numbers from the advertising exchange with monitor data in order to construct a report that would then be used to calculate the figures needed by executive staff. After instructing employees as to how he would like the report to look, the manager jokingly said, "Imagine a future. Just imagine. There's a waterfall. The sun is shining and [this system] is generating reliable information." Here, a basic form of organizational sensemaking (counting inventory) cannot be performed by technology and so technology becomes a vehicle for skill deployment.

Inventing a workaround, employees demonstrated what Paolo Virno terms "virtuosic" (2004, p. 54) or virtuoso-like deployments of interpretative and problem-solving skills. These skills require general, flexible knowledge of ICTs rather than codified knowledge (e.g., computer programming, woodworking, machining, etc.). Keep in mind that no AdOps workers had technical backgrounds. Rather than a technical background, analytics work requires a generic capacity for thinking and problem solving developed over the course of lives spent interacting with ICTs outside of work (e.g., smartphones, personal computers, televisions, videogames).

Statements from management confirm this need for workers with generic, yet self-directed skills. As one hiring manager stated, he seeks to find "real-time self-starters" capable of performing a variety of "ad-hoc" tasks. Illustrating a characteristically post-bureaucratic definition of "freedom as potential" (Maravelias, 2003), another executive stated that he simply wanted to "empower" people to do what they wish. Workers are given autonomy to develop what he termed "innovative" solutions[3] or, as several other managers said, "to be creative." Though I have no in-depth interviews from Obsession, workers in comparable digital media jobs reported that "to be creative" and self-directed were the most enjoyable aspects of work.

Along with this invitation to "be creative," employees experience immersion in routine tasks. I found myself staying late to solve data problems, often losing track of time and skipping breaks. Lost in the cloud, I experienced what informants called "worm-holing" or, more often, "deep-diving." An analytics employee at another firm said that she experiences "zen" in these moments. She explained, "I just put my head down and just zoom in. It's like I'm putting a zoom lens on my brain" and added "I'm very focused. You could say zoned out." During these moments, I lost track of time, staying well past my shift's scheduled end or working through lunch breaks.

Feeling immersed in a data-filled screen ought to be a familiar experience for quantitative social scientists that spend hours inside the windows of STATA or SPSS. For me, this felt comparable to a videogame – albeit a crudely designed one. This sort of immersion – often linked to creativity and job satisfaction (Amabile et al., 2005) among both expressive (Hesmondhalgh & Baker, 2011) and routine (Siciliano, 2016) creative industry workers – provides one of the relative satisfactions of routine immaterial labor.[4]

In order to secure profits, Obsession and similar organizations depend upon workers to assemble disparate data into a stable, immaterial product: impressions. After the above processes solidify impression inventory, AdOps workers "release" inventory for sale by algorithmic systems and sales personnel. The production of audience commodities requires generic capacities for problem-solving based on general knowledge of ICTs and these skills are needed to develop improvised workarounds. As such, analytics employees at Obsession appear skilled, autonomous, and free to "be creative" – albeit in a rather circumscribed way. Management encourages and expects these workers to autonomously plan and execute their immediate work tasks. Extending beyond the organization to infrastructure, however, reveals a cloud-based separation of planning and execution that runs counter to managerial goals.

SEPARATING MEASUREMENT FROM INTERPRETATION

Continuing to illustrate how calculative cloud-based ICTs shape this routine, immaterial labor process, I now present data that illustrates analytics employees' perception of ICTs as inscrutable blackboxes. As above, my fieldwork suggests a paradox: workers appear empowered by management while in thrall to calculative cloud systems. The planning and execution of measurement occurs outside the organization while worker interpretation and improvisation remains free or "creative." The effects of changes in calculative cloud infrastructure reveal themselves in an example of changes in measurement that occurred during fieldwork.

Like many digital firms that sell audience commodities, Obsession uses cloud-based, calculative systems (monitors, ad-servers, and ad-exchanges) owned and operated by ICT infrastructure providers. Though companies such as Amazon and Microsoft provide similar cloud infrastructures, Google is the largest of these providers. In reference to these calculative systems, Katherine said, "Well, Google owns those." Hanna interjected, "Yeah and they'll probably buy the ones that they don't own soon enough. They're buying everything. That's how we get screwgled!"[5] Regardless of the truth of Katherine's claim, these comments indicate the degree to which employees perceive their work to be bound up in forces beyond their control and the control of management.

In November 2013, Google adjusted measurement calculations for mobile internet audiences. Mobile refers to audiences that access Obsession's blogs via smartphones and tablet computers. Google collapsed calculations of tablet and smartphone impressions into a single measure. Prior to this, Obsession sold tablet and smartphone impressions as differently priced products. In order to translate impressions generated by mobile audiences into separate products, the organization requires independent measures of smartphone and tablet impressions. This change in the cloud rendered Obsession's strategy difficult, if not wholly impossible. Though it may seem ridiculous that such a simple figure could not be calculated separately, one analytics employee recounted her interactions with Google as follows:

> I asked them how tablet [pageviews] could be calculated and the woman said 'well, this is better because it's one metric for all of your mobile traffic' which is fine for them I guess, they like that, but we need separate tablet reporting. Anyway, I asked how the system is tracking that information and the woman said, "Well, that's a good question. I'll look into that." They have like, in their training they have specific things that they're told to say to us in those situations [and avoid answering my question].

In the above example, the worker's desire for information or "structure of wanting" (Cetina & Bruegger, 2000, p. 152) does not correspond to the structure of information provided by the system. These mismatches of desire and data structure tend to be associated with what I term acute frustration[6] – emerging proximally from interactions with technology – rather than the immersive pleasure found in other studies of ICTs and knowledge workers.

Another example of employees interacting with calculative cloud-based ICTs comes from Marcus, a content-uploader and web-traffic analyst at another firm.

> Say we have this [page] that gets all these crazy views, like suddenly, like out of nowhere. [The views] were low on the weekend and [then] they get all these views. We look and say, "this looks odd to us, why are they getting all these views?" We'll look at where these views are coming from and we'll see that there's a large number of views coming from Kazakistan [sic] which is odd. We'll go to [Google-owned] YouTube and say "Hey we're noticing [an odd trend], can you tell us if something odd is going on" and they'll say "We can't really tell you, but your instincts are probably on the money."

Again, the data provided by these systems may or may not be usable. The organization and its employees have no way of knowing or gaining access to the principles that structure data production. From the workers' perspective, this data is structured in accordance with the cloud-owner's inscrutable interests. Obsession and its employees simply execute their interpretive and analytic tasks. Rather than immersive pleasure – disappearing into the screen – workers experience acute frustration. As another data analyst said:

> If we're just talking about the interfaces that I work on, you know, there's times when you feel great about it. [The cloud provider] finally put all the proper tools in there and it's functioning properly and it's easy and it's great. Then two weeks later, [the cloud provider] goes 'Hey, check out our new interface" and it's a mess. Functionalities are gone! Names have changed. You know, those times can be frustrating.

In other cases, workers experience cloud-level changes as positive. As another informant said, "Yeah, those changes happen. Usually it's because it's better. It's always changing, always getting better." Positive or negative, these illustrate an affective connection to technology *and* a dynamic experience of work linked to ever-evolving ICTs that enable and constrain the deployment of skill while increasing uncertainty. As described earlier, workers improvise and develop workarounds for unexpected situations such as this one.

Grappling with upstream, metric reconfiguration, Obsession's analytics workers attempted to translate restructured traffic data into saleable inventory. Hanna decided to use data that tracks particular models of smartphones and tablets in order to generate counts of tablet computer and smartphone users. This requires the generation of reports that list mobile device model identification numbers for devices used by mobile media audiences. These reports often contain more than 3,000 rows and require employees to research and determine whether the identification numbers correspond to smartphones or tablets.

After translating these reports, data may become usable estimates of smartphone and tablet audiences. At this point, the data remains unsellable as inventory. In order to turn these data into saleable inventory, analytics employees instruct a different system to interpret the above-mentioned identification numbers as either "smartphone" or "tablet" users. This requires labor-intensive, non-automatable, manual entry of this information rather than the instantaneous, non-mediated use of "big" data that has so often been depicted in popular industrial discourse and news media.

In another instance, Isaac, a sales supervisor asked Jamie, an analytics employee, how to use another calculative cloud system to properly track impressions. The system should generate targeting "tags" that track and calculate impressions, however, AdOps employees stated that this system does not typically work as expected. They explained that attempts to fix this issue came to nothing. Isaac said "… the person that had emailed me from Google, telling me to call them for training on the product, that person doesn't even exist there. [Google] just said 'that person, that name doesn't exist here'." Jamie responded to Isaac's comment and said, "That company is too big. I think someone should take them down and get rid of like, a few hundred, 150,000 people. Right?" Isaac, the manager, said "I called [Google] Adwords and they asked me if I was an advertiser, 'you're an advertiser, would you like to place ads with us?' I was like hold on Google, hold on with that. No." Jamie sympathetically said, "Yeah, they're terrible." Worth mentioning again is Google's dependence upon global advertising sales as a primary source of revenue (Hern, 2016) and Google's position as owner of much of the cloud infrastructure used to sell online advertisements. As such, Google's revenue structure and position within the field suggest an obvious vested interest and a disproportionate power to structure this data.

In another conversation, Isaac (sales manager) and Hanna (AdOps supervisor) discussed common discrepancies between these multiple, equally "perfect" data sources. In the following excerpt of typical office chatter, Hanna and Isaac briefly discuss two conflicting reports from one of the monitors and one of the ad-servers.

H: It says 700,000 [impressions] here and 250,000 here. This 700 is right, but…

I: Damnit!

H: Right.

I: Well if that continues we'll be asking for our money back [from the cloud software provider]

Here, Hanna refers to reports that measure impressions that Obsession sells to advertisers. Her statement regarding the correctness of one figure over another may appear puzzling insofar as neither of these figures can be linked to physical objects. Instead, Hanna's statement refers to the triangulation of this figure with multiple reports from other systems. Obviously, the higher figure is preferable because a larger saleable inventory possesses more potential revenue. Conflicting measurements call Obsession's inventory into question and thus confound the organization's ability to sell product. Similarly, another analytics worker stated, "[Google and YouTube] didn't use to do that, but [now] they're constantly re-evaluating. So you could have a 100,000 views today and check back tomorrow and it's down to 50,000." In a heated exchange among analytics and sales employees, Isaac emphatically suggested that the employees simply "lie" about the impressions in light of contradictory information. Though in all likelihood no one provided false information, the manager's response highlights the difficulties produced by temporally delayed and conflicted data. This data tends to be structured by technologies that have been configured by actors external to the organization. Control over the labor process lies, partially, in the cloud – not as technologically embedded convention (Damarin, 2013), but as perpetually in-flux measurement planned and executed upstream.

Competing measures fluctuate from day-to-day and thus further confound the employees' and organization's capacity for economically rational action. Fluctuation occurs frequently with measurements differing by as much as ±300%. An historical example of improper ICT inventory measurement seems comparatively small with variations being under 20% (Gasser, 1986). At Obsession, cloud-generated inventory calculations refer to immaterial objects and improper measurement cannot be easily confirmed. Even reports of past impression sales and blog-traffic tended to yield different results depending on the day on which the report had been generated. As one employee said, "The impression estimates are always changing because [the systems] are sampling. It doesn't stay the same from day-to-day." Katherine, another analytics employee, explained her understanding of this situation as follows:

K: Those don't even pull numbers correctly! Like, it should be able to tell me how many people viewed an advertisement, but it varies. It should give a static number! It's not a projection! How many times was the ad accessed by the ad-server? It's a simple thing and still it gives me different numbers for the same time period every time I access it. If I pull Q3's [3rd fiscal quarter] numbers today, it might be different next week and there's no reason for that.

Author: So it's sampling and estimating then?

K: Yeah, yeah it must be, but how?! I don't know. We don't know and [the cloud-owners] don't tell you!

This excerpt highlights employee experience of these technologies as black-boxes. While enabling calculability of immaterial objects, these technologies frequently do so in unpredictable, unreliable, and acutely frustrating ways. Thus, employees experience unpredictable fluctuations in data as raw material and data as product (inventory) — as if workers' tools and the definition of pieces in a piece rate system were both subject to change from moment-to-moment. These fluctuations cannot be easily linked to actions of other humans or technology's internal practices. Above, the proximal cause of employees' acute frustration (bad information) stems from changes in cloud-based systems located upstream, autonomous from workers and management.

A manager at another firm recounted a similar experience: "This one time, we had been getting a lot of views from this one module that was on YouTube and then [Google] deleted that. They said 'well we don't need that anymore, so we deleted it' and all of our views left with that module. Yeah, that happens all the time." These fluctuations in calculative cloud-based ICTs reduce workers' ability to sell immaterial inventory and so these changes reduce Obsession's ability to produce revenue. At the organizational level, workers may autonomously and inventively analyze data, however, the planning and execution of measurement remains separate, in the cloud. In this case, the technical microstructures of information gathering — planned and designed elsewhere — complicate, if not thwart economic action.

A concluding example comes from a tumultuous week that included executive-level changes and heavy lay-offs. Directly confronted with the precariousness of their standard employment, many workers cried in the open office. An AdOps manager yelled, "All of our revenue comes from the sale of ads!" This came after she had explained a recent technological problem resulting from the algorithmically controlled ad-exchanges. These systems indicated that Obsession had sold all estimated impressions for the fiscal quarter. Despite this, the company had not achieved its estimated level of profit. Hanna suspected that the algorithmically managed system had been using up inventory for less profitable advertisements.

Rather than selling more profitable advertising space to global brands, Hanna suspected that the system sold impressions to "remnant" sources. Remnant refers to common, text-based advertisements found on blogs and other portions of the internet such as web-based email. Remnant advertisements take up little space on a website and lack images or video components. Impressions sold to remnant advertisers earn only fractions of a cent as opposed to nearly two cents per impression for other advertisements. Still, Hanna and the rest of the analytics team had no way of knowing why or how this had occurred. More importantly, the employees had no way of fixing or adjusting the process because algorithmically controlled ad-exchanges sell impressions autonomously. Here, the actions of blackboxes heighten uncertainty as managers hold employees accountable for unacceptable gaps between revenue projections and actual earnings.

Controlled from on high, employees experience algorithmically controlled processes as blackboxes located upstream. These calculative, cloud-based ICTs structure measurement calculations in accord with cloud-owners' interests and so cloud-based, calculative systems directly affect both an employee's capacity to perform work and the organization's ability to produce revenue. These technologies that rationalize the measurement of audiences (Napoli, 2008) produce uncertainty. Insofar as Obsession's impression inventory depends upon these systems, employees experience acutely frustrating, rapid change within the labor process that adds to already precarious, standard employment.

DISCUSSION

I now briefly restate my argument before highlighting contributions to discussions within the sociology of work regarding technology, skill, autonomy, and management/worker relations. In the workplace described above, technology − as microstructure that both enables and constrains skill − controls work by separating the planning and execution of measurement from autonomous, creative interpretation conducted downstream. The calculative procedures embedded in cloud-based, calculative systems remain unknowable to the organization and its employees. The blackboxed technical content of these calculative systems appears to serve the interests of the cloud-owner (Google, in this case) or the ideal-typical users for which the software has been configured (Grint & Woolgar, 1997).

Calculative cloud-technologies enable workers to engage in inventive or "creative" acts of information processing. While the necessary skills for work (cognitive capacities, problem-solving) may be forever a part of the worker, organizations require ICTs in order to activate these skills. Without these systems they cannot "be creative" and as such, creativity at work appears bounded by ICT affordances.[7] By "being creative" and negotiating these technologies, employees render the information provided by calculative cloud ICTs usable for the organization by translating information as raw material into information as saleable immaterial product (impressions, a type of audience commodity). Additionally, workers appear affectively bound at all times to their glass screens. Insofar as upstream decisions affect their working day, analytics workers lack control and instead appear in thrall to cloud-based, calculative ICTs. While my findings may not be probabilistically generalizable, these findings appear theoretically generalizable to a wide range of workers and organizations that appear structurally similar vis-à-vis calculative cloud-based ICTs. Below, I highlight theoretical implications of these findings.

Labor Process Theory and Control over Skill

Labor process theory tends to presuppose relatively stable technologies that control work by regulating tasks (Edwards, 1979) or surveilling workers (Aneesh, 2009). Recent studies suggest new modes of technological control predicated upon employees' intellectual, affective, and aesthetic attachments (Cetina & Bruegger, 2000; Rennstam, 2012; Siciliano, 2016) and the constraint of skill (Damarin, 2013). Though similar, my findings suggest crucial differences with regard to studies of labor processes and relations between ICTs, skill, autonomy, and labor/management relations. These differences lie in the *source* of control, the *quality* of negotiation, and the *speed*, *scope*, and *scale* of change.

This case suggests that the *source* of control over worker skill lies neither in some inherently capitalist tendency, nor in organization-level variables (i.e., workplace culture, relations in production, unionization). Instead, skill appears affected by organization-level variables as mediated by the structural relationship between an organization and owners of technology. Thus control stems, in part, from the interests of cloud-based ICT providers. From the perspective of the worker and the organization, cloud-based ICT providers' interests appear inscrutable and often in conflict with worker and organizational interests.

While workers may still appeal to management for more autonomy or control over work, power over technology lies outside the organization. Thus, organizational and worker autonomy appear always already bounded by a socio-technical network in constant flux. Others have noted the role of technology's designers (see, e.g., Grint & Woolgar, 1997) and the uneasy, conflicted relationships between management and new technology. Zuboff (1989), for example, quotes a manager struggling with technology vendors to "... leave the design flexible enough so that it does not preclude the uses we want to make of it" (1989, p. 414). As my data suggest, cloud-based, calculative ICTs appear as blackboxes to workers and system owners appear inscrutable.

In terms of the *quality* of these relations, control does not appear as a relatively stable "convention" (Damarin, 2013) to which workers may refer or even a stable object that can be clearly resisted. Based upon observed conflict between cloud-based ICT providers and Obsession, organizations and workers do not appear to possess a power of appeal. For theories of labor mobilization wherein autonomy and constraint affect the militancy of labor (Low-Beer, 1978), it no longer appears clear whom workers would, should, or could mobilize against in efforts to gain control over technology.

Neither the separation of planning and execution, nor the negotiation of technology's implementation is "new" to the study of work, technology, and skill (see, e.g., Adler, 1988; Gasser, 1986). Similar to classic deskilling (Braverman, 1974), planning and execution appear separate. Analytics workers do not plan how the raw information is generated and algorithmically controlled measurement systems act autonomously. Illustrating the paradoxical quality of work, management explicitly seeks out "creative," autonomous, and flexible workers and the organization depends upon worker creativity in order to bring technology in line with organizational interests.

With regard to *speed*, *scale*, and *scope* of change, calculative cloud-based ICTs differ fundamentally from ICTs of previous decades. As stated by scholars in the neighboring field of communication, technology that operates with proprietary algorithms "can be easily, instantly, radically, and invisibly changed" (Gillespie, 2014, p. 178; see also Gillespie, Pablo, & Kirsten, 2014). The ethnographic data presented above illustrates how the rapidity and invisibility of such changes affect a routine, immaterial labor process. Relatedly, unstable technologies problematize coherent documentation of particular work processes, potentially circumventing codification associated with professionalization (Bridges & Villemez, 1991). This suggests a state of perpetual learning or "permanent pedagogy" (Sallaz, 2015), but not the skill extraction found in the study of workplace "wikis" or web-based task documentation (Griffith, Sawyer, & Neale, 2003).

Affectively Binding Technology

Empirical research suggests that ICTs focus attention and elicit passionate attachment to work by way of pleasurably immersive experiences associated with acting within ICTs (Cetina & Bruegger, 2000; Kaiser et al., 2007; Rennstam, 2012; Siciliano, 2016). More speculative theories of cognitive capitalism suggest that interactions with ICTs affectively bind employees to work, providing pathways or "vectors" that "suggest, enable, solicit, prompt, encourage, and prohibit certain actions, thoughts, and affects" (Lazzarato, 2014, p. 30). Above-presented data support, yet complicate these descriptions of worker experience by showing how positive affects associated with ICTs depend upon the provision of useful information that afford pathways to action. Above, technology focuses attention upon particular kinds of information while placing limits upon work processes. No less affectively bound to technology, pathways afforded by cloud-based, calculative systems acutely frustrate Obsession's workers due to the aforementioned speed and invisibility of technological change. This case highlights how socio-technical networks shape the everyday experiences of immaterial labor and how experiences of immersion or "flow" are shaped by structures of ownership within these networks.

Measuring Skill

This study suggests that the aggregate measure of skill may be more complicated than previously thought. In the case presented here, workers may appear autonomous and skilled based on job descriptions and daily task-content. Simultaneously, they lack control over and knowledge regarding technical processes that structure work. While there have already been criticisms of aggregate measures of workforce skill (see Vallas, 1990), my findings suggest that the aggregate measure of skills may cancel out or simply go unmeasured. Relatedly, this presents a problem in measuring the effect of calculative cloud-based ICTs similar to problems noted by Barley (1986) in measuring the effects of technology upon social structures at work. In contexts wherein the demands of technology and management differ, it may be difficult to observe technology's effects outside of participant observation.

CONCLUSION

This chapter presented a case in which a structural source of post-bureaucratic control lies outside the organization — serving the interests of cloud-based ICT providers. Rather than being normative, reputational, or strictly social (Anderson-Gough et al., 2006; Barley & Kunda, 2011; Kunda, 1992; Osnowitz, 2006), control over skill stems from socio-technical networks in which work and organizations are embedded. I make three key points. First, as organizations exteriorize and digitalize calculative and immaterial production processes, managers' and workers' interests appear subordinate to the interests of ICT providers. Thus, technology alters the relations between capital and labor by establishing a hierarchy based on a political economy of information flows. Second, pleasurable immersion found in other cases appears interrupted by control imposed from outside the organization. Supporting aspects of theories of cognitive capitalism, technical control over skill and the subjective experience of work descend from the cloud to the firm rather than from managerial offices to the shopfloor. Last, findings suggest that labor process studies must continue to extend further outward — beyond the community, the state, the organizational field, or even stable ICTs — to the ever-evolving, dense socio-technical networks of infrastructures and human actors in which contemporary work is embedded.

NOTES

1. Digital publishing networks — like television networks — organize and distribute media content produced by both "O&O" (owned-and-operated) and independent production companies. As with all forms of advertising-supported media, Obsession — a pseudonym — sells advertising on those media properties in order to generate revenue.
2. In the United States, median wages for "creative" or information industry occupations (i.e., media, arts, engineering, computer, finance, and education) tend to be higher than other industries (U.S. Bureau of Labor Statistics, 2013).
3. Here I focus on reactions to technological systems, however, it was equally common for employees to discuss creative strategies for bending audiences to the company's will by way of these same technological systems. For example, workers

were also devising ways by which Obsession could generate new revenue streams by placing more advertisements into blogs.

4. Given claims about the aestheticization of work (Hancock, 2003) and "mobile lifestyles" that depend upon work technologies (Gregg, 2011), it is worth noting that immersion metaphors are common in philosophical and anthropological writings on aesthetic experience (see, e.g., Adorno, 2004 [1970]; Dewey, 2005 [1934]; Gell, 1998; Kant, 2000 [1790]).

5. Here, the informant makes reference to both her feelings about Google, but also the popular "screwgled" internet meme and "Scroogled," an anti-Google campaign sponsored by Microsoft. In fact, the team frequently made sense of their everyday experiences by making explicit references to popular, digital media content and popular culture in general.

6. All work contains general, structural sources of frustration such as various forms of wage inequality, lack of benefits, or lack of career prospects to name just a few. An *acute* frustration should be understood as an interaction-present source of frustration, similar to an annoying co-worker. In this case, the technical source of acute frustration is both interaction present and a structural feature of work.

7. All work might be said to be dependent upon technology or techniques. Certainly, one might argue that the nail that sticks up cannot be hammered down without a hammer and yet, a resourceful person may use a rock for the same task. Here, cloud technology appears qualitatively different insofar as the raw materials and products only exist inside of the technology.

ACKNOWLEDGMENTS

For encouraging, thoughtful, and critical comments on earlier drafts of this chapter, I would like to thank Ching Kwan Lee, Christopher Kelty, Edward Walker, Pat Reilly, Alexandra Lippman, Christine Williams, Steven Vallas, Hannah Landecker, Kyle Nelson, Neil Gong, Steven Tuttle, and anonymous reviewers at *Research in the Sociology of Work*.

REFERENCES

Abbott, A. (1988). *The system of professions: An essay on the division of expert labor*. Chicago, IL: University of Chicago Press.

Adler, P. S. (1988). Automation, skill and the future of capitalism. *Berkeley Journal of Sociology, 33*, 1–36.

Adler, P. S. (2001). Market, hierarchy, and trust: The knowledge economy and the future of capitalism. *Organization Science, 12*(2), 215–234.

Adorno, T. W. (2004). *Aesthetic theory*. London: Continuum International Publishing Group.

Amabile, Teresa M., Barsade, Sigal G., Mueller, Jennifer S., & Straw, Barry M. (2005). Affect and creativity at work. *Administrative Science Quarterly, 50*(3), 367–403.

Anand, N., & Peterson, R. A. (2000). When market information constitutes fields: Sensemaking of markets in the commercial music industry. *Organization Science, 11*(3), (Special Issue: Cultural Industries: Learning from Evolving Organizational Practices), 270–284.

Anderson-Gough, F., Grey, C., & Robson, K. (2006). Professionals, networking and the networked professional. *Professional service firms* (Vol. 24, pp. 231–256). Research in the Sociology of Organizations. Bingley, UK: Emerald Group Publishing Limited. Retrieved from http://www.emeraldinsight.com/doi/abs/10.1016/S0733-558X%2806%2924009-6. Accessed on January 20, 2016.

Aneesh, A. (2009). Global labor: Algocratic modes of organization. *Sociological Theory, 27*(4), 347–370.

Arthur, M. B., & Rousseau, D. M. (2001). *The boundaryless career: A new employment principle for a new organizational era.* Oxford: Oxford University Press.

Attewell, P. (1987). The deskilling controversy. *Work and Occupations, 14*(3), 323–346.

Attewell, P. (1990). What is skill? *Work and Occupations, 17*(4), 422–448.

Baker, P. (1991). *Bored and busy: An analysis of formal and informal organization in the automated office.* New York, NY: Peter Lang International Academic Publishers.

Barley, S. R. (1986). Technology as an occasion for structuring: Evidence from observations of CT scanners and the social order of radiology departments. *Administrative Science Quarterly, 31*(1), 78–108.

Barley, S. R., & Kunda, G. (2011). *Gurus, hired guns, and warm bodies: Itinerant experts in a knowledge economy.* Princeton, NJ: Princeton University Press.

Becker, H. S. (1984). *Art worlds.* Berkeley, CA: University of California Press.

Boltanski, L., & Chiapello, È. (2005). *The new spirit of capitalism.* London: Verso.

Boutang, Y. M. (2011). *Cognitive capitalism.* Malden, MA: Polity Press.

Braverman, H. (1974). Labor and monopoly capital: The degradation *of work in the twentieth century.* New York, NY: Monthly Review Press.

Bridges, W. P., & Villemez, W. J. (1991). Employment relations and the labor market: Integrating institutional and market perspectives. *American Sociological Review, 56*(6), 748–764.

Burawoy, M. (1998). *The extended case method.* Berkeley, CA: University of California Press.

Buzzard, K. (1990). *Chains of gold: Marketing the ratings and rating the markets.* Metuchen, NJ: Scarecrow Press.

Castells, M. (2010). *Rise of the network society: Volume 1 of the information age: Economy, society, and culture.* Oxford: Wiley-Blackwell.

Caves, R. E. (2000). *Creative industries: Contracts between art and commerce.* Cambridge, MA: Harvard University Press.

Cetina, K. K., & Bruegger, U. (2000). The market as an object of attachment: Exploring post-social relations in financial markets. *The Canadian Journal of Sociology, 25*(2), 141–168.

Cetina, K. K., & Bruegger, U. (2002). Global microstructures: The virtual societies of financial markets. *American Journal of Sociology, 107*(4), 905–950.

Choi, S., Leiter, J., & Tomaskovic-Devey, D. (2008). Contingent autonomy: Technology, bureaucracy, and relative power in the labor process. *Work and Occupations, 35*(4), 422–455.

Chun, W. H. K. (2005). On software, or the persistence of visual knowledge. *Grey Room, 18*, 26–51.

Csikszentmihalyi, M. (1990). *Flow: The psychology of optimal experience.* New York, NY: Harper Perennial.

Damarin, A. K. (2006). Rethinking occupational structure: The case of web site production work. *Work and Occupations, 33*(4), 429–463.

Damarin, A. K. (2013). The network-organized labor process: Control and autonomy in web production work. In S. Mcdonald (Ed.), Networks, work and inequality (Vol. 24, pp. 177–205). *Research in the Sociology of Work.* Bingley, UK: Emerald Group Publishing Limited.

Deuze, M. (2007). *Media work.* Malden, MA: Polity.

Dewey, J. (2005). *Art as experience.* New York, NY: The Berkeley Publishing Group.

Edwards, R. C. (1979). *Contested terrain: The transformation of the workplace in the twentieth century.* New York, NY: Basic Books.

Ettema, J. S., & Whitney, D. C. (Eds.). (1994). *Audiencemaking: How the media create the audience.* Thousand Oaks, CA: Sage.

Florida, R. L. (2002). *The rise of the creative class.* New York, NY: Basic Books.

Fuchs, C. (2011). Cognitive capitalism or informational capitalism? The role of class in the information economy. In M. A. Peters & E. Bulut (Eds.), *Cognitive capitalism, education and digital labor* (pp. 75–122). New York, NY: Peter Lang.

Gallie, D. (1991). Patterns of skill change: Upskilling, deskilling or the polarization of skills? *Work, Employment & Society, 5*(3), 319–351.

Gasser, L. (1986). The integration of computing and routine work. *ACM Transactions on Information Systems, 4*(3), 205–225.

Gell, A. (1998). *Art and agency: An anthropological theory.* Oxford: Clarendon Press.

Gillespie, T. (2014). The relevance of algorithms. In T. Gillespie, P. J. Boczkowski, & K. A. Foot (Eds.), *Media technologies: Essays on communication, materiality, and society* (pp. 167–193). Cambridge, MA: The MIT Press.

Gillespie, T., Pablo, J. B., & Kirsten, A. F. (Eds.). (2014). *Media technologies: Essays on communication, materiality, and society.* Cambridge, MA: The MIT Press.

Gitlin, T (1983). *Inside prime time.* New York, NY: Pantheon Books.

Gregg, M. (2011). *Work's intimacy.* Hoboken, NJ: Wiley.

Griffith, T., Sawyer, J., & Neale, M. (2003). Virtualness and knowledge in teams: Managing the love triangle of organizations, individuals, and information technology. *Management Information Science Quarterly, 27*(2), 265–287.

Grint, K., & Woolgar, S. (1997). *The machine at work: Technology, work and organization* (1 ed.). Malden, MA: Polity Press.

Hancock, P. (2003). Aestheticizing the world of organization – Creating beautiful untrue things. In A. Carr & P. Hancock (Eds.), *Art and aesthetics at work* (pp. 174–193). Basingstoke: Palgrave Macmillan.

Hardt, M., & Negri, A. (2001). *Empire.* Cambridge, MA: Harvard University Press.

Harvey, D. (1989). *The condition of post-modernity.* Cambridge: Blackwell.

Hern, A. (2016). How alphabet became the biggest company in the world. *The Guardian,* February 2. Retrieved from http://www.theguardian.com/technology/2016/feb/01/how-alphabet-made-google-biggest-company-in-the-world. Accessed on February 27, 2016.

Hesmondhalgh, D., & Baker, S. (2011). *Creative labour.* Abingdon: Taylor & Francis Group.

Heydebrand, W. V. (1989). New organizational forms. *Work and Occupations, 16*(3), 323–357.

Huws, U. (2014). *Labor in the global digital economy: The cybertariat comes of age.* New York, NY: New York University Press.

Kaiser, S., Müller-Seitz, G., Lopes, M. P., & e Cunha, M. P. (2007). Weblog-technology as a trigger to elicit passion for knowledge. *Organization, 14*(3), 391–412.

Kant, I. (2000). *The critique of judgment.* Amherst, NY: Prometheus Books.

Kotamraju, N. P. (2002). Keeping up: Web design skill and the reinvented worker. *Information, Communication & Society, 5*(1), 1–26.

Kunda, G. (1992). *Engineering culture: Control and commitment in a high-tech corporation.* Philadelphia, PA: Temple University Press.

Lazzarato, M. (2014). *Signs and machines: Capitalism and the production of subjectivity.* Los Angeles, CA: Semiotext.

Lingo, E. L., & O'Mahony, S. (2010). Nexus work: Brokerage on creative projects. *Administrative Science Quarterly, 55*(1), 47–81.

Low-Beer, J. R. (1978). *Protest and participation: The new working class in Italy.* Cambridge: Cambridge University Press Archive.

Maravelias, C. (2003). Post-bureaucracy – Control through professional freedom. *Journal of Organizational Change Management, 16*(5), 547–566.

Marazzi, C. (2011). *Capital and affects: The politics of the language economy.* Los Angeles, CA: Semiotext.

Mears, A. (2011). *Pricing beauty: The making of a fashion model* (1st ed.). Los Angeles, CA: University of California Press.

Napoli, P. M. (2003). *Audience economics: Media institutions and the audience marketplace.* New York, NY: Columbia University Press.

Napoli, P. M. (2008). *The rationalization of audience understanding.* McGannon Center Working Paper Series (25).

Napoli, P. M. (2011). *Audience evolution new technologies and the transformation of media audiences.* New York, NY: Columbia University Press.

Osnowitz, D. (2006). Occupational networking as normative control collegial exchange among contract professionals. *Work and Occupations, 33*(1), 12–41.

Piore, M., & Sabel, C. (1984). *The second industrial divide.* New York, NY: Basic Books.

Quinn, R. W. (2005). Flow in knowledge work: High performance experience in the design of national security technology. *Administrative Science Quarterly, 50*(4), 610–641.

Reich, R. B. (1991). *The work of nations.* New York, NY: Knopf.

Rennstam, J. (2012). Object-control: A study of technologically dense knowledge work. *Organization Studies, 33*(8), 1071–1090.

Ross, A. (2004). *No-collar: The humane workplace and its hidden costs.* Philadelphia, PA: Temple University Press.

Salganik, M. J., Dodds, P. S., & Watts, D. J. (2006). Experimental study of inequality and unpredictability in an artificial cultural market. *Science, 311*(5762), 854–856.

Sallaz, J. J. (2015). Permanent pedagogy: How post-fordist firms generate effort but not consent. *Work and Occupations, 42*(1), 3–34.

Scholz, T. (Ed.). (2013). *Digital labor: The internet as playground and factory.* New York, NY: Routledge.

Sennett, R. (2000). *The corrosion of character: The personal consequences of work in the new capitalism* (1st ed.). New York NY: W. W. Norton & Company.

Sewell, G. (2005). Nice work? Rethinking managerial control in an era of knowledge work. *Organization, 12*(5), 685–704.

Siciliano, M. (2016). Disappearing into the object: Aesthetic subjectivities & organizational control in routine cultural work. *Organization Studies*, (January), 1–22. [Online First]

Simpson, R. L. (1985). Social control of occupations and work. *Annual Review of Sociology*, *11*(1), 415–436.

Smythe, D. (1977). Communications: Blindspot of western Marxism. *Canadian Journal of Political and Social Theory*, *1*(3), 1–27.

Tolbert, P. (2001). Occupations, organizations, and boundaryless careers. In M. B. Arthur & D. M. Rousseau (Eds.), *The boundaryless career: A new employment principle for a new organizational era* (pp. 331–345). Oxford: Oxford University Press.

U.S. Bureau of Labor Statistics. (2013). *May 2013 national occupational employment and wage estimates United States*. Retrieved from http://www.bls.gov/oes/current/oes_nat. htm#13-0000. Accessed on November 15, 2014.

Vallas, S. P. (1990). The concept of skill a critical review. *Work and Occupations*, *17*(4), 379–398.

Vallas, S. P. (1999). Rethinking post-fordism: The meaning of workplace flexibility. *Sociological Theory*, *17*(1), 68–101.

Virno, P. (2004). *A grammar of the multitude: For an analysis of contemporary forms of life*. Cambridge, MA: MIT Press.

Winter, S., Berente, N., Howison, J., & Butler, B. (2014). Beyond the organizational 'container': Conceptualizing 21st century sociotechnical work. *Information and Organization*, *24*(4), 250–269.

Zammuto, R. F., Griffith, T. L., Majchrzak, A., Dougherty, D. J., & Faraj, S. (2007). Information technology and the changing fabric of organization. *Organization Science*, *18*(5), 749–762.

Zuboff, S. (1989). *In the age of the smart machine: The future of work and power* (Reprint ed.). New York, NY: Basic Books.

THE LIMITS OF CONTROL IN SERVICE WORK: INTERACTIVE ROUTINES AND INTERACTIONAL COMPETENCE

Brian Ott

ABSTRACT

Service work is often differentiated from manufacturing by the interactive labor workers perform as they come into direct contact with customers. Service organizations are particularly interested in regulating these interactions because they are a key opportunity for developing quality customer service, customer retention, and ultimately generation of sales revenue. An important stream of sociological literature focuses on managerial attempts to exert control over interactions through various techniques including routinization, standardization, and surveillance. Scripting is a common method of directing workers' behavior, yet studies show that workers are extremely reluctant to administer scripts, judging them to be inappropriate to particular interactions or because they undermine their own sense of self. This paper examines a panoptic method of regulating service workers, embodied in undercover corporate agents who patrol employee's adherence to scripts. How do workers required to recite scripts for customers respond to undercover control?

Research in the Sociology of Work, Volume 29, 155–183
Copyright © 2016 by Emerald Group Publishing Limited
ISSN: 0277-2833/doi:10.1108/S0277-283320160000029022

What does it reveal about the nature of interactive labor? In-depth interviews with interactive workers in a range of retail contexts reveal that they mobilize their own interactional competence to challenge the effects of the panoptic, as they utilize strategies to identify and adapt to these "mystery shoppers," all the while maintaining their cover. The paper shows the limits on control of interactive workers, as they maintain their own socialized sense of civility and preserve a limited realm of autonomy in their work.

Keywords: Surveillance; control; scripts; resistance; service work

INTRODUCTION

The growth of the service sector along with increased competition has led many food and beverage based service businesses to devise new approaches to managing the service encounter (Albrecht & Zemke, 1985; Lohr, 2014; Macdonald & Sirianni, 1996). Businesses treat the frontline service interaction as an opportunity to cultivate a unique brand image or customer experience that remains consistent across all visits (Fuller & Smith, 1996; McCammon & Griffin, 2000; Pettinger, 2004). Leading this charge is a focus on the customer (Du Gay & Salaman, 1992); however, service firms face a bind of meeting customer expectations of quality service while also maintaining control over the behavioral components of the employee-customer interaction, what Korczynski (2009) has termed the "customer-oriented bureaucracy." Businesses have responded by attempting to control the consistency of employee-customer interactions in order to provide quality service, retain customers, and ultimately to increase revenue. One example of this control is through routinization, including requiring standardized scripts, or rules dictating how employees should sound (Butler, 2014; Eustace, 2012) and what they should say in each customer interaction (Leidner, 1993, 1996; Ritzer, 2004; Walsh, 2000). Scripts typically include specific requirements outlining how to greet the customer, introduce and explain products or promotions, or request future business, but most often scripts involve requirements to directly market products through suggestive selling (Finn, 2001; Leidner, 1993; Ritzer, 2004; Victorino, Verma, & Wardell, 2008). Research has shown that requiring frequent suggestive selling can increase a business' revenue by nearly 20%

(Johnson & Masotti, 1990; Martinko, White, & Hassell, 1989; Milligan & Hantula, 2005; Squires et al., 2007). By requiring employees to follow scripts that are focused on selling, employers treat the service interaction as an opportunity to extract more revenue from customers. However, because rules (scripts) cannot account for all possible interactional contingencies or customer variation, employees are expected to adhere to script require- ments by ignoring these contingencies and acting like "judgmental dopes," or blind rule followers without the ability to interpret a situation and exert agency (Garfinkel, 1967; Heritage, 1984).

Standardizing the behavioral components of the frontline service interac- tion exposes the difficulty of traditional methods of control. As manage- ment is unable to watch over each employee during every frontline service encounter they have had to use alternative management strategies, often involving customers, to surveil employees and encourage compliance with the rules (Du Gay & Salaman, 1992; Fuller & Smith, 1996). One way that employers attempt to control the service interaction is by monitoring script adherence through the use of mystery shoppers (Fuller & Smith, 1996). Mystery shoppers are individuals contracted by a business to anonymously visit their store, appearing as real customers, in order to evaluate employ- ees' performances including their adherence to behavioral requirements dic- tated by scripts (Wilson, 1998, 2001). Fuller and Smith (1996) speculate that mystery shoppers may work to control employee behavior through the enactment of a panopticon. Adapted from Foucault's (1995) description of Bentham's prison design, in theory a panoptic method of surveillance is based on perfect knowledge/information; it describes a situation where sub- jects self-monitor because they assume the constant potential of observa- tion. Because employees are made aware of the use of mystery shoppers during training but do not know when they will actually be under their observation, it is expected that they will police themselves and follow the required procedures at all times.

Sociologists of labor increasingly point to strategies for controlling employee behavior in frontline service interactions, including forms of scripting (Butler, 2014; Eustace, 2012; Leidner, 1993; Ritzer, 2004) and observational management strategies, such as mystery shoppers, technolo- gical monitoring, or direct manager observation, to ensure workers follow rules (Fuller & Smith, 1996; Marx, 1999; Salzinger, 2003; Sewell & Wilkinson, 1992). Other scholars have questioned the reach of strict control in service settings and have argued that they are overly deterministic and do not allow room for agency (Bain & Taylor, 2000). Bolton and Boyd (2003), for example, in a critique of Hochschild's (1983) separation of public and private forms of emotional labor, question the extent of control over the behavioral characteristics in organizations that require emotional labor. They argue that laborers enter the workplace with prior emotional training that they rely on as a resource to "calibrate" their emotional performance flexibly, from interaction to interaction (Bolton & Boyd, 2003, p. 294). In this vein, I show how frontline service workers rely on their interactional competence to strategically subvert the control strategies of standardized scripts and mystery shoppers. In doing so, I demonstrate the flexibility in alliances between frontline laborers and customers or management depending on the perceived threat of mystery shopper observation or managerial sanction. I argue that these laborers utilize their interactional competence, not as outright forms of resistance, but as coping strategies that allow them to maintain dignity and an identity as a competent interactant. I seek to identify what Prasad and Prasad (1998, p. 227) call the "more pervasive," often "invisible," "unplanned," and everyday practices of workplace resistance that are more characteristic of frontline service work, but less likely to drastically alter structural conditions than traditional forms of more overt resistance such as strikes or sabotage.

CONTROLLING EMPLOYEE BEHAVIOR IN FRONTLINE SERVICE WORK

Researchers who study frontline service labor have focused a good deal of attention on the themes of standardization, deskilling and dehumanization, the interactional characteristics of frontline service work, cultural or identity reorganization, and monitoring/surveillance practices. The focus of these themes has shifted from technological determinism to the limits of standardization, often including forms of employee resistance. By breaking up the production process into several small pre-defined tasks, similar to a Taylorist model of production, businesses rely on a low skilled, non-professional workforce to accomplish these tasks for low pay to increase profit (Braverman, 1974; Leidner, 1993; Macdonald & Sirianni, 1996; Ritzer, 2004). Braverman (1974) warned of the "deskilling" of labor in recognizing that "the rationalization of skills in the end destroys these skills" (p. 370). Deskilling is also a result of the limited mental work or agency exerted in a rationalized process that prevents employees from realizing their full potential (Form, 1987).

The incomplete realization of employee potential and the limited ability to exert agency in the face of a rigidly standardized labor process has led some to conclude that this type of labor is also dehumanizing (Ritzer, 2004). However, these arguments have been criticized for being too technologically deterministic (Jones, 1989), for not giving fair attention to employee resistance (Hodson, 2001; Thompson & Ackroyd, 1995; Vallas, 1990), and for the ability of workers' resistance to play a part in shaping the labor process (Burawoy, 1979; Roy, 1959; Smith, 1994). Lopez (2007) provides evidence of resistance to standardization shaping the labor process in his analysis of nursing home employees. He finds that laborers work together with management and residents to develop "mock routinization," completing tasks without following every component of the requirements (Lopez, 2007).

Another approach to understanding standardization and its effects on workers deals with the interactional component of service work, specifically with the standardization of employee speech. Garfinkel (1967, p. 68) found that in order for rules, such as standardized scripts, to dictate action an actor must act like a "judgmental dope," or one who unthinkingly acts out pre-established rules or courses of action. He argued that people cannot act like judgmental dopes and still be regarded as competent interactants. Instead, as Heritage (1984, p. 121) states, rules must be applied "to specific configurations of circumstances which may never be identical." People always face contingencies in interaction that require individual common-sense reasoning or tacit knowledge to manage actions that the rules do not address.

In support of Garfinkel (1967), Lavin and Maynard (2001), in their study of laughter and rapport in the standardized telephone survey, observed that complete interactional standardization is not entirely possible. They found that respondent laughter is a contingency that interviewers were not taught how to handle (Lavin & Maynard, 2001). In order to manage contingencies, individuals must use "tacit knowledge," which refers to the ability of interactants to "supplement rules" by relying on their ethnomethodological competence to have a meaningful interaction (Lavin & Maynard, 2001; Maynard & Schaeffer, 2002, p. 9). In their study of call centers, Whalen, Whalen, and Henderson (2002, p. 257) recognize that scripting is "used during singular encounters that are locally organized and thus necessarily contingent." The emphasis on the interactions being "locally organized" highlights that scripts are pre-constructed, distanced from the actualities of particular situations, and open to variation.

Both call center employees (Houlihan, 2000) and McDonald's employees (Leidner, 1993, 1996) do not follow all of the scripts they are required to use. In her study of call centers, Houlihan (2000, p. 230) questioned the totalness of control of the standardized script, and observed that many workers would "edit scripts according to interpretive knowledge." Similarly, Leidner (1993, 1996) observed that some McDonald's employees enjoy following a standardized routine due to the comfort a predictable work routine provides, or the helpfulness of relying on a script when dealing with rude or irate customers. Even with this apparent comfort with the script, many employees refrained from adhering to certain aspects of the script that they disliked; this was especially the case with suggestive selling (Leidner, 1993). The use of a script in frontline interactions relies on customer conformity to the script, but customer behavior cannot always be predictable (Leidner, 1993, 1996). Customers may be uncomfortable feeling like the interaction is inauthentic and might respond in ways that the script does not address; therefore, employees as well as customers may attempt to exert their own control over the work process (Leidner, 1993, 1996). In other words, laborers and customers have found ways to resist strict standardization.

CONTROL STRATEGIES OF SERVICE ORGANIZATIONS

In an effort to regain control over service laborers many businesses turn to different management strategies including cultural organization through teamwork and identity regulation, or surveillance strategies such as electronic monitoring or using customers as observers, such as is the case with mystery shoppers. The development of new control strategies reflects a broader transition in attempts to control the service encounter. Frontline service-based businesses face what Korczynski (2009) calls the "customer-oriented bureaucracy," or the bind of providing customer service (giving the customer what they want), while also keeping control over employees, all while maintaining low overhead. While these new forms of control may appear less coercive than prior forms of industrial-centered technological control, they are still typically aimed at achieving increased productivity and efficiency at low cost (Sewell, 1998).

Bureaucratic control measures have been characterized as unable to produce continual improvement in employee performance, especially in a post-Fordist labor market (Alvesson & Willmott, 2002; Du Gay & Salaman, 1992). Building from Leidner's (1993) recognition that workers face so much variability in customer interactions that there is "no manageable set of routines [that] could encompass them all," Sallaz (2015) identifies a form of indirect management, what he calls "permanent pedagogy," that relies on workers using their own interactional competence to continually develop new ways to best take control of interactions. He argues that call center workers use "flexible problem-solving skills" to gain mastery over a computer-based call documentation system. Instead of the computer program, with set parameters for how to gather and enter customer information, controlling employee interactions, management relies on employees using their interactional competence to control the interactions to most productively navigate the computer program. Sallaz (2015, p. 17) identifies the potential to view the computer system as controlling the interactions, but he warns against this interpretation and instead posits that employees engage in an "autonomous learning game" that provides workers a "sense of mastery," while also benefitting the organization by achieving increased effort.

Another response to the limits of bureaucratic management strategies involves organizations using measures of cultural or symbolic control to govern employee subjectivities. These views, utilizing Foucault's concept of governmentality, explain how organizations attempt to shape organizational discourse to get employees to fall in line with managerial objectives of increased effort, creativity, and self-regulation (Alvesson & Willmott, 2002; Du Gay, 1996; Du Gay & Salaman, 1992). Alvesson and Willmott (2002, p. 622) argue that treating the "employee as identity worker," benefits organizations by aligning "managerial discourses into narratives of self-identity." By offering a stable identity anchor in corporate identity discourse, employees may be less likely to "engage in organized forms of resistance" (Alvesson & Willmott, 2002). Similarly, Du Gay and Salaman (1992) argue that organizations have turned to "cultural reorganization" as a more totalizing effort at managing the "behavior, values, and attitudes" of employees in order to encourage "them to believe they have control over their own lives" (Du Gay & Salaman, 1992, pp. 622, 625). By relying on a discourse of the "enterprise of the self," organizations seek to govern laborers by blurring the lines between consumer and producer through the creation of a "sovereign customer," resulting in an even more total form of control than that proposed by Alvesson and Willmott (2002). For Du Gay and Salaman (1992, p. 628), the reach of regulation does not exist solely in identification within one's managerial interests, but instead involves the "application of 'market forces' and 'entrepreneurial principles' to every sphere of human existence." In other words, it is expected that this form of identity regulation will produce rational, individual entrepreneurs who seek fulfillment through continued improvement and success within the organization. By treating all individuals as entrepreneurs, organizations create a totalizing mechanism of control that produces increased productivity and performance, one that establishes the rooting of identity in a market, while simultaneously instilling the belief of individual freedom of creativity and control.

Further utilizing Foucault's concept of governmentality, Knights and McCabe (2003) argue that management strategies of developing teams or a team-focused mentality could reorient employee subjectivities to fall in line with team-oriented goals, thereby meeting management aims of increasing productivity. However, Knights and McCabe (2003) leave more room for agency than the previously mentioned analyses of cultural regulation. Similar to Bolton and Boyd's (2003) critique of Hochschild's (1983) separation of private and organizational selves, Knights and McCabe (2003) state that employees may recognize a tension between their workplace and private selves and in response, resist managerial attempts to shape their personalities. In contrast to Alvesson and Willmott (2002), Du Gay and Salaman (1992), and Du Gay (1996), Knights and McCabe's (2003) contribution complicates the totaltity of control by demonstrating how resistance to governmentality can arise due to a conflict of managerial and employee orientations to identity; management approaches workplace control through a primary focus on workplace identity, while employees may more strongly value retaining their own conception of their private self and not so easily succumb to the identity proposed by the organization.

EMPLOYEE CONTROL THROUGH PANOPTIC SURVEILLANCE

Along with attempts to control employee behavior through cultural and identity regulation, another form of control over employee behavior can be found in different kinds of surveillance strategies, often involving customers (Fuller & Smith, 1996). As customer-employee interactions are difficult to monitor, and knowing that employees often subvert interactional script usage, many service firms have instituted the use of mystery shoppers as a mechanism to regain control over the frontline service interaction. Mystery shoppers are individuals hired by businesses who pretend to be real customers in order to evaluate the service experience (Fuller & Smith, 1996; Wilson, 2001). The use of mystery shopping has been the most prominent way to monitor the behavioral aspects of workers' service performance, such as how customers are greeted upon entering a store, if they are asked if they need assistance, or if sales clerks ask them to add on to a purchase (Finn & Kayandé, 1999; Wilson, 2001). Mystery shoppers evaluate worker adherence to the standardized procedures required in each interaction, including standardized scripts (Wilson, 1998).

The Mystery Shopping Providers Association (MSPA) is the main organization of the mystery shopping industry in the U.S. According to an MSPA report, "the mystery shopping industry had an estimated value of nearly $600 million in the United States in 2004" and was recently valued at around $1.5 billion (MSPA, 2009a, 2009b, 2013). The MSPA estimates that there are over 1.5 million individuals employed as mystery shoppers.

Businesses normally inform workers during training of the potential for mystery shopping, but employees are not told when mystery shoppers will be present (Ford, Susan, & Myron, 1997). Once a particular business has been "shopped," management is soon notified and supplied with a detailed report. Employers typically use the results for evaluation purposes. Good evaluations can lead to promotions, raises, or simple congratulatory recognition; poor evaluations may result in various forms of discipline, including having one's mistakes pointed out in front of co-workers, suspensions, missing out on a pay raise, or in extreme cases may result in firing (Fuller & Smith, 1996). Businesses contract mystery shopping companies for multiple visits to gauge over time how workers measure up to workplace standards.

For employers, the benefits of mystery shopping revolve mainly around its cost-effectiveness in comparison to other methods of assessing employee performance such as customer surveys, the ability to monitor employee adherence to standardized procedures, and in helping to highlight areas in need of improvement (Wilson, 1998). Mystery shopping is believed to be objective due to its reliance on standardized measures, as opposed to other methods that are based on customer opinion (Finn, 2001; Finn & Kayandé, 1999; MSPA, 2009; Wilson, 1998).

Research on the effects of mystery shoppers on service employees follows the technologically deterministic view that mystery shoppers will control worker behavior and enforce adherence to scripts, either because employees choose to take control and follow the behavioral requirements, or because they constantly fear the potential of observation so they will always follow the rules. In the first case, it is acknowledged that the "objectivity and reliability" of mystery shopping may be compromised due to variability in the characteristics of individual customers (Wilson, 1998, p. 414).

However, this view holds that if workers adhere to the required standardized procedures, no matter how the interaction unfolds, then each customer should, in theory, be treated in the exact same way; "differences between customers should have little or no impact on the processes and procedures followed" by the workers (Wilson, 1998, p. 417).

On the other hand, the threat of mystery shoppers may control worker behavior through invoking the panopticon. According to Fuller and Smith (1996) mystery shopping invokes the power of the panopticon in its potential to control behavior through the constant possibility of observation (Fuller & Smith, 1996). "The knowledge that [mystery] shoppers may be there at any time may continuously constrain workers' actions," thereby exhibiting the effect of the panopticon (Fuller & Smith, 1996, p. 85). However, this argument remains only at the level of speculation, Fuller and Smith's (1996) research focused mainly on the effects of customer control strategies on managers, not on frontline service laborers.

Bain and Taylor (2000) critique the technological determinist approach of other labor scholars in applying Foucault's analysis of the panopticon as an inescapable system of surveillance. They argue that uses of Foucault often involve a limited reading and interpretation of his work. In order to challenge the overly deterministic approach of other Foucauldian analyses of labor, they examined employee agency in the face of observational management strategies. While they mention the use of mystery shoppers, they did not analyze their impact, instead in their analysis of call center workers, they focus on the use of "remote observations," or the supposedly covert recording of worker calls used for training and disciplinary purposes (Bain & Taylor, 2000, p. 11). However, instead of discovering perfect surveillance and control, they found that workers recognize patterns in manager behavior that could clue them in to the potential that they were under observation; these strategies included recognizing a manager plugging into their computer or even receiving a call from a manager who would check if they were at their station. While management at service firms have attempted new forms of managerial control, researchers have found that in no case does total control over employee's self and behavior occur.

CURRENT RESEARCH

Much of the prior research on the control of the behavior of frontline service laborers has revolved around analyses of often totalizing forms of control, such as standardized scripts (Ritzer, 2004), identity regulation

(Alvesson & Willmott, 2002), cultural reorganization (Du Gay & Salaman, 1992), or forms of panoptic surveillance (Fuller, & Smith, 1996). In each of these cases, other researchers have responded by complicating these characterizations as technologically deterministic and missing elements of resistance (Bain & Taylor, 2000; Knights & McCabe, 2003; Leidner, 1993) or game play (Sallaz, 2015). Leidner (1993) and more recently Sallaz (2015) each identify the shortcomings of strict behavioral control in frontline service work, but in very different ways. Leidner (1993) finds that employees will often drop standardized scripts in instances that make them uncomfortable, such as in suggestive selling. Employees in these cases form alliances with customers to subvert managerial rules for scripting. Sallaz (2015) argues that, in a situation not involving scripts, but instead with a computer system that is in place to regulate employee-customer interactions, employees will rely on their interactional competence to try to master the computer system in the form of a game. What they share, however, is an introduction into how frontline service laborers do not respond to control strategies in a uniform way, even from interaction to interaction. Instead, frontline service laborers demonstrate flexibility in the face of unpredictable interactions. Knowing that these laborers are faced with such variability in interactions moment-to-moment throughout their work day, I seek to uncover their flexibility in alliances and maintenance of their own agency, while also facing two different kinds of control mechanisms: standardized scripts and mystery shopping. I seek to answer these questions: (1) How do frontline service workers manage following a standardized script while also facing interactional contingencies that the script does not address?; (2) How do frontline service employees manage their job requirements with the knowledge that they could be under observation by a mystery shopper?; (3) What strategies do employees use to exert agency or provide resistance?

METHODS

To answer these questions, I conducted face-to-face, semi-structured, in-depth interviews with twenty frontline service workers, ten females, ten males, ranging in age from 18 to 27.[1] All names have been changed to protect confidentiality. I recruited interviewees via a snowball sampling method. Each interviewee worked for a major foodservice chain store in a medium sized city in either the U.S. Midwest or Pacific Northwest;[2] seven were counter workers at fast food restaurants and cafés, nine were servers from chain sit-down restaurants, and four were retail salespeople. Six of these employees had also worked their way up to shift manager positions. By looking across businesses, I was able to account for a wider range of experiences (Williams & Connell, 2010). At the time of their interview all interviewees were employed for at least one year, with job tenure ranging between 1 and 10 years, and median tenure at 4 years. As a requirement of participation in this study, each interviewee had to work in a job where they were required to follow a set of standardized procedures, including standardized scripts, in each customer interaction. Each of their employers also had to use the services of a mystery shopping company to monitor the employees' adherence to the standardized procedures.

Interviews covered training procedures, script requirements, experience with mystery shoppers, and examples of situations where following a script was difficult. Interviews followed an interview guide, but were semi-structured to allow for further probing as the interview unfolded. Each interview was conducted outside of the work setting so that interviewees could speak freely about their experiences without the chance of being overheard by co-workers or managers. Interviews ranged from 45 minutes to 1½ hours in length and were digitally audio-recorded. After interviews were completed, verbatim transcripts were created. To begin immersing myself in the data, initial coding was performed (Lofland & Lofland, 1995). In initial coding, I created line by line codes of interviewee responses. After initial coding was completed for each interview, "focused coding" followed in order to pull out broader themes from the initial ones occurring across the interviews [descriptions of competing requirements, recognizing contingencies, managing mystery shoppers] and to examine their similarities and differences (Esterberg, 2001; Lofland & Lofland, 1995).

FINDINGS

Script Requirements

Before describing the ways in which employees manage the scripted service encounter, I first describe in greater detail the general requirements of scripted interaction. I also identify the behavioral components of the employee-customer interaction that employees are aware are monitored by mystery shoppers; this information stems from the reports provided by mystery shoppers to management that are then typically shared with employees (as discussed in detail further below).

Although the substance of the script varied for each interviewee, similarities existed in the structural elements of the interactions that are scripted. For example, each employee was required to vocalize a greeting, suggestive sale, and closing remark in every customer interaction. Paula described the greeting she was required to give at the beginning of each interaction. She had to thank the customer for choosing that particular business, state her name, and then ask how she could serve the customer. The greeting Paula was required to say is typical of most required greetings reported by the interviewees who are counter workers. "We're just supposed to say 'Hi, thank you for choosing Burger Time. My name is so and so. How can I be of service?'" A variation of this greeting was reported by Emily, where a suggestive sale is embedded within the greeting, "Welcome to Burger Time. Would you like to try our new iced mocha today?"

After the greeting, every interviewee had multiple suggestive sale scripts they had to follow. The most common involved upselling to larger sizes of already purchased items, with others including suggesting dessert, or in a few cases, suggesting a store membership card. Louie explained a typical interaction where he received an order, in this case for a medium caramel machiatto:

> Let's say they get a medium caramel machiatto, and I would say "for thirty cents more you could upsize that to a large. Would you like that?" Then you would ask them towards the end of the transaction, "do you have a Big Box Bookstore membership card? That would save you ten to twenty percent on your transaction." And if they say "no, I do not." "Would you like one, to sign up for one today? It costs twenty five dollars and we can get that started for you." You go on to say "would you like anything from the dessert bar, or dessert menu?"

Along with the specific suggestive sale scripts, the servers had been instructed by management to directly market to customers by trying to "upsell everything." Dan explained:

> Upselling they always want to do ... if something was on sale, or just like some better choice for the customer, offer that or desserts, just try to upsell everything you can.

The most extensive requirements were outlined by Sylvia who had to not only follow a script, but also follow time requirements. Sylvia explained that the grading criteria for the secret shop mirrored the standardized requirements. She said that the requirements for each interaction follow a "20 step process," which is "basically the secret shop," or the elements of her interaction that would be evaluated by a mystery shopper. She explained:

> It's like a twenty step process, it's basically the secret shop. What you have to do is greet the guest within 45 seconds, and then introduce yourself, suggest an upsell drink, so not like Pepsi, like "do you want a margarita?" And then you have three minutes to

get back to the table with the drink, and then you have to ask for an appetizer, and then put that in, if they're not ready to order you have two minutes to get back to take their order .... And then at the end of the meal you have to ask if they'd like a dessert, you have to name a specific dessert. Then you have five minutes to get the dessert out. At the end of the meal ... you have to thank them by their name on the credit card if they give you a credit card. And then you have to suggest, or point to and explain the email signup club, then you have to ... suggest gift cards.

The bulk of each of the scripts centered on upselling. As Leidner (1993) observed, frontline service workers were uncomfortable with suggestive sale scripts and sometimes left them out of the interaction. Sylvia's recognition that the requirements are "basically the secret shop" provides a clear tie between the script and the use of mystery shoppers as an enforcement mechanism.

While each employee had a set of script requirements that were supposed to be followed for each interaction, sometimes they were not able to adhere to the rules. This will be explored more fully in the next section, where interviewees explain contingencies that the script did not account for, as well as situations where customers resist the role of frontline service workers as direct marketers.

Recognizing Interactional Contingencies

Many participants recognized a conflict between the requirements of their jobs and the ways the interactions actually unfolded. A contingency that Louie recognized is that a customer may order a meal and say "that's it" after their order, therefore making a suggestive sell nonsensical, or making him appear as if he ignored the customer. Louie explained:

They'll tell you "that's it." So a guy came up to me ... "I want a medium latte and that's it. I don't want anything else." He will let you know that. So it conflicts with what I need to do for the job. What they [employers] require me to do and what this guy actually wants.

Louie sets up a clear imbalance of the different parties here and he is at the center of making a decision of where to ally. His identity presentation is at stake. Other interviewees described similar situations where customer behavior prevented the required script from making interactional sense and placed the employee in a position where they had to choose which requirement to fulfill: making sense or following the script and suggestively selling.

Emily was required in each customer interaction to welcome them with a specific greeting and to make a suggestive sale. She also described the difficulty of implementing suggestive selling with customers who marked their orders as complete. Emily explained:

> Customers will come like "I only want dadadada, I just want this, that's all".... I remember I had customers, I would just start to say it [suggestive sell] and they would be like "no no, don't want that, I just want my cup of coffee," or "I just want."

Emily felt that customers were aware of the script and that they could become irritated and provide resistance; they know what their order is and they do not want to hear the further suggestive sale scripts.

This discrepancy was not only described by counter workers, but by table servers, as well. Diane elaborated on Louie's and Emily's descriptions of customers marking their orders as complete with a statement such as "that's it." She recognized a conflict between the rules of the script and implicit rules of interaction; she stated that it was hard to follow the script in a situation where the customer had "already made up their mind." Diane realized the script established a pre-defined turn-by-turn organization for the interaction, and adhering to the script pressured the customer to adhere to this particular organization. This organization can clash with the contingencies of the interaction that often arise due to a conflicting understanding of the worker's role as direct marketer/non-direct marketer. As she explained:

> You'll try to start your little routine [script] and they're just like "no I want," you know, "a water, and this is what I want to eat, that's it, now go away." So, like in that situation it's hard to ... do that kind of stuff (use script and upsell) because they've already made up their mind what they're getting and we're trying to just get them to do something else.

From the customer's viewpoint, once they place their order, the goal of this portion of the interaction has been reached: the meal has been ordered. Diane was placed in a position where she must either break the rules by deviating from the script and treating the interaction as complete, or continuing the interaction according to her script requirements, by suggestively selling and appearing nonsensical, or ignoring the customer's stated desires. By adhering to the script, Diane indicated that conflicts can arise between requirements of scripted and everyday interactions.

Workers were not the only ones who recognized conflicts in the requirements they are supposed to follow. Customers also sometimes recognized scripts and even questioned them. As Sylvia described:

> If you just go through the routine, sometimes people will [say] "they ask you to say that right?" Like about gift cards ... especially, they're like, "I don't want any, but they make you say that.".... People recognize certain things that seem forced.

Customer awareness of scripts is another contingency that standardized scripts do not address. Louie provides an additional example of customer recognition of a script. He described an instance where a customer who regularly frequented the café was so aware of the script that instead of following it through, he would address the questions he knew were going to be asked before Louie had an opportunity to ask them. Louie explained:

> This guy would say "I don't want anything else," and "that's it." He would even say like "I don't want a membership card," or ya know, "I don't want to upsize my drink." He's been there so many times that he knows the script.

When a customer displays awareness of the use of a script, the frontline service worker faces pressure to not use more scripts in the interaction. To continue following the script in such instances, workers appear to ignore customers and behave nonsensically or like judgmental dopes (Garfinkel, 1967). On the other hand, not following through with the script, employees ignore their job requirements and risk being sanctioned by management.

When customers question the script, acknowledge scripted questions before they are asked, and cut off the script before the worker completes it, they demonstrate their resistance to the worker as direct marketer, or salesperson, identity. This serves as evidence that the customers, employees, and management have incompatible understandings of the employee's "relevant identity" in the interaction (Sacks, 1972, 1992; Schegloff, 1991). By requiring suggestive selling, management proposes the identity of employee as salesperson. The identity proposed by management can come into direct conflict with an employee's own sense of self, or a customer's expectations of the employee. Customers, in this case, do not simply accept the managerially imposed identity of the worker, as Alvesson and Willmott (2002) and Du Gay and Salaman (1992) propose. Instead of customers accepting frontline service workers as salespeople, they propose their own local definition by orienting to workers as simply an intermediary to get what they want.

Managing Interactional Contingencies

By not adhering to the script, one increases the risk of reprimand from their employer and of potentially not obtaining a pay increase during employee reviews. On the other hand, following the script in times where remaining a competent interactant would involve cutting it off, the worker increases their risk of defying the customer's wishes or ignoring the customer, and causing more stress for both the customer and the employee.

All interviewees reported deviating from the script to stop bothering customers and working against their wishes. The interviewees stated that they typically align with the customer's orientation to the purchase and deviate from the script to avoid conflict and retain a sense of dignity (Hodson, 2001); workers use "alternative procedures" as a form of coping mechanism that helps interactions run more smoothly (Hodson, 1995, p. 89). They did this even in the face of potential reprimands, such as losing points on a mystery shop, not obtaining an ideal schedule, or not receiving a pay increase during employee evaluation.

Louie further described not challenging customer wishes and retaining a sense of dignity in the interaction. Louie explained:

> If I already know that this guy's annoyed before I even say anything, I cut it off, I don't say anything. Just to make his experience more pleasant ... [The] customer comes first and I really don't care about the company .... Even though I might be ... getting screwed with pay increases .... I might be doing discredit to the company but .... I look at the customer and I don't want them having a bad time or bad experience because of something someone's forcing me to do, because the customer doesn't know maybe that the company is forcing me to do this. And it's kind of like my face, I'm the company, so if they have a problem, they are gonna deal with it with me.

Louie framed this discussion as one between the company on one side and the customer and himself on the other. The locally organized face-to-face interaction with the customer is treated with more priority than the employee-employer relationship. Louie's explanation clearly demonstrates that he separated himself "from the script" for customers. He recognized that he would be seen as "the company." Similar to Knights and McCabe's (2003) finding that call center workers resisted manager attempts to reshape their self-identity, Louie similarly resisted managerial shaping of his identity. Louie stated that when he departed from the script, he took the risk of maybe "doing discredit to the company." Even though he may be breaking the rules, he may actually be restoring dignity to both himself and the company by retaining interactional competency in the eyes of the customer.

Thus far I have demonstrated the limits of strict standardized control of worker behavior by demonstrating how workers will resist when their interactional competence is threatened. Similarly, Leidner's (1996) work on scripting frontline service interactions treated the script as the control mechanism. However, since Leidner's (1996) research, organizations have developed new surveillance measures for monitoring and enforcing compliance with scripts. The next section looks at how workers deal with the knowledge that they could potentially face a panoptic situation, where a mystery shopper could be observing and evaluating their script adherence.

Servers' Recognition of Mystery Shoppers and Mystery Shop Potential

The logic behind using mystery shoppers as a form of panoptic control is that they appear to be ordinary customers, and therefore, workers should not be able to tell whether they are under observation. Because they cannot tell when they are under observation, they are expected to assume that observation is always possible and will follow the required procedures in every interaction. The interviewees, however, said that they had strategies for deciding the potential observation of a mystery shopper. Table servers recognized repeat mystery shoppers and also believed that they recognized differences between mystery shoppers' behavior and ordinary customers' behavior. They reported having the ability to sometimes gauge whether they were under observation, thus taking away the anonymity of mystery shopping and allowing them the flexibility of adhering to the script when they perceived that they were under observation, or dropping portions of the script when they believe they are not being evaluated. Counter workers also reported increased awareness of mystery shopper potential as they were often aware of when mystery shoppers would arrive. They reported knowing the time of month they usually occur, or receiving a warning from a manager of an impending mystery shop.

Table Servers

No interviewee claimed to know every time that they were under observation, but they did reported strategies, or clues that could tip them off, to determine if they were dealing with a mystery shopper. Employees could confirm if they had been observed by a mystery shopper once the mystery shopper report was filed. Interviewees reported that after a mystery shopper had graded them they were typically notified by management within a week. When the store received the mystery shopper report, the manager would notify the workers, as Tricia reported:

> We were given a sheet, when we are graded we are given a sheet that is supposedly very similar to what the mystery shoppers get.

And Sylvia:

> We have regular shoppers and like, they tell you on the printout that you get, with the questions. [They] tell you what time they came in, what they ordered, and like you remember. "Oh, I remember them!" — Sylvia,

Instead of keeping elements of the mystery shoppers anonymous, like what day or time the mystery shopper arrived and what they ordered, interviewees reported that the grading sheet aided them in recognizing who mystery shoppers were.

In addition to receiving the graded mystery shopper printouts, some interviewees also reported identifying when they were going to be interacting with a mystery shopper because a mystery shopper would have their notes visible. As Charlie stated:

> I've come up behind a person, he was a shopper, and he was doing it on his phone. I thought he was texting and I happened to walk up behind him and get a glance at his phone and realized he was taking notes. So I dropped off the food and my entire demeanor changed.

And Tricia:

> Some of them [mystery shoppers] are really obvious. They'll have like a really long piece of paper with them that they kind of hide in their purse a little bit and they're like checking stuff off and it's like, "you're a mystery shopper."

By learning after they were graded by a mystery shopper or by recognizing a mystery shopper taking notes, both servers and counter workers had experience identifying who were mystery shoppers, allowing them the ability to compare their experiences with mystery shoppers to those who they knew were not.

Dan discussed how often the exact same mystery shoppers would visit the restaurant each month. He stated that after a while, servers were able to recognize the mystery shoppers, eliminating the "mystery." Whereas ordinary customers may appear less recognizable, Dan, a shift manager, reported that not only were the same mystery shoppers grading his restaurant, but their behaviors were organizationally distinct from regular customers due to their aim of fulfilling the grading procedures they were hired to carry out. As Dan explained:

> After a while we were able to recognize who the mystery shoppers were .... It was a couple .... They always had a particular spot they liked to sit .... If I was the manager I would sometimes assign particular servers to that table that I know would do everything they were supposed to .... They're [servers] the ones that would also come up to me and say they were mystery shoppers, "that's a mystery shopper." There's a huge incentive for that, if you got everything right and got a hundred percent on a mystery shop they [employers] gave you a hundred dollars.

It is in the interest of service workers to be able to distinguish between mystery shoppers and ordinary customers. In this case, and also reported by other interviewees, the business had a monetary incentive for receiving a perfect mystery shop. The incentive was created by upper-management in order to encourage adherence to the script, however, Dan, a shift manager, described how the reward had been undermined and instead used as an incentive for employees to recognize mystery shoppers. Shift-managers, in this case Dan and their fellow employees aligned their interests to subvert the mystery shop. For Dan, he would alert his employees if a mystery shopper was present and assign particular servers to take the table. It would be in both the shift-manager and the server's interest as the shift-manager appears as a competent manager and the server could receive a bonus. By distinguishing between mystery shoppers and ordinary customers, workers can strategically adhere to and drop the script depending on the perceived mystery shopper threat. This also allows them the ability to appear to be following procedures when they think they are being graded, and to break the rules when they believe they are not under mystery shopper observation.

Similar to Dan, Sylvia also explained how often the same mystery shoppers graded the store, allowing recognition by workers and prompting changes in their behavior. In Dan's description, there was one couple that would perform mystery shops at his restaurant each month, but in Sylvia's restaurant, there were "a lot of regular shoppers" that they recognized. This shows that even when multiple mystery shoppers are used, as the MSPA recommends, workers can still remember repeat shoppers and adjust their behavior accordingly. Sylvia explained:

> We have a lot of regular shoppers and we know who they are. Everything for them will be like, completely different. We will make sure everything goes out right, they'll make sure the manager talks to them. Like we know who they are, you make sure you know what you are doing. It affects it, like, you make sure you hit your points .... When I got shopped I didn't know. They were like not regulars at all. But you can tell. But when you can tell, and you know, everyone acts different.

Sylvia's reference to "you hit your points" refers to the procedural and script requirements on the mystery shop. Her orientation to the requirements as "points" highlights the strictly procedural characteristic of the job requirements in her eyes. This reveals a difference in approach to the service encounter between workers and ordinary customers due to the use of mystery shoppers. As the worker orients the objective of the interaction to receiving points, the ordinary customer's orientation lacks this reference. In further support of the difference in orientation to the scripted service interaction by customer and worker is Sylvia's awareness of the change in worker behavior when a customer is recognized as a mystery shopper; in these instances, everyone works to adhere to the standardized procedures.

Sylvia stated that "they were like not regulars at all ... but you can tell." Even when mystery shoppers were not recognized as repeat shoppers, servers often noticed differences within the interactions that influenced whether workers would determine if a customer was a mystery shopper or an ordinary customer. Joanna reported that she could tell the difference between mystery shopper and ordinary customer behavior by the way the interaction took shape. Joanna:

> You can tell like who the average customer is, they just tell you their order .... "we want this, this, and this, that's it." They're like "we don't want this, and we don't want that." Like if you start talking they'll interrupt you like "oh we don't want soup." Like you'll tell them the soups of the day and they'll be like "we don't want soup" .... Like if you're having a mystery shopper they won't interrupt you. They'll let you say everything because they're grading you.

Interviewees reported that they believed that mystery shoppers allow the worker to follow their script without interruption. Joanna attributed this to the fact that they are grading employees on their script adherence and interrupting them would interfere with their own requirement of grading. On the other hand, she realized that ordinary customers have no grading requirement, leaving them to freely interrupt the script as they please.

Worker descriptions of the differences in the behaviors of mystery shoppers and ordinary customers reveal their perception of the observable variation in orientations between the different actors in the service interaction. While the workers and mystery shoppers orient to the required script, as Charlie notes, mystery shoppers are perceived by these laborers to be "checking to make sure you're following the script and you're making sure you're following the script," while they assume ordinary customers approach the interaction with their own needs, regardless of the script. The interviewees reported that they believe that mystery shoppers have their own set of rules to follow in order to evaluate employees; in other words they are also expected to act like judgmental dopes (Garfinkel, 1967) by simply adhering to their own set of interactional rules established by the mystery shopper grading requirements. This study is admittedly limited in its analysis of mystery shopper behavior, as it relies solely on interviews with frontline service laborers. Despite this limitation, some insight into mystery shopper behavior can be gleaned, including varied mystery shopper practices where some will poorly conceal their note taking, while others were less easy to readily detect at a glance. Further analysis of mystery shopper behavior and skill-development would provide a fuller picture.

The inability for rules to dictate action points to the limitations of both scripting employee speech and policing scripted behavior. By recognizing behavioral differences, workers have one strategy for recognizing surveillance potential. Contrary to Fuller and Smith's (1996) assumption, instead of being controlled by mystery shoppers and forced to adhere to the script at all times, they are able to selectively choose to follow the script when they are aware that they are being observed and drop aspects of the script when they perceive that the threat of mystery shopper evaluation is minimal. This is similar to Leidner's (1993) finding that McDonald's employees would often use the script like a shield to hide behind when faced with difficult customers. In addition to Leidner, I demonstrate that employees can not only exert agency and use the script when dealing with problem customers, but that they can also choose to adhere to the script in order to appear to be following the required procedures when they believe that they are under observation, or to drop the script when they believe that they are not interacting with a mystery shopper. Whether the attempt to control worker behavior lies in required scripts or in their monitoring by mystery shoppers, workers will rely on their interactional competence to recognize when they can strategically subvert workplace rules.

Counter Workers

Counter workers were also able to limit the effectiveness of control because managers forewarned them of a mystery shop. This advance warning works in both the manager's and the counter worker's interest, as a bad mystery shop would reflect poorly on both. This suggests that store managers and counter workers might align interests in order to appear to upper-management to be following the rules. Louie explains how a low mystery shop score can look bad for management because it appears as if they have not done an adequate job of training their employees:

> Your manager looks bad and, you know, other people within the organization look bad .... They don't get their goals met because they obviously aren't teaching you something, and they're teaching you something wrong.

In order to prevent a poor evaluation, managers monitored the potential for a mystery shop and warned their employees to act accordingly. Managers were often aware of a heightened potential for mystery shoppers because they kept schedules of when they had arrived in the past. In Emily's case, mystery shoppers typically arrived at the end of the month. Her manager would warn her that a mystery shopper may be coming soon, and she explained how they subsequently changed their behavior to be in compliance with the requirements. Emily explained:

> Knowing that the mystery shop was coming I really made sure to say [the script]. As soon as [managers] are saying "hey we think we're gonna get a mystery shop" ... people are smiling more, they're making sure to, you know, [say] "hi there ... can I get you anything else?"

Emily described how she had been working to adhere to the script a bit more consciously toward the end of the month when the threat of a mystery shop was present. After the mystery shop occurred, she explained that she began to deviate from the script:

> After we got the mystery shop I noticed that I didn't say it [the script] as much cause I was like, "well we already got the mystery shop and I feel dumb saying this and I hate saying this and this is stupid" so I really didn't.

After the mystery shopper left, she was able to cut an aspect of the script that she did not particularly care for; that is, saying "have a nice day, stop by again" at the end of the interaction. She had difficulty with this part of the script, because customers often would respond with "thank you, you too." She thought "stop by again" felt awkward and decided to cut it after the threat of a mystery shop had passed. This serves as a further illustration of how workers alter their behavior in relation to the threat of a mystery shop.

This section shows that managers play a key role in counter workers' ability to limit the full realization of a panopticon by warning them of an impending mystery shop. Differing from the experience of table servers, managers in counter work establishments would keep schedules and forewarn employees of an impending mystery shop. Workers adhere to the script until the threat of a mystery shop has passed, and then they often immediately drop the script. This collusion allows employees to exercise tacit knowledge and still achieve high mystery shop scores which make managers appear competent to their superiors. In no instances did counter workers report that managers would alert them when a mystery shopper had entered the store. This is most likely due to the greater rapidity of interactions that counter workers faced.

DISCUSSION

The frontline service workers interviewed share similar approaches to facing the competing requirements of adhering to a standardized script while managing customer variation that the script does not address. They not only recognize competing requirements in the scripted service encounter, which they frame in terms of a choice between (1) following interactional norms by dropping the script and appearing sensical and (2) adhering to job requirements and appearing nonsensical or like judgmental dopes. They also take conscious risks, in the form of "routine resistance" (Prasad & Prasad, 1998), in order to maintain interactional competence and dignity (Hodson, 2001) in the encounters.

In support of Lopez (2007), and Leidner's (1993) findings, this research calls into question the breadth of the impact of behavioral standardization. In particular, frontline service laborers are expected to identify and comply with managerial expectations for adherence to behavioral scripts. However, it has been demonstrated that these laborers only strategically comply with managerial behavioral expectations. Additionally, this research builds from Sallaz's (2015) findings of the flexibility workers display in facing variance in the way every interaction takes shape. We both find that the preservation of interactional competence is often prioritized over strict rule following and can result in a form of a game that benefits both the organization and the employee. Differing from Sallaz, however, I examine a setting of face-to-face interactions where employees experience a form of direct control (whereas Sallaz examines the indirect control of "permanent pedagogy") through the requirements of standardized scripts and observation by mystery shoppers. In this case, one might expect that employees would be more limited in their ability to subvert managerial control of employee behavior and/or identity (Alvesson & Willmott, 2002; Du Gay & Salaman, 1992; Ritzer, 2004). Instead, I demonstrate that in the case of the face-to-face frontline service interaction, the alliances between employees, customers, and management are more fluid, changing moment-to-moment depending on how the interactions unfold. Employees are not controlled by an imposed workplace identity, but instead exhibit flexibility based the contingencies presented in each interaction. Like Bolton and Boyd's (2003, p. 294) finding that emotional laborers bring with them their own emotional competence and have the ability to "calibrate how much feeling is invested into the performance," I demonstrate that frontline service employees who are required to follow standardized scripts rely on their own interactional competence to take strategic risks in choosing when they are less likely to receive a sanction for subverting the rules. I outline how workers align with customers in some situations in order to maintain interactional competence and their own personal identity over the management imposed identity. I also show how in other instances workers align with management in order to achieve a satisfactory mystery shop score, undermining the control of this customer observation method by still appearing to follow the rules.

I argue that the strategies developed by frontline service employees are not those of organized resistance, but are instead an example of "ambiguous accommodation," a form of "routine resistance" where the "appearance of consent and cooperation … conceals resistance (Prasad & Prasad, 1998, p. 238). Because frontline service employees cannot fully adhere to standardized scripts, but they are required to do so for their jobs, they respond to these circumstances by taking calculated risks, thus limiting the control of their behavior by standardization. These laborers show interactive dexterity in their ability to navigate interaction to interaction, much like emotional laborers (Bolton & Boyd, 2003). By exerting agency, frontline service workers subtly provide resistance to the rigidity of standardization in order to retain dignity (Hodson, 2001), and to maintain the workplace as a negotiated, instead of fixed, order (Prasad & Prasad, 1998). Similar to the findings of Burawoy (1979) and Lopez (2007), however, while workers may be subverting official rules, their routine resistance may also work to the benefit of the organization as a form of "making out" (see also Hodson, 1991). By maintaining interactional competence, workers maintain a competent face for the organization and align with customers to keep them happy.

The larger effect that these subtle subversions have on the structure of the work environment and on the development of standardized procedures is unclear. The immediate result is that it is clear that frontline service employees can strategically exert individual agency in the face of strict standardized scripting requirements and a panoptic management strategy. Due to this agency, standardized scripts and mystery shoppers are prevented from completely controlling worker-customer interactions. It is also clear that workers believe that they can recognize when they are under observation in order to appear to be following the rules, only to drop uncomfortable aspects of the script when they perceive that the threat of observation is not present. Interactional competency is preserved by workers and serves as an aspect of self that is out of reach of standardization and observational control.

NOTES

1. In addition to the initial interviews, one follow-up interview was conducted with Emily, the first interviewee, who had experienced changes in the scripted speech requirements in her job after the initial interview.
2. I moved during the middle of this project from the U.S. Midwest to the Pacific Northwest. I had completed 10 interviews in the Midwest and was cognizant of regional variation, but after completing 10 interviews in the Northwest, a regional difference has not presented itself. This could have to do with the fact that interviewees work for large national chain stores with identical employee requirements in all stores.

REFERENCES

Albrecht, K., & Zemke, R. (1985). *Service America!: Doing business in the new economy*. Homewood, CA: Dow Jones-Irwin.

Alvesson, M., & Willmott, H. (2002). Identity regulation as organizational control: Producing the appropriate individual. *Journal of Management Studies, 35*, 619–644.

Bain, P., & Taylor, P. (2000). Entrapped by the 'Electronic Panopticon'? Worker resistance in the call centre. *New Technology, Work and Employment, 15*, 2–18.

Bolton, S. C., & Boyd, C. (2003). Trolley Dolly or skilled emotion manager? Moving on from Hochschild's managed heart. *Work, Employment, & Society, 17*, 289–308.

Braverman, H. (1974). *Labor and monopoly capital: The degradation of work in the twentieth century*. New York, NY: Monthly Review Press.

Burawoy, M. (1979). *Manufacturing consent: Changes in the labor process under monopoly capitalism*. Chicago, IL: University of Chicago Press.

Butler, C. (2014). Wanted—straight talkers: Stammering and aesthetic labour. *Work, Employment, and Society, 28*, 718–734.

Du Gay, P. (1996). *Consumption and identity at work*. London: Sage.

Du Gay, P., & Salaman, G. (1992). The cult[ure] of the customer. *Journal of Management Studies, 29*(5), 615.

Esterberg, K. G. (2001). *Qualitative methods in social research*. Boston, MA: McGraw-Hill.

Eustace, E. (2012). Speaking allowed? Workplace regulation of regional dialect. *Work, Employment, and Society, 26*, 331–348.

Finn, A. (2001). Mystery shopper benchmarking of durable-goods chains and stores. *Journal of Service Research, 3*, 310–320.

Finn, A., & Kayandé, U. (1999). Unmasking a phantom: A psychometric assessment of mystery shopping. *Journal of Retailing, 75*, 195–217.

Ford, R. C., Susan, A. B., & Myron, D. F. (1997). Methods of measuring patient satisfaction in health care organizations. *Health Care Management Review, 22*, 74–89.

Form, W. (1987). On the degradation of skills. *Annual Review of Sociology, 13*, 29–47.

Foucault, M. (1995). *Discipline and punish: The birth of the prison*. New York, NY: Vintage Books.

Fuller, L., & Smith, V. (1996). Consumers' reports: Management by customers in a changing economy. In C. L. Macdonald & C. Sirianni (Eds.), *Working in the service society* (pp. 74–90). Philadelphia, PA: Temple University Press.

Garfinkel, H. (1967). *Studies in ethnomethodology*. Malden, MA: Blackwell Publishing.
Heritage, J. (1984). *Garfinkel and ethnomethodology*. Cambridge: Blackwell Publishers.
Hochschild, A. R. (1983). *The managed heart: Commercialization of human feeling*. Berkeley, CA: University of California Press.
Hodson, R. (1991). The active worker: Compliance and autonomy at the workplace. *Journal of Contemporary Ethnography, 20*, 47–78.
Hodson, R. (1995). Worker resistance: An underdeveloped concept in the sociology of work. *Economic and Industrial Democracy, 16*, 79–110.
Hodson, R. (2001). *Dignity at work*. New York, NY: Cambridge University Press.
Houlihan, M. (2000). Eyes wide shut? Querying the depth of call centre learning. *Journal of European Industrial Training, 24*, 228–240.
Johnson, C. M., & Masotti, R. M. (1990). Suggestive selling by waitstaff in family-style restaurants: An experiment and multisetting observations. *Journal of Organizational Behavior Management, 11*, 35–54.
Jones, B. (1989). When certainty fails: inside the factory of the future. In S. Wood (Ed.), *The transformation of work? Skill, flexibility, and the labour process* (pp. 44–58). London: Unwin Hyman.
Knights, D., & McCabe, D. (2003). Governing through teamwork: Reconstituting subjectivity in a call centre. *Journal of Management Studies, 40*, 1588–1619.
Korczynski, M. (2009). Understanding the contradictory lived experience of service work: The customer-oriented bureaucracy. In M. Korczynski & C. L. Macdonald (Eds.), *Service work: Critical perspectives* (pp. 73–90). New York, NY: Routledge Press.
Lavin, D., & Maynard, D. W. (2001). Standardization vs. Rapport: Respondent laughter and interviewer reaction during telephone surveys. *American Sociological Review, 66*, 453–479.
Leidner, R. (1993). *Fast food, fast talk: Service work and the routinization of everyday life*. Berkeley, CA: University of California Press.
Leidner, R. (1996). Rethinking questions of control: Lessons From McDonald's. In C. L. Macdonald & C. Sirianni (Eds.), *Working in the service society* (pp. 29–49). Philadelphia, PA: Temple University Press.
Lofland, J., & Lofland, L. H. (1995). *Analyzing social settings: A guide to qualitative observation and analysis*. Belmont, CA: Wadsworth Publishing Company.
Lohr, S. (2014). Unblinking eyes track employees: Workplace surveillance sees good and bad. *The New York Times*, June 21. Retrieved from http://www.nytimes.com/2014/06/22/technology/workplace-surveillance-sees-good-and-bad.html. Accessed on November 9.
Lopez, S. H. (2007). Efficiency and the fix revisited: Informal relations and mock routinization in a nonprofit nursing home. *Qualitative Sociology, 30*, 225–247.
Macdonald, C. L., & Sirianni, C. (1996). The service society and the changing experience of work. In C. L. Macdonald & C. Sirianni (Eds.), *Working in the service society* (pp. 1–26). Philadelphia, PA: Temple University Press.
Martinko, M. J., White, J. D., & Hassell, B. (1989). An operant analysis of prompting in a sales environment. *Journal of Organizational Behavior Management, 10*, 93–107.
Marx, G. T. (1999). Measure everything that moves: The new surveillance at work. *Research in the Sociology of Work, 8*, 165–189.
Maynard, D. W., & Schaeffer, N. C. (2002). Standardization and its discontents. In D. W. Maynard, H. Houttkoop-Steenstra, N. C. Schaeffer, & J. van der Zouwen (Eds.), *Standardization and tacit knowledge: Interaction and practice in the survey interview* (pp. 3–45). New York, NY: Wiley.

McCammon, H. J., & Griffin, L. J. (2000). Workers and their customers and clients: An editorial introduction. *Work and Occupations, 27*, 278–293.

Milligan, J., & Hantula, D. A. (2005). A prompting procedure for increasing sales in a small pet store. *Journal of Organizational Behavior Management, 25*, 37–44.

Mystery Shopper Provider's Association (MSPA). (2009a). *Mystery shopping industry estimated at nearly $600 million in Unites States, according to market size report.* Retrieved from http://www.mysteryshop.org/news/article_pr..php?art_ID = 69. Accessed on April 13, 2009.

Mystery Shopper Provider's Association (MSPA). (2009b). *Mystery shopper Q and A.* Retrieved from http://www.mysteryshop.org/news/MSPA_Shopper_QA.pdf. Accessed on April 13.

Pettinger, L. (2004). Brand culture and branded workers: Service work and aesthetic labour in fashion retail. *Consumption, Markets, and Culture, 7*, 165–184.

Prasad, A., & Prasad, P. (1998). Everyday struggles at the workplace: The nature and implications of routine resistance in contemporary organizations. *Research in the Sociology of Organizations, 15*, 225–257.

Ritzer, G. (2004). *The McDonaldization of society: Revised new century edition.* Thousand Oaks, CA: Pine Forge Press.

Roy, D. F. (1959). Banana time: Job satisfaction and informal interaction. *Human Organization, 18*, 158–168.

Sacks, H. (1972). An initial investigation of the usability of conversational data for doing sociology. In D. Sudnow (Eds.), *Studies in social interaction* (pp. 31–74). New York, NY: The Free Press.

Sacks, H. (1992). *Lectures on conversation.* Cambridge, MA: Blackwell Publishers.

Sallaz, J. J. (2015). Permanent pedagogy: How post-fordist firms generate effort but not consent. *Work and Occupations, 42*, 3–34.

Salzinger, L. (2003). *Genders in production: Making workers in Mexico's global factories.* Berkeley, CA: University of California Press.

Schegloff, E. (1991). Reflections on talk and social structure. In D. Boden & D. H. Zimmerman (Eds.), *Talk and social structure* (pp. 44–70). Cambridge: Polity Press.

Sewell, G. (1998). The discipline of teams: The control of team-based industrial work through electronic and peer surveillance. *Administrative Science Quarterly, 43*, 397–428.

Sewell, G., & Wilkinson, B. (1992). 'Someone to Watch Over Me': Surveillance, discipline and the just-in-time labour process. *Sociology, 26*, 271–289.

Smith, V. (1994). Braverman's legacy: The labor process tradition at 20. *Work and Occupations, 21*, 403–421.

Squires, J., Wilder, D. A., Fixsen, A., Hess, E., Rost, K., Curran, R., & Zonneveld, K. (2007). The effects of task clarification, visual prompts, and graphic feedback on customer greeting and up-selling in a restaurant. *Journal of Organizational Behavior Management, 27*, 1–13.

Thompson, P., & Ackroyd, S. (1995). All quiet on the workplace front? A critique of recent trends in British Industrial Sociology. *Sociology, 29*, 615–633.

Vallas, S. P. (1990). The concept of skill: A critical review. *Work and Occupations, 17*, 379–398.

Victorino, L., Verma, R., & Wardell, D. G. (2008). *Service scripting: A customer's perspective of quality and performance.* Cornell Hospitality Report 8:20.

Walsh, M. W. (2000). When 'May I Help You' is a labor issue; The customer-service assembly line. *The New York Times*, August 12. Retrieved from http://www.nytimes.com/2000/08/12/business/when-may-i-help-you-is-a-labor-issue-the-customer-service-assembly-line.html?src = pm&pagewanted = 1. Accessed on November 9, 2014.

Whalen, J., Whalen, M., & Henderson, K. (2002). Improvisational choreography in teleservice work. *British Journal of Sociology*, *53*, 239–258.

Williams, C. L., & Connell, C. (2010). "Looking Good and Sounding Right": Aesthetic labor and social inequality in the retail industry. *Work and Occupations*, *37*, 349–377.

Wilson, A. M. (1998). The role of mystery shopping in the measurement of service performance. *Managing Service Quality*, *8*, 414.

Wilson, A. M. (2001). Mystery shopping: Using deception to measure service performance. *Psychology and Marketing*, *18*, 721–734.

PART III
GENDER, SEXUALITY
AND PRECARITY

THE WALK-IN CLOSET: BETWEEN "GAY-FRIENDLY" AND "POST-CLOSETED" WORK

David Orzechowicz

ABSTRACT

Since the 1950s, the closet has been the chief metaphor for conceptualizing the experience of sexual minorities. Social change over the last four decades has begun to dismantle some of the social structures that historically policed heteronormativity and forced queer people to manage information about their sexuality in everyday life. Although scholars argue that these changes make it possible for some sexual minorities to live "beyond the closet" (Seidman, 2002), evidence shows the dynamics of the closet persist in organizations. Drawing on a case study of theme park entertainment workers, whose jobs exist at the nexus of structural conditions that research anticipates would end heterosexual domination, I find that what initially appears to be a post-closeted workplace is, in fact, a new iteration: the walk-in closet. More expansive than the corporate or gay-friendly closets, the walk-in closet provides some sexual minorities with a space to disclose their identities, seemingly without cost. Yet the fundamental dynamics of the closet − the subordination of homosexuality to heterosexuality and the continued need for LGB workers to manage information about their sexuality at work − persist

Research in the Sociology of Work, Volume 29, 187−213
ISSN: 0277-2833/doi:10.1108/S0277-283320160000029023

through a set of boundaries that contain gayness to organizationally desired places.

Keywords: Heteronormativity; homonormativity; organizations; sexuality; the closet; work culture

INTRODUCTION

The social status of sexual minorities has rapidly changed over the last 40 years. Public opinion toward lesbians, gays, and bisexuals[1] (LGB) has improved since the 1970s (Hicks & Lee, 2006), signaling greater social tolerance and acceptance. Improved public opinion has unfolded alongside increased media visibility (Gross, 2001; Walters, 2001) and expanded state support (Seidman, 2002). The prohibition of sexuality-based housing and employment discrimination (Hunter, 2000), decriminalization of sodomy (*Lawrence v. Texas*, 2003), hate crime legislation (Jenness & Grattet, 2001), and marriage equality (*Obergefell v. Hodges*, 2015) signal a rolling-back of anti-gay policies at the federal and state level. Such change leads Seidman (2002) to argue that post-closeted life is now possible for some sexual minorities.

Structural changes that dismantle the workplace closet are particularly important. Anticipated and experienced discrimination impacts sexual minorities' choice of vocation, ability to secure work and career advancement, social isolation at work, and comparably higher levels of work-related stress and depression (Croteau, 1996; Schneider & Dimito, 2010; Woods & Lucas, 1993). Discrimination also restricts the potential talent available to organizations (Tilcsik, Anteby, & Knight, 2015) and diminishes the productivity of LGB workers who expend time and energy to conceal their queer identities (Hall, 1986; Woods & Lucas, 1993). Here, too, we find important changes as organizations adopt queer-inclusive nondiscrimination policies, extend benefits to same-gender partners, and advance diversity training in an effort to reduce workplace heterosexism (Giuffre, Dellinger, & Williams, 2008; Raeburn, 2004; Williams, Giuffre, & Dellinger, 2009). Although scholars demonstrate that these changes produce a new iteration of the workplace closet (Rumens & Kerfoot, 2009; Williams et al., 2009) and thus fail to offer sexual minorities the same degree of inclusion found in gay-owned or gay-community-based organizations (Ward, 2008; Weston & Rofel, 1984), there is nevertheless evidence that the closet is being dismantled at work.

But is post-closeted work in a large company possible? The literature on organizational sexuality details the social structures that (re)produce different iterations of the workplace closet. It therefore anticipates the conditions under which post-closeted work might exist. The Entertainment division at Wonderland,[2] an American theme park, operates under these conditions, offering a case study to assess the potential for a post-closeted workplace. At first glance, Wonderland Entertainment seems to illustrate post-closeted work: employing a large number of openly gay men and characterized by a gay masculinity all men were expected to embody on-the-job, gay men are not silenced or tokenized (Hall, 1986; Williams et al., 2009; Woods & Lucas, 1993), but dominant and normative in the workplace. Yet upon deeper inspection we find the dynamics of the closet persist, albeit in less immediately limiting ways. The result is a *walk-in closet* characterized by the constrained permissibility of LGB sexuality, demonstrating the potential for and limits on post-closeted work under some of the most ideal organizational conditions.

BACKGROUND

Since the 1950s, the closet has been *the* dominant lens for understanding the social experiences of sexual minorities in Western societies (Seidman, 2002). The term references the dynamic of heterosexual domination and gay subordination that produces "a 'life-shaping' pattern of homosexual concealment ... with family, friends, and at work" (Seidman, 2002, p. 25). The hegemony of the closet, circa 1950s–1980s, was founded upon "aggressively enforced" (Seidman, 2002, p. 218, f10) heteronormativity and compulsory heterosexuality (Escoffier, 1997) policed by multiple institutions and legitimated by the state (Seidman, 2002; Seidman, Meeks, & Traschen, 1999). To navigate concerted heterosexual domination, LGB people often manage information to render invisible any queer interests, activities, and identities (Escoffier, 1997). State-legitimated oppression and wide-spread cultural stigma heighten the stakes around the closet: one can either "come out" and risk violence from individuals and institutions, or "stay in" and live a life of isolation and internalized stigma (Escoffier, 1997; Seidman, 2002).

Traditionally, this "pattern of homosexual concealment" manifests on-the-job as the corporate closet (Woods & Lucas, 1993), where sexual minorities face a decision to either stay in the closet and do the necessary dramaturgical work to pass as straight, or come out and risk the social and professional costs of systemic homophobia. These costs include stress over being outed at work, time and energy spent on feeling and information management related to sexual identity, isolation from coworkers, and diminished career opportunities (Hall, 1986; Rofes, 2000; Woods & Lucas, 1993).

Associated with jobs in business, medicine, law, and education, the corporate closet is produced and sustained by a confluence of social forces. This includes, in part, occupational expectations for professionalism. The myth of professionalism − that it demands an asexual worker and removes sexuality from organizations − obscures how it legitimates heteronormativity (Burrell & Hearn, 1989; Connell, 2014; Rumens & Kerfoot, 2009; Woods & Lucas, 1993). Ideal-typical professionalism implicitly imagines a heterosexual man (Grey, 1998), which reinforces the closet by normalizing and privileging heterosexual masculinity.

Specific organizational structures − that is, company policies and formal hierarchy − further (re)produce the corporate closet. The absence of nondiscrimination policies and diversity training, and the exclusion of same-gender partners from access to healthcare and other work-related benefits reinforce the heterosexism that sustains the corporate closet (Woods & Lucas, 1993). Research likewise demonstrates that the absence of minorities at higher levels of an organization's hierarchy sustains hegemonic forms of normativity and exclusion (Scott, 2005). Scholars also document the role of heterosexist work idiocultures (Hall, 1986; Rumens & Kerfoot, 2009; Ward & Winstanley, 2003, 2006; Williams et al., 2009; Woods & Lucas, 1993) − that is, the set of practices, discourses, and interests shared by an interactive group of coworkers (Fine, 1979) that assert and police heteronormativity − in sustaining heterosexual domination and gay subordination.

Evidence also suggests that the power of the corporate closet is reinforced by a "traditional" model of organization. Characterized by rigid hierarchy, a high proportion of benefit-receiving jobs, loyalty-based advancement, and the expectation one's career should unfold within a single company (Williams, 2013), traditional work organizations prize the "organizational man" (Whyte, 1956). This unidimensional worker seamlessly conforms to homogenous corporate life, striving to blend in rather than stand out (Fleming, 2009). When one's career is expected to unfold within a single company, where benefits and advancement may depend on the assessments of homophobic superiors, the potential to experience discrimination is high. The high the stakes of disclosure make the corporate closet the most viable survival strategy for LBG workers.

Historically, these forces came together against a backdrop of homophobia and the hegemony of the closet in the public sphere (Griffith & Hebl, 2002), which further extended the risks of being out (or outed) at work to all areas of one's life. Yet the closet is a "product of historically specific

social dynamics" (Seidman, 2002, p. 218f10), not a static set of social relations. The conditions that supported the hegemony of the closet during the
1950s–1980s – media censorship (Gross, 2001; Walters, 2001), medicaliza-
tion, and criminalization by the state (Foucault, 1980) – have changed,
diminishing its prominence in U.S. society (Seidman, 2002). This reduced
hegemony is evidenced in the ways LGB people have embraced and
integrated queerness into their daily lives (Seidman et al., 1999).
Fragmentation of the closet's hegemony further allows some sexual minorities to live "beyond the closet" (Seidman, 2002), without the information
management required to pass as straight *or* the internalized stigma of a
deviant sexual identity.

Although the corporate closet may still characterize the work experiences of some sexual minorities, the fracturing of the closet's hegemony
produces a new experience: the "gay-friendly" closet (Williams et al., 2009).
Some organizations attempt to reduce on-the-job heterosexism (Giuffre
et al., 2008; Raeburn, 2004; Williams et al., 2009). These organizations
tolerate – even celebrate – sexual minorities as important sources of organizationally valued diversity. Yet visibility comes at a price: out employees
experience tokenization and pressure to be the model sexual minority
(Williams et al., 2009). This gay-friendly closet continues to force sexual
minorities to manage information and downplay socially undesirable details
about their "openly" queerly life (Williams et al., 2009; Yoshino, 2002).

Critical to the emergence of the gay-friendly closet is company-wide
adoption of LGB-inclusive policies – for example, sexuality-based sensitivity
training and nondiscrimination policies, and the availability of benefits to
employees' partners, regardless of gender identity – that address heteronormativity and diminish the stakes of disclosing a queer identity at work
(Rumens & Kerfoot, 2009; Williams et al., 2009). New or "neoliberal" organizational practices (Williams, 2013), produced by pressure from the new
economy, additionally reduce the risks around disclosure. The shift to contingent, temporary, and flexible labor eliminates expectations for a single-
company career and diminishes workers' access to benefits (Williams, 2013).
The new ideal employee displays their "authentic self" (Fleming, 2009), celebrating individuality and a degree of diversity that, however limited, is not
permissible for the "organizational man." These changes displace the corporate closet in favor of the gay-friendly closet (Fleming, 2007). As companies
adopt neoliberal models of organization, the stakes for "coming out" and
claiming a non-heterosexual identity at work diminish.

Yet changes to organizational structure does not necessarily translate to
an inclusive work culture. Workplace idioculture – as an emergent feature

of interactive groups within an organization (Fine, 1979) – creates a back-door through which heteronormativity can enter a company and reproduce the dynamics of the closet. It also shapes sexual minorities' experiences of inclusion or exclusion. Research on the gay-friendly closet evidences the persistent role that informal, heterosexist work culture plays forcing sexual minorities to manage information regarding their sexuality, even as they are "out" at work (Giuffre et al., 2008; Rumens & Kerfoot, 2009; Williams et al., 2009). In fact, the everyday efforts made by straight coworkers to dismantle heterosexism are phenomenologically more important for the workplace inclusion of queer youth than any structural changes made by management (Willis, 2009). So long as work idiocultures assert heteronormativity, the dynamics of the closet persist.

This begs the question: Is post-closeted work possible? Can organizations provide sexual minorities with environments that eliminate the dynamics of the closet, that is, end heterosexual domination and gay subordination? Building on the literature, we can anticipate the potential conditions under which post-closeted work is likely to emerge. This includes occupations with a high concentration of gender-atypical workers (Baumle, Compton, & Poston, 2009; Ueno, Roach, & Peña-Talamantes, 2013) and weak expectations for professionalism. Tilcsik et al. (2015) additionally show that the type of work tasks associated with different occupations may increase the concentration of queer workers and diminish the closet's power. Jobs with high task independence decrease the need to engage in routine information management regarding sexuality at work, while jobs that require high levels of social perceptiveness, that is, the ability to anticipate and read others' reactions, capitalize on a historically critical skill needed to navigate the threat of violence that sustains the closet (Tilcsik et al., 2015). These occupational characteristics potentially weaken heteronormativity by encouraging increased concentrations of LBG workers.

Post-closeted work is similarly likely to exist in organizations with gay-friendly policies (e.g., nondiscrimination policies, benefits for same-gender partners, and sensitivity training) and visible representation of sexual minorities among management. Workplaces characterized by "neoliberal" organizational practices that venerate the "authentic self" also potentially undermine hegemonic heteronormativity and further dismantle the closet. Finally, we would anticipate post-closeted work in places characterized by *homonormative* – and not heteronormative – work idiocultures.

By homonormative, I mean the ideas, discourses, and practices that render a particular style of queerness the "morally-endorsed ideal" (Wade, 2010) within a bounded social space. This definition builds on and departs from dominant uses of the term. In its initial conceptualization (Duggan, 2002) and subsequent use (Connell, 2014; Puar, 2006; Ward, 2008), homonormativity labels and critiques a particular set of sexual politics and identities. Specifically, it references gays and lesbians who — their same-gender interests aside — embody "the good sexual citizen" (Duggan, 2002; Seidman, 2002; Seidman et al., 1999), consumer, and patriot (Puar, 2006). Although critical of contemporary gay politics — as assimilationist, not liberationist (Seidman, 2002), and benefitting some identities over others — current use of the term privileges the role of states and corporations in defining normative sexualities (Brown, 2012). It thus fails to capture the ways in which sexual identities can be normative, (i.e., morally endorsed ideals) in local contexts. Corporations and the state are well-positioned to shape societal-level *hegemonic* constructions of normativity. But just as state definitions of sexual harassment get modified in local contexts, with group members negotiating what constitutes "inappropriate" sexual activity (Dellinger & Williams, 2002), so, too, are hegemonic ideas about normative sexualities modified or challenged in local settings. Bears, radical fairies, and leathermen, for example, assert three styles of gay masculinity that are morally endorsed and privileged within the spaces these subcultures claim (Hennen, 2008). So in bounded settings, variations of and alternatives to hegemonic ideas about what constitutes morally endorsed sexuality emerge. It is this contextualized, embedded sense of homonormativity that I reference throughout the paper.

Wonderland Entertainment operates under these social conditions and, initially, seems to demonstrate post-closeted work. The two departments in which I worked — Parades and Characters — employ many openly gay men and are characterized by a particular homonormativity that renders stereotypical gay masculinity and gay male sexuality the morally endorsed ideal at work. All men — regardless of their sexual identity and performance of masculinity *outside* of work — must "do" this particular masculinity on-the-job if they want to be fully socially integrated into the workplace. Yet deeper inspection reveals the persistent dynamics of the closet. Although not characterized by isolation, stigma, tokenization, or stress associated like the corporate or gay-friendly closets, sexual minorities in Wonderland Entertainment must still engage in information management about their sexuality at the boundaries of Entertainment-specific spaces.

The dynamics resemble a walk-in closet. This is a space where certain styles, interests, and activities often associated with gay men are shared and where the accoutrement of a stereotypically gay masculinity can be taken up and set aside without costs. Yet, though spacious, there are still boundaries that constrain when, where, and what queerness can be enacted in the organization. Entertainment had a ceiling that set an upper limit for homonormativity within the company's hierarchy; it had walls that marked the limits of everyday enactments of homonormativity with coworkers and park-goers; and it had a floor that continued to marginalize and exclude other forms of queerness. The walk-in closet thus illustrates the potential for and limitations to post-closeted work in a large organization.

METHODS

My discussion of the walk-in closet builds on 17 months of fieldwork as an entertainer in Wonderland, a Disney-like, American theme park. This includes over 2,000 hours of on-the-job fieldwork and many informal conversations with entertainers. Wonderland offers an array of attractions and entertainment for adults and children delivered with a middle-class aesthetic that presents the "popular" (i.e., low-brow, mass-produced culture) in a clean, manicured, and friendly atmosphere. Similar to other parks, Wonderland organizes entertainers into three jobs in two departments. Parade performers, tasked with enacting choreographed movement while traversing a set route through the park at a slow pace on or in-procession with motorized floats, are part of the Parade Department, simply called "Parades." Choreography is done to short, two- to three-minute songs, and repeated dozens of times in a typical 40-minute show. The Character Department, also known as "Characters," includes two in-park entertainment jobs. Character performers portray Wonderland's branded characters in interaction with park-goers, while Companions speak for masked characters, set lines, prepare fans for autographs, and help take pictures. As both a parade performer and a Companion, I observed and experienced the walk-in closet in both departments.

There were roughly equal numbers of men and women in both departments. Performers were predominantly white; nonwhite performers were primarily Latino and Asian/Pacific Islander, with Black/African-American performers consistently underrepresented. Approximately fifty percent of men in Characters openly identified as gay, as did about eighty percent of men in Parades. These estimates come from conversations I had with entertainers about the gay-to-straight-male ratio. Performers often guessed a percentage, although my coworkers and I did a few informal counts based on men's declared sexual identity. This means that any men whose straight identity was considered suspect by other entertainers was counted as heterosexual, despite some performers' firm, contrary beliefs. More accurate estimates were not possible, as injuries and employee turn-over kept the population of entertainers in flux. While male homosexuality was openly performed and discussed, women's homosexuality or bisexuality was not: Less than five percent of women in Parades openly identified as lesbian or bisexual, or privately confided same-gender interests to me, and I knew even fewer queer-identified women in Characters. It is possible that more women identified as lesbian or bisexual, but the visibility of these identities was exceptional in Entertainment.

My estimates of the sexual composition of Entertainment was additionally constrained by my position in the field. Wonderland – like most theme parks – has ties to larger organizations and media conglomerates through ownership and licensing agreements. This required that I do covert fieldwork. Corporate power and resources present scholars with a dilemma common to "studying up": how to research entities with extensive control over access and representation (Galliher, 1980; Nader, 1972). Although I did not disclose my status as a researcher, I also avoided deliberate misrepresentation (Spicker, 2011): I was "out" as a sociology graduate student. Similarly, although the covert nature of my fieldwork constrained my ability to directly pursue certain questions – including performers' sexual identity – being an "out" sociology grad student allowed me to investigate how performers came to and experienced Wonderland Entertainment. Sexuality was a common topic of conversation among performers, which made it easier to informally discuss the division's homonormativiy.

THE WALK-IN CLOSET: GAY WORK CULTURE AND THE LIMITS OF POST-CLOSETED WORK

Characterizing Wonderland Entertainment as a walk-in closet highlights (1) the centrality of homonormative masculinity to everyday work and (2) the ways in which gayness was rendered benign in an organization that sold tales of heteronormative gender roles. Parades and Characters were structured such that a particular gay masculinity was permissible – even desirable – to enact, yet relegated to select organizational spaces. Instead of the isolation and stress of the corporate closet (Woods & Lucas, 1993) or the tokenization and pressure to be the model sexual minority characteristic of the gay-friendly closet (Williams et al., 2009), gay men found a place where their sexuality could be shared, enjoyed, and celebrated; a space where a style of gay masculinity could be picked up and "tried on" with friends, so long as it was set down and left behind at organizationally desired times.

I develop the idea of the walk-in closet by building the concept from the inside out. I begin by briefly identifying the social conditions of Wonderland Entertainment that, based on the existing literature, anticipate a post-closeted workplace. I then describe Entertainment homonormativity to establish the dominant style of gay masculinity engendered, and illustrate how it was "tried on" by male performers – evidence that suggests a workplace that elevates gay men and gay masculinity beyond mere acceptance (i.e., the gay-friendly closet) to a normative status that seemingly eliminates the dynamics of the closet (i.e., post-closeted work). Finally, I delineate the boundaries placed around this homonormativity that inhibit a truly post-closeted workplace: the ceiling or upper-organizational limits on its permissibility, the walls that constrain its everyday enactment and the floor that marginalizes, stigmatizes, or excludes other styles of queerness.

Wonderland Entertainment operates at the nexus of the social conditions most likely to support post-closeted work. Theme park entertainment involves highly performative and expressive interactive service work, that is, feminized work that potentially decreases the enforcement of heteronormativity for men. There are low expectations for conventional professionalism, additionally diminishing pressure to conform to heteronormativity. These jobs also demand social perceptiveness and involve a moderate degree of task independence: most formal job tasks that require performers to interact with coworkers occur in-park, where personal discussions are discouraged and often impossible. This potentially weakens heteronormativity by drawing more LGB identified people into the workforce.

Wonderland has a number of gay-friendly policies that further undermine organizational heteronormativity, including a nondiscrimination policy that protects sexual minorities, benefits for fulltime employees' partners regardless of gender identity, and mandatory diversity training. Openly gay men are visible among Entertainment management, displacing heterosexuality's prominence among performers' immediate supervisors. The park additionally employs a number of "neoliberal" organizational practices (Williams, 2013) that potentially decrease the stakes of coming out. Performers are primarily a contingent, flexible labor force, who must re-audition 2–3 times a year to keep their job. Few achieve fulltime status, and thus cannot access company benefits. This means performers have potentially less to lose by being out at work. In the absence of job security and benefits, Wonderland attempts to secure workers' consent by promoting a "fun" work culture where employees can "be your [authentic] self" – ideals the company espouses in orientation and training. Combined, these reduce expectations that performers must conform to the heteronormative "organizational man" that characterized the traditional workplace, and increase the odds that post-closeted work will emerge.

Inside the Walk-In Closet

Under these structural conditions, we find a workplace that initially appears to be "beyond" the closet. Workers in and out of Entertainment often refer to Characters and Parades as the "gayest" departments in Wonderland. This is because, unlike the majority of documented organizational cultures (Hall, 1986; Rumens & Kerfoot, 2009; Ward & Winstanley, 2003, 2006; Woods & Lucas, 1993), that which is "gay" is not marginalized or excluded in Entertainment, but central and dominant. Parades and Characters are characterized by a style of *homonormativity* that, at first glance, suggests a post-closeted workplace. This includes ironic use of gendered language, like when men call each other "girl," reference themselves and others as "she" and "her," and describe close gay-male friends as "sisters." It also incorporates slang associated with gay culture. New performers to learn whether a parade was "sexual!" (a good thing) or "a hot mess" (a bad thing), discover how to "get it" (i.e., enact a noteworthy performance) during a shift, and say "fierce" in place of "cool" or "exceptional and without flaw." Fashionable attire and music featuring female divas are often discussed at work. Drag is another common topic of conversation, and many popular performers have drag personas outside of work. Men openly objectify and discuss the male body, describe recent or favorite sexual activity, or talk about their current crushes and significant others. Flirtatious comments and advances are also common between men, as is intimate touch. Men grope, cuddle, and hold hands with other men in break areas and changing rooms.

The ubiquity of Entertainment homonormativity is evident in the widely shared belief that men are "gay until proven straight;" that is, all men in Entertainment are assumed to be gay. Some men and women in the department expanded this belief to claim, with various degrees of sincerity, that Wonderland Entertainment actually "made" men gay. Justin, Wonderland's head Companion trainer and a veteran entertainer, was the first to explicitly state that if you were a guy "[a]t Wonderland, you're gay until proven straight," then admitted that this primarily applied to Entertainment. He added, "I've known some guys where you're like, 'Really? Really?!? You're straight?'"

Justin then illustrated why people assume that all men are gay with a story about Brandon, a young man who claimed a straight identity when he first started working in Wonderland as a character performer. According to Justin, "everyone" thought Brandon was actually gay. "So I went up to him one day and said, 'Are you sure [you're straight]?' and he's like, 'I'm straight! I have a girlfriend!' Then I run into him a couple months later and say to him that he would make a really great gay guy. And he says, 'You know I'm here with my boyfriend, right?' And I was like [*J makes a face: eyes pop wide open and his jaw drops*]. 'But a month ago you had a girlfriend!' And he's like, 'I know. I broke up with her.'"

For Justin, this story legitimates the "gay until proven straight" rule. Brandon's change in publicly stated sexual identity validates others' perceptions that he was "always" gay, despite early claims to the contrary. Having established the "gay until proven straight" rule, Justin went further to insist that lots of men "become" gay while working as Wonderland entertainers, starting off with a straight identity and then "coming out" as gay. He joked that Entertainment "makes" people gay, dryly quipping, "Wonderland made me gay. That's what I tell people sometimes."

I heard other performers comment on Entertainment's power to "make" men gay. These were often flippant remarks, with a tongue-in-cheek attitude regarding the homonormative masculinity deeply embedded in both departments. While no one seemed to seriously believe that Entertainment inculcated men with a gay identity, people openly grappled with the claim's veracity. Teresa, a veteran character performer, vented about her father's belief that "gayness" is contagious, something that could be caught like the common cold. Though we both laughed at the idea, she went on to add, "But he's sorta right," explaining the she has seen a number of men "become" gay while working in Entertainment. Teresa's comments reveal a struggle to understand men's sexuality at work. Although her father's belief that gayness was infectious is laughable, she still sensed something unusual at play in Entertainment, something that defied common expectations of work that she could not articulate.

The belief that Wonderland Entertainment "makes" men gay essentializes and obscures a more complex set of social processes. By normalizing and "naturalizing" a particular style of homonormative masculinity, Wonderland Entertainment provides young men with a safe, interactive space to play around with and "try-on" non-heteronormative identities and gender performances. Men that supposedly evidenced how Entertainment "made" workers gay were usually between the ages of 18 and 21, the normative coming out age in early twenty-first century America (Williams, 2010); a time when a number of young Americans grapple with issues of sexuality. They came to the park exposed to heteronormative organizations — schools or previous jobs — where queer interests were stigmatized or marginalized. But in Wonderland Entertainment, they find a space where new identities can be tested and tried-on before adoption.

Newly identified are not the only ones to engage in, take up, and enjoy Entertainment's homonormativity. Openly gay performers described feeling "at home" when they first arrived in the department, while straight men confessed appreciation that they did not have to worry about trying to be "macho." Straight women also seemed to enjoy the dynamics of the walk-in closet. The objectification of men and privileging of the feminine (e.g., pronouns, nicknames, popular musicians) normalized and naturalized a familiar style of femininity, thus better incorporating some women into the social hierarchy of work.[3]

Some men come to Entertainment familiar with this style of homonormativity, while others only become acquainted with it through work. This acquisition illustrates how Entertainment acts as a *walk-in* closet. "Trying-on" some of the accoutrement of homonormativity can lead to habituation, making it difficult to leave behind. Take, for example, Nicholas, a veteran straight-identified parade performer. By his own admission, Nicholas came into Parades knowing some of the performers, but not necessarily familiar with its gay work culture. When I asked him what it was like to be a straight man in Parades, he told me that it had been a time of personal growth, though there were certain things he wished he had not picked up. "Like 'fierce,'" he explained. "I wish I could get rid of it. But sometimes it's just the most appropriate word." *Fierce* is only "the most appropriate word" when one is familiar with a culturally specific meaning. Having "tried it on" and developed a comfortable affinity for the term, *fierce* became part of Nicholas's cultural repertoire; and like a well-loved pair of jeans worn past their prime, he could not easily discard it.

Men creatively played with Entertainment homonormativity. Flirtation was a common choice. Even straight men who were initially defensive toward a gay coworker's flirtatious advances eventually welcomed such attention, and even initiated playful homoerotic flirtations of their own. But other strategies are also employed. Dustin, a straight-identified, veteran entertainer, once jokingly complained about the constraints of heteronormative masculinity, saying, "You know, guys need an ego boost, too. So I should be able to say, 'That is a *nice* penis.' And have it be a straight thing to say. [*emphasis his*]" This comment, met with laughter, pushes the boundary of heteronormative masculinity and reflects a sensibility many straight men in Entertainment shared around "doing" gender (West & Zimmerman, 1987) backstage. In contemporary American culture, there are few spaces where men can openly gaze at and compliment other men's bodies — especially sexualized parts like the penis. To first call attention to another man's penis and then positively assess it in aesthetic terms would, too often, injure public perceptions of one's masculinity. At the heart of Dustin's humorous comment is a willingness to play with the boundaries of heteronormative masculinity to allow aesthetic appreciation of men's bodies. Though a highly unusual joke to make — few straight-identified men expressed an interest in viewing and appreciating other men's genitalia — the underlying belief that heteronormative rules for intimacy between men could be set aside illustrates how straight men played with sexuality in Entertainment. Because the closet rests upon heteronormativity (Seidman, 2002), its displacement initially suggests a post-closeted workplace.

Bounding the Walk-In Closet

Evidence of a *walk-in closet* becomes clear, however, when we investigate the limitations for displacing heteronormativity. Despite the ease with which most male performers engaged with homonormativity — picking up or "donning" the interests, tastes, references, and interactional scripts of this work idioculture — they could not enact gay masculinity with impunity. Workers and management collectively maintained a set of boundaries that contained homonormativity to backstage areas of the park. These boundaries work to prevent the disclosure of queer interests and identities to park-goers and management, force queer performers to continue to engage in information management, and thus reproduce gay oppression and heterosexual domination beyond Entertainment-only spaces.

I distinguish between three boundaries: the ceiling, the walls, and the floor. The first of these separates Entertainment homonormativity from upper management, thus preserving heteronormativity at higher levels of the company. The second boundary — the walls — delineates which everyday work spaces permit or forbid homonormativity. Finally, the floor excludes other queer interests and identities from Entertainment's homonormative work idioculture.

Ceiling

The closet ceiling is the limit to which one could be upwardly mobile in the organization while embodying Entertainment homonormativity. Being dramatic, campy, and expressive is fine among frontline entertainment workers, but as men climb the organizational ladder it becomes increasingly incompatible with expected, "appropriate" work behavior. Character and Parade management seemed to be the highest position a man could hold and still enact Entertainment homonormativity. During my time in the field, all male Parade managers and most male choreographers, Character managers, and Entertainment assistant managers frequently participated in this work idioculture. But they only engaged with it to interact with each other and their subordinates, not their superiors.

Few of my coworkers expressed interest in moving up into park management. Most approached Wonderland Entertainment as a fun college job or as part of a broader performance career rather than a chance to start a career with the park. Few, then, cared about the possibility of an organizational ceiling placed on homonormativity, making it difficult to judge how aware they were of its presence. Its existence was most salient when Michael, a veteran performer with more than eight years of experience in Characters and Parades when I entered the field, decided to apply to the company's management training program. Michael's strong candidature earned him an interview, conducted by several high-level park managers. He later described how he meticulously selected his outfit, conscientious of the image he wanted to present. He contemplated wearing a fashionable pink tie to the interview, but ultimate decided against it, explaining he did not want the panel of interviewers to think he was "too gay" for the job. "I mean, if they ask [about my sexual identity], I'd tell them," Michael confided over lunch during one of my post-employment park visits, reassuring me he would not fake a straight identity. But he was not comfortable presenting himself with a potentially overt sign that he was gay. He chose instead a red-patterned tie, "Because red is a power color." A couple months later, Michael was offered a spot in the training program and within a year became a Character Manager.

Michael's admission that he did not want to be seen as "too gay" evidences an upper boundary on Entertainment homonormativity. This limit is, in part, a product of who dominates the upper echelons of management: straight-identified men. But it also reflects Michael's attempt to move deeper into the core personnel of the park where professionalism and the traditional model of organization — a corporate ladder to climb, salaried work, benefits, and greater job security — were the strongest. With more at stake

to gain or lose, Michael set down Entertainment homonormativity to
advance his career.

Walls

There were also walls placed around Entertainment homonormativity via
the generally accepted belief that these enactments of masculinity should be
kept backstage and out of the park. While Wonderland's in-park aesthetic
demands theatricality, male performers must avoid the camped femininity
so common backstage. Policing of this boundary began in my first shift, a
rehearsal for a new medieval parade. The cast, predominantly newly hired
men, hung out in the Parades building while we waited for rehearsal to
begin. Three gay-identified men entertained the rest of us with jokes and
some dramatic, flamboyant catwalks up and down the hallway. They were
interrupted by Gavin, our show director and choreographer. He quickly
introduced himself in a friendly but short tone before explaining, "When
you guys are out there, you need to be strong and serious. I don't care how
you act back here. Trust me," he said with a courtesy, right hand in the air
as if swearing an oath, a gesture met with laughter, "I'm with you. But out
there, you need to be manly. Remember, you're soldiers. You're just back
from battle." Here, Gavin explicitly draws boundaries around the catwalks
he interrupted, acknowledging that "back here" such behavior was accepta-
ble, while "out there," in the park we needed to embody a more traditional
masculinity.

Management reinforced these boundaries whenever men's in-park performances were too feminine. Gideon, one of the gay men who started
working in Parades with me, received a string of critiques about his embodiment of masculinity on the parade route shortly after he started his second show. Choreographers repeatedly criticized his hand-on-hip placement
during one section of chorography. The desired look and "proper" choreography had Gideon's open palm resting on his hip, elbow straight out to
his side. But he was often caught rolling his wrist into his body so that only
his thumb, forefinger, and the connecting joint rested on his hip while his
other fingers splayed out from his waist. Every time Gideon received a note
about his hand-on-hip placement, it was framed the same way: he needed
to look "more masculine." This suggests that his performance was too
effeminate, too "gay," to appropriately embody the park's image. Maybe
the rolling of the wrist is too closely associated with the stereotypically
limp-wristed gay man, an association that threatened to undermine
Wonderland's safe, non-aggressive version of heteronormative masculinity
in the park; or perhaps his splayed fingers were too expressive, failing to

achieve the bodily control that heteronormative masculinity demands. Whatever the reason, this one action became a concern for Parade management who rarely critiqued the execution of choreography at this level of detail.

Performers find management's boundary between good and bad expressivity to be subjective, a source of frustration, and an object of ridicule. One evening, a dancer entered the men's changing area and loudly announced that Bobbie, a new, gay-identified performer in his late teens, was told he was "too gay" on the parade route today. Everyone burst out laughing at the irony: there were only three straight-identified dancers currently in that particular show.[4] I later saw Bobbie standing by his locker, and asked him about the note.

> I was told [by the choreographer] to "butch it up." That I was "too hip-ee," he explained with a note of exasperation in his voice. "I was like, 'Seriously?!?'" Richard, a gay-identified veteran performer in his late forties, voiced the opinion that all entertainment parades "are gay." Bobbie nodded in agreement. "It's like, 'Smile! Smile! Smile! Smile! But butch,'" his voice shifting from an overly enthusiastic, high-pitched, perky "Smile!" to a lower-pitched, more serious "butch" to emphasize the gendered expectations with his tone. He waved his hand dismissively as if dusting the note away with his fingers. "I'm over it."

Like Gideon, Bobbie's in-park performance of masculinity was challenged for being too expressive, too feminine and, by extension, too "gay." Bobbie and other performers found irony in this critique, especially in light of the lack of straight-identified men cast as dancers. Yet management controlled men's bodies by reasserting symbolic and spatial boundaries around appropriate performances of masculinity. The campy, effeminate, expressive masculinity of Entertainment was fine backstage, but not on the parade route. Out there, men were still expected to engage in information management, covering homonormativity from park-goers' eyes.

Choreographers and managers do not regulate the walls of the closet alone. Performers police themselves, assessing men's performance of gender and criticizing anyone deemed "too gay." During an overnight rehearsal, I sat with two gay-identified veteran performers who had a combined ten years of experience in three different parks. While we waited for our turn to perform, they critiqued Ben, another gay-identified performer with three years of experience, who was in the middle of a run-through. "He's so gay," Edward said with a chuckle. Buck agreed, pointing out the wrist-on-hip pose Ben had just struck. They decided that both the pose and Ben's flamboyant masculinity were inappropriate, and continued to criticize him for the rest of his run-through.

Backstage, Edward and Buck both — like Ben — "do" Entertainment's homonormative masculinity: they interact with flamboyant gesture, are facially expressive, and reference men with feminine language. So their critique of Ben is not about his performance of gender and sexuality in general, but whether or not it is appropriate in the park. In other words, does his gender performance cross a tacitly understood boundary? Both ultimately agree that Ben is too flamboyant to suitably embody Wonderland's aesthetic. I heard similar assessments of other performers whose coworkers saw them as "so gay" or "too gay," meaning that they embodied Entertainment homonormativity more than most of their coworkers. Comments like these were rarely made to a man's face, so the boundary work does not necessarily involve the violator. But these assessments still police the closet walls, reminding oneself and others that gay masculinity was not appropriate in the park.

Performers sometimes *directly* police the walls of the walk-in closet, playfully calling attention to a man's inappropriate embodiment of masculinity in the park. I was changing after work one evening when Jason, a veteran performer with six years of experience in four theme parks, walked into the changing area and announced, "I've finally found someone gayer than PJ!"[5]

"Who?" Anthony, another gay veteran, asked.

"Rubin," Jason responded with a large grin. "She was swinging her hips walking on route today." He went on to explain that one of the male characters had also noticed Rubin's hip-sway and started mimicking him during the parade. The three of us chuckled at the idea.

When Rubin joined us a couple minutes later, Jason gave him a hard time. He again described the walk, adding an impersonation. His hips swung left to right with each step.

"I do *not* walk like that," Rubin said defensively [emphasis his].

"Yes you do," Jason insisted. "Walking around out there like she thinks she's a diva."

Rubin, who had been making his way to the bathroom, stopped in his tracks. Popping one hand into the air, palm out as if to stop the conversation, he said, "Thinks she's a diva? THINKS?!?" His head bobbed back and forth a little to punctuate the attitude he tossed Jason's direction.

"I said 'thinks,'" Jason replied, so unfazed by Rubin's tone or attitude that he did not even look up from the sweat-soaked parade clothes he was gathering up. "We all know she's not."

Rubin's swaying hips are twice sanctioned in this tale. First, one of the characters in the parade calls attention to Rubin's walk, parodying it before park-goers and performers alike. The parody works by highlighting the movement as "inappropriate" for the body, a feminized movement on a male-presenting figure. Drawing attention to the "inappropriate" performance of gender through humor, the character is able to simultaneously acknowledge the violation and bracket it as exceptional: it is only Rubin who sways on route, and only his violation of the symbolic boundary of how to "do" gender and sexuality in the park that deserves playful commentary.

Rubin's performative breach is reaffirmed when Jason brings up the parody after the parade. By marking Rubin as someone "gayer than PJ," Jason tries to convey the degree of Rubin's transgression to those of us in the changing area. Jason goes on to reproduce the movement, both out of and in Rubin's presence, to illustrate what is "wrong" with the performance. These enactments reassert a symbolic boundary around homonormative masculinity to keep it backstage.

Unlike Bobbie and Gideon's performances of masculinity, which came under management scrutiny, Rubin finds himself directly critiqued by coworkers and friends. These critiques take a more playful form and tone than management's performance notes, but they still police the walls of the walk-in closet. Male performers are ultimately reminded that Entertainment's homonormative masculinity may be the morally endorsed ideal backstage, but not in the park. In the presence of park-goers, men are subject to the traditional logics and demands of the closet.

In Characters, it was often women who policed the walls of the closet through their expressed concerns regarding their boyfriends' engagement with Entertainment's homonormativity. After several weeks of working exclusively in Characters, Topher — a straight man who was initially hired for the same medieval parade as me — complained that the department [Characters] was "too much drama ... they all say Parades is drama, but they're worse." He went on to explain, in a tone of exasperation, that a lot of the drama stemmed from one issue: "All the girls worry that their boyfriends are going to go gay." Between friendships with gay male coworkers, engagement with the homonormative work idioculture, and a shared belief that Wonderland Entertainment "made" men gay, some women expressed concerned about the stability of their boyfriends' sexual identity. So while women generally seemed to enjoy Entertainment's homonormativity, there was tension with regards to dominant ideas and expectations about how straight or gay men "ought" to act that left some women uncomfortable and threatened.

Consider, for example, Gina and Adam's relationship. Gina, a straight veteran entertainer in her early twenties with a five years of experience in

Characters and Parades, met Adam shortly after he was hired. Adam came to Wonderland embodying a nontraditional masculinity. In high school theatre, he developed a physically and facially expressive presentation of self that fit the park's aesthetic. Backstage and at home, Adam comfortably draped his arm around or cuddled-up with other men in Characters. He was unafraid to playfully flirt with, grope, or be groped by men in Entertainment, and he did not shy away from explicit conversations about gay sex. Adam's closest straight male friends at work similarly played with masculinity, even joking amongst themselves that "[I]t's not gay if you like it!"

Gina was already familiar with Entertainment's homonormativity when she and Adam started dating. She had her own group of gay-identified coworkers who she treated like "the girls," openly discussing sex and men with them. In fact, I rarely saw her spend time backstage with straight men. But she was around them often enough to see them engage in Entertainment homonormativity.

About nine months after they started dating, Gina and Adam's relationship became strained. Gina began criticizing Adam's performance of masculinity, telling him to "man it up." She confessed to nightmares where he cheated on her with a guy, and forbade him from hanging out with gay-male performers outside of work. These things all upset Adam, who expressed frustration that she could not accept that he was both straight and friends with gay men; heterosexual, but homonormatively masculine. They eventually decided they needed space and broke up.

Gina and Adam's experience illustrates another dimension to the everyday limits of homonormativity. On the one hand, the presence of a large number of gay men created a unique space for straight women, where the dominance of certain feminized interests enabled feminine-identified women's greater inclusion in the workplace. But the normative masculinity and the opportunities it created for young men to "come out" at work also created uncertainty regarding their male romantic partners' sexuality. So while all men were expected to participate in Entertainment's gay work culture, straight men's engagement was more heavily policed and constrained.

Floor

Finally, Entertainment's walk-in closet had a floor, a boundary that excluded things explicitly or implicitly understood as profane to the culture. Like the culture of any interactive group (Fine, 1979), the homonormativity of Parades and Characters fit the social hierarchy of the departments. The styles, practices, and discourse that comprise this culture align with the

interests and sensibilities of the entertainers who enjoy social and/or organizational positions of prestige: popular gay-male performers and depart-
mental managers.

The closet floor reproduces familiar workplace inequalities. Despite being
a space where men can openly objectify other men and discuss gay sexual acts
and preferences, promiscuity is still stigmatized. Rumor and gossip involving
slut-shaming was not uncommon when entertainers sought to disparage the
character of coworkers. The use of slut-shaming discourse was particularly
surprising given that the majority of male performers − regardless of sexual
identity − confessed to casual hook-ups with coworkers. Some gay men took
a sex-positive stance, comfortably talking about their sexual conquests the
way one might expect some straight men to brag in a locker room. But men
who did were too often described by coworkers as "such a hoe."

The most potent form of slut-shaming focused less on sexual activity and
more on stigmatized badges of promiscuity: who had − or was rumored to
have − a sexually transmitted infection (STI). During my time in the field, I
heard performers exchange words of warning about who had genital warts,
herpes, scabies, and other STIs. Greetings like "We were *missing* STDs at
our table," and comments about guys so sexually active that "He must have
something growing in him," (i.e., he must have some STI) were posed as
jokes. But they ultimately reinforce a particular style of homonormativity
that shames sexual activity by reinforcing stigma around STIs as signs of
promiscuity. That the amount of sex one has is unrelated to the protection
one uses was seemingly irrelevant. The boundary was so strong that when
one friend and former coworker learned they had seroconverted (i.e., they
tested positive for HIV) after I had left the field, he made it very clear to me
that he would not be disclosing that information to other people in
Entertainment. This was not something that could be "out" at work. So
even though seroconversion is not an exclusively queer experience, it is still
subject to the traditional dynamics of the closet: isolation, internalized
stigma, and invisibility.

Parades and Characters are also widely understood − by workers in and
out of Entertainment − to be gay *male* spaces. Women's same-gender
interests and desires are rendered invisible. There were a few bi- or lesbian-
identified women among performers, their limited presence paired with a
limited degree of openness. The homonormativity of Entertainment, which
valorized "campy" femininity, reinforced the conflation of biological fema-
leness with heterosexuality.

This association silences lesbianism. Heterosexuality is still the morally
endorsed ideal for women in Entertainment, which continues to pressure

women to silence their own non-heterosexual interests. A few women quietly confided same-gender crushes to me, not wanting it to get around the department, while openly queer women found it difficult to act on or discuss these same-gender attractions. "It's hard being a lesbian here," one woman admitted with resignation, frustrated that few women shared her interests. So although Entertainment culture challenges the marginalization of male homosexuality, women continued to work within the confines of the traditional closet.

There is also little room for performers – especially men – to claim a bisexual identity. Men are categorized as gay or straight. Rarely did performers directly disavow male bisexuality. Instead, it was discredited through suggestion, like when a gay performer casually remarks that a man "*says* he's bi*,*" with an eye roll, tone, or inflection that silently adds a "but" disclaimer. Bisexuality is interpreted as confusion or a place of transition rather than a legitimate sexual identity – a stance that reproduces hegemonic biphobia.

Both women and men are quick to sort new men into gay- or straight-categories, and can be quite direct in the labeling process. During my first three months working in Wonderland, I was approached by women on three separate occasions, each striking up a conversation that eventually led to a point-blank question: Are you straight or are you gay? The gay/straight binary was so embedded in Wonderland Entertainment that even the first woman who directly inquired about my sexuality, a Character performer who self-identified as bisexual, still only offered me two options: gay or straight. It was as if the prospect that I was a bisexual *man* was impossible, despite her own identity. Everyone – particularly men – must be sorted into one of the two categories, reproducing an essential dynamic of the closet.

Entertainment's walk-in closet also marginalizes other forms of queerness. To the best of my knowledge, none of my coworkers were gender-queer or trans-identified performers. If anyone did identify as gender-nonconforming, they felt the need to keep such identities invisible. Even if management hired an openly trans-identified performer – and I am skeptical they would – Entertainment homonormativity, particularly use of the transphobic term "tranny" to reference drag and drag performers, would continue to marginalize trans-identities. Furthermore, because this work culture draws on and subsequently reifies popular associations between flamboyant effeminacy and "gayness," it excludes other gay masculinities. Bear-, radical faery-, and leather daddy-masculinities (Hennen, 2008) are as subordinated as queer femininities and women's same-gender interests.

CONCLUSION

In Wonderland Entertainment, we see another iteration of the closet: the walk-in closet. The constrained permissibility of gay masculinity makes these departments feel like gay havens and initially appear to be post-closeted workplaces. Unlike heterosexist (Hall, 1986; Ward & Winstanley, 2003, 2006; Woods & Lucas, 1993) or gay-friendly (Giuffre et al., 2008; Rumens & Kerfoot, 2009; Williams et al., 2009) workplaces, there are few consequences for enacting homonormative masculinity in Entertainment. In fact, there is an expectation that men in these departments will actively "try on" and play around with the elements of gay work culture in order to enjoy full membership. This changes the phenomenological experience of work: many men and women described freedom, comfort, or enjoyment that stemmed from hegemonic masculinity's displacement.

But Entertainment homonormativity is bounded, limiting its potential to challenge heteronormative masculinity in the organization, the theme park, and American society. Advancement in the organization requires an abdication of homonormativity, thus leaving heteronormativity at higher levels of management and the company intact. Boundaries on the day-to-day enactments of gay masculinity; where management and workers police when, where, and how it can be "done-preserve heteronormativity in the park." Finally, while a stereotypical gay masculinity may flourish, the walk-in closet continues to marginalize, silence, and exclude other sexual identities and expressions of gender. So while Entertainment's walk-in closet moves beyond the gay-friendly closet to make a type of gay man not just *normal* but *normative*, it fails to be a truly post-closeted workplace.

I can only speculate what social forces produce the walk-in closet rather than post-closeted work. Persistent heteronormativity in Wonderland's leadership – evident in the professionalism Michael feels he must perform to become management – helps produce the ceiling. Pressure to cover queer interests and be the model sexual minority at higher levels of the organization are reinforced by the traditional model of organization that characterizes the experiences of "core" personnel (Smith, 2002; Williams, 2013). With benefits, job security, and the promise of advancement on the line for management, more may be gained by downplaying one's "authentic self" to be more like the "organizational man" (Fleming, 2007, 2009).

The closet walls are sustained in part by Wonderland's narratives of heteronormative masculinity and femininity. Like other theme parks, Wonderland's branded characters are canonically straight men and women. Portrayal of these characters must protect these narratives. The park's heteronormative aesthetic is additionally reinforced among unbranded roles, like the pairing of male and female dancer partners in Parades. The walls are also supported by consumer-producer relationships and the "generalized other" consumer (Mead, 1934). So long as management imagines an abstracted target consumer invested in hegemonic heteronormativity, they are unlikely to produce queer characters or an aesthetic that makes queerness the morally endorsed ideal in the park. Social constructions of children as vulnerable populations, especially in regards to sexuality (Connell, 2014), further buttress in-park heteronormativity and the walk-in closet walls.

Hegemonic ideas of gender and sexuality similarly produce the closet floor. The gendering of Entertainment work renders emphasized femininity and a feminine masculinity normative, opening up the workplace for gay men while closing it off to queer women. Additionally, performers bring forms of sexual stigma found in dominant culture into Entertainment's homonormative work idioculture. This reinforces the closet floor by marginalizing and silencing other forms of queerness.

The walk-in closet, then, illustrates a new stage in the dismantling of the closet at work. If the gay-friendly closet marks LGB workers as normal, albeit tokenized, the walk-in closet takes this a step further to make certain LGB identities *normalized*. Yet this iteration of the closet reminds us that organizations and organizational sexuality exist in a broader social context. The workplace closet is sustained by more than just organizational practices and culture; it is also a product of hegemonic ideas about sexuality found outside of organizations. So long as narrow social constructions of the "good sexual citizen" (Seidman, 2002; Seidman et al., 1999) dominate the public sphere, sexual minorities will continue to be expected to engage in information management and navigate some form of the closet if they want to maintain their position or advance in the workplace.

NOTES

1. The absence of any "out" trans-identified workers coupled with evidence that transgender people navigate a different set of workplace experiences (Schilt, 2010) means that I focus on the experiences of LGB workers. I use the terms LGB, sexual minorities, and queer interchangeably throughout the paper.

2. All names in this paper have been changed.

3. For more discussion of how men and women experienced Entertainment's homonormativity, see Orzechowicz, 2010.

4. The other straight men held non-dancer roles, e.g., stilt-walkers and character performers.

5. PJ was often called, by friends and coworkers, the "gayest" man in Parades, a title he alternately embraced and contested.

ACKNOWLEDGMENTS

I would like to thank Laura Mora, Desiree Naseath, Madina Salahi, Vanessa Solis, and Andrew Vieira for their research assistance, as well as Vicki Smith, Courtney Caviness, members of the Power & Inequalities Workshop, Laura Grindstaff, Christine Williams, Steve Vallas, and the reviewers for their feedback and guidance.

REFERENCES

Baumle, A. K., Compton, D., & Poston, D. L., Jr. (2009). *Same-sex partners: The social demography of sexual orientation*. Albany, NY: SUNY Press.

Brown, G. (2012). Homonormativity: A metropolitan concept that denigrates "ordinary" gay lives. *Journal of Homosexuality, 59*(7), 1065–1072.

Burrell, G., & Hearn, J. (1989). The sexuality of organization. In J. Hear, D. L. Sheppard, P. Tancred-Sheriff, & G. Burrell (Eds.), *The sexuality of organization* (pp. 1–28). Newbury Park, CA: Sage Publications Inc.

Connell, C. (2014). *School's out: Gay and lesbian teachers in the classroom*. Berkeley, CA: University of California Press.

Croteau, J. M. (1996). Research on the work experiences of lesbian, gay, and bisexual people: An integrative review of methodology and findings. *Journal of Vocational Behavior, 48*(2), 195–209.

Dellinger, K., & Williams, C. L. (2002). The locker room and the dorm room: Workplace norms and the boundaries of sexual harassment in magazine editing. *Social Problems, 49*(2), 242–257.

Duggan, L. (2002). The new homonormativity: The sexual politics of neoliberalism. In R. Castronovo & D. D. Nelson (Eds.), *Materialising democracy: Towards a revitalized cultural politics* (pp. 175–194). Durham, NC: Duke University Press.

Escoffier, J. (1997). The political economy of the closet: Notes towards an economic history of gay and lesbian life before Stonewall. In A. Gluckman & B. Reed (Eds.), *Homo economics: Capitalism, community, and lesbian and gay life* (pp. 123–134). New York, NY: Routledge.

Fine, G. A. (1979). Small groups and culture creation: The idioculture of little league baseball teams. *American Sociological Review, 44*, 733–745.

Fleming, P. (2007). Sexuality, power and resistance in the workplace. *Organization Studies, 28*, 239–256.

Fleming, P. (2009). *Authenticity and the cultural politics of work: New forms of informal control*. Oxford: Oxford University Press.

Foucault, M. (1980). *The history of sexuality: An introduction* (Vol. 1). New York, NY: Pantheon.

Galliher, J. F. (1980). Social scientists' ethical responsibilities to superordinates: Looking upward meekly. *Social Problems, 27*(3), 298−308.

Giuffre, P. A., Dellinger, K., & Williams, C. L. (2008). 'No retribution for being gay?' Inequality in gay-friendly workplaces. *Sociological Spectrum, 28*, 254−277.

Grey, C. (1998). On being a professional in a "Big Six" firm. *Accounting, Organizations and Society, 23*(5), 569−587.

Griffith, K. H., & Hebl, M. R. (2002). The disclosure dilemma for gay men and lesbians: "Coming out" at work. *Journal of Applied Psychology, 87*(6), 1191−1199.

Gross, L. P. (2001). *Up from invisibility: Lesbians, gay men, and the media in America*. New York, NY: Columbia University Press.

Hall, M. (1986). The lesbian corporate experience. *Journal of Homosexuality, 12*, 59−74.

Hennen, P. (2008). *Faeries, bears, and leathermen: Men in community queering the masculine*. Chicago, IL: University of Chicago Press.

Hicks, G. R., & Lee, T. (2006). Public attitudes toward gays and lesbians: Trends and predictors. *Journal of Homosexuality, 51*, 57−77.

Hunter, N. D. (2000). Sexuality and civil rights: Re-imagining anti-discrimination laws. *NYL Sch. J. Hum. Rts, 17*, 565−587.

Jenness, V., & Grattet, R. (2001). *Making hate a crime: From social movement to law enforcement*. New York, NY: Russell Sage Foundation.

Lawrence v. Texas, 539 U.S. 558 (2003).

Mead, G. H. (1934). *Mind, self, and society from the standpoint of a social behaviorist*. Chicago, IL: University of Chicago Press.

Nader, L. (1972). Up the anthropologist − Perspectives gained from studying up. In D. Hymes (Eds.), *Reinventing anthropology* (pp. 284−311). New York, NY: Vintage Books.

Obergefell v. Hodges, 135 S. Ct. 2584 (2015).

Orzechowicz, D. (2010). Fierce bitches on Tranny Lane: Sexuality, culture, and the closet in theme park parades. *Research in the Sociology of Work, 20*, 227−252.

Puar, J. K. (2006). Mapping US homonormativities. *Gender, Place and Culture, 13*(1), 67−88.

Raeburn, N. C. (2004). *Changing corporate America from inside out: Lesbian and gay workplace rights*. Minneapolis, MN: University of Minnesota Press.

Rofes, E. (2000). Bound and gagged: Sexual silences, gender conformity and the gay male teacher. *Sexualities, 3*(4), 439−462.

Rumens, N., & Kerfoot, D. (2009). Gay men at work: (Re)constructing the self as professional. *Human Relations, 62*(5), 763−786.

Schilt, K. (2010). *Just one of the guys?: Transgender men and the persistence of gender inequality*. Chicago, IL: University of Chicago Press.

Schneider, M. S., & Dimito, A. (2010). Factors influencing the career and academic choices of lesbian, gay, bisexual, and transgender people. *Journal of Homosexuality, 57*(10), 1355−1369.

Scott, E. K. (2005). Beyond tokenism: The making of racially diverse feminist organizations. *Social Problems, 52*, 232−254.

Seidman, S. (2002). *Beyond the closet: The transformation of gay and lesbian life*. New York, NY: Routledge.

Seidman, S., Meeks, C., & Traschen, F. (1999). Beyond the closet? The changing social meaning of homosexuality in the United States. *Sexualities*, *2*(1), 9–34.

Smith, V. (2002). *Crossing the great divide: Worker risk and opportunity in the new economy.* New York, NY: Cornell University Press.

Spicker, P. (2011). Ethical covert research. *Sociology*, *45*, 118–133.

Tilcsik, A., Anteby, M., & Knight, C. R. (2015). Concealable stigma and occupational segregation toward a theory of gay and lesbian occupations. *Administrative Science Quarterly*, *60*(3), 446–481.

Ueno, K., Roach, T., & Peña-Talamantes, A. E. (2013). Sexual orientation and gender typicality of the occupation in young adulthood. *Social Forces*, *92*(1), 81–108.

Wade, L. (2010, July 8). *Norms, normality, and normativity.* Retrieved from http://thesociety-pages.org/socimages/2010/07/08/norms-normality-and-normativity/

Walters, S. D. (2001). *All the rage: The story of gay visibility in America.* Chicago, IL: University of Chicago Press.

Ward, E. J. (2008). *Respectably queer: Diversity culture in LGBT activist organizations.* Nashville, TN: Vanderbilt University Press.

Ward, J., & Winstanley, D. (2003). The absent presence: Negative space within discourse and the construction of minority sexual identity in the workplace. *Human Relations*, *56*, 1255–1280.

Ward, J., & Winstanley, D. (2006). Watching the watch: The UK fire service and its impact on sexual minorities in the workplace. *Gender, Work, and Organization*, *13*, 193–219.

West, C., & Zimmerman, D. H. (1987). Doing gender. *Gender & Society*, *1*(2), 125–151.

Weston, K. M., & Rofel, L. B. (1984). Sexuality, class, and conflict in a lesbian workplace. *Signs*, *9*, 623–646.

Whyte, W. H. (1956). *The organization man.* New York, NY: Simon & Schuster.

Williams, C. L. (2013). The glass escalator, revisited gender inequality in neoliberal times. *Gender & Society*, *27*(5), 609–629.

Williams, C. L., Giuffre, P. A., & Dellinger, K. (2009). The gay-friendly closet. *Sexuality Research and Social Policy*, *6*, 29–45.

Williams, R. (2010, November 15). People coming out as gay at younger age, research shows. *The Guardian.* Retrieved from www.guardian.co.uk/world/2010/nov/15/gay-people-coming-out-younger-age/print

Willis, P. (2009). From exclusion to inclusion: Young queer workers' negotiations of sexually exclusive and inclusive spaces in Australian workplaces. *Journal of Youth Studies*, *12*, 629–651.

Woods, J. D., & Lucas, J. H. (1993). *The corporate closet: The professional lives of gay men in America.* New York, NY: Free Press.

Yoshino, K. (2002). Covering. *Yale Law Journal*, *111*, 769–939.

WORKPLACE REGULATION OF SEXUAL HARASSMENT AND FEDERAL AND STATE-LEVEL LEGAL ENVIRONMENTS

Julie A. Kmec, C. Elizabeth Hirsh and Sheryl Skaggs

ABSTRACT

This study investigates how federal and state-level laws designed to reduce workplace sexual harassment relate to the content of sexual harassment training programs in a sample of private U.S. companies. To gauge the effect of the law on the regulation of sexual harassment, we draw on unique data containing information on federal and state-level legal environments, formal discrimination charges filed with the federal Equal Employment Opportunity Commission, and establishment-level sexual harassment training initiatives. State-level legal regulation of sexual harassment at work is linked to more elaborate sexual harassment training programs, even when federal legal regulations are not. Our findings underscore the importance of state-level legal regimes in the

Research in the Sociology of Work, Volume 29, 215–240
ISSN: 0277-2833/doi:10.1108/S0277-283320160000029024

workplace regulation of gender-based rights and provide an example for future studies of work inequality and the law.

Keywords: Sexual harassment programs; state-level legal environment; federal law; gender; organizations

Researchers have produced compelling evidence that workplaces adopt equal employment policies and structures that protect workers' rights in response to pressures stemming from equal employment opportunity (EEO) policies and court jurisdictions (see Stainback & Tomaskovic-Devey, 2012, for a review). Pressures associated with sex-based anti-discrimination legislation provide one example of how employers may come to create and implement policies that promote equal opportunities in terms of hiring, promotion, pay, and job assignment. Although scholars largely agree that federal legal environments exert influence on workplaces, less is known about the impact of state-level legal environments on EEO-related policy adoption.[1] Even less is known about the ways in which federal and state-level legal environments operate in tandem, especially when the issue at hand is related to employment rights. In this paper, we explore how both federal and state-level environments influence one potential indicator of employers' progress toward gender equality at work – the adoption and content of sexual harassment (SH) training programs – among a sample of private work establishments.

Theoretically, our focus on legal environments and EEO policy adoption engages and extends current perspectives in organizational inequality in two key ways. First, recent research on workplace gender (and race) inequality demonstrates the importance of local context in contemporary gender (and race) inequality regimes for understanding organizations' progress toward equality. In their exhaustive book on EEO law and inequality since the Civil Rights Act, Stainback and Tomaskovic-Devey (2012, p. 293) argue that contemporary gender and race inequality and employment practices reflect "locally negotiated status orders," rather than the deeply entrenched system of white male advantage characteristic of the pre-Civil Rights era. That is, gender and race inequality – and any organizational policies designed to combat it – differ considerably across contemporary work establishments, reflecting variation in workplaces' local cultural context. Although Stainback and Tomaskovic-Devey (2012) focus on industry, sector, and local labor markets as the primary drivers of the local cultural context, we view the state-level legal environment (vis-à-vis state-level employment law) as a crucial element of this local environment and, accordingly, a determinant of policies related to gender equality (see also Skrentny, 2006). Thus, our analysis allows us to assess the importance of state law for structuring workplaces' protection of sex-based rights.

Second, our research builds on institutional approaches to law and organizations. As institutionalists have long noted, policies designed to guarantee workers' rights — such as anti-harassment policies — can serve largely ceremonial purposes in organizations, decoupled from everyday practices and/or substantive outcomes (Edelman, 1990, 1992; Kalev, Dobbin, & Kelly, 2006; Meyer & Rowan, 1977). In the analysis of EEO practices in particular, research suggests that organizations adopt policies to appear responsive to their external legal environments and demonstrate their commitment to broad ideals of equal opportunity rather than alter workplace practices, routines, or behavior (Bisom-Rapp, Stockdale, & Crosby, 2007; Dobbin & Kelly, 2007; Edelman & Petterson, 1999; Edelman, Uggen, & Erlanger, 1999; Kelly & Dobbin, 1998, 1999). In assessing the impact of legal environments on the *content* of SH training programs, we examine how legal environments affect the adoption of training programs that range from the largely symbolic to the more substantively meaningful.

The present analyses represent an effort, then, to understand the joint impact of federal and state-level legal environments on the *elaboration* of SH regulations in private work establishments. Specifically, we ask: To what extent are federal and state-level legal environments related to the features of workplace SH training programs? We provide a novel data collection strategy — combining original establishment-level survey data containing information on the content (not mere presence) of workplace policies, with workplace-level composition data from the Equal Employment Opportunity Commission's (EEOC's) EEO-1 database, discrimination charge data also from the EEOC, and original data on state-level adoption of gender-equity laws — to address a timely workplace problem. While the cross-sectional nature of our data prevent us from investigating the process of workplace adoption of SH training policies, we explore the extent to which variation in the content of SH training programs relates to workplaces' federal and state-level legal environments, an important investigation in its own right due to prevalence of the problem of SH at work (McDonald, 2012).

We begin with a discussion of the theoretical relevance of incorporating federal and state-level legal environments in examining the presence and elaboration of workplace SH and EEO-related policy more generally.

Following this, we highlight the significance of studying the content of SH training programs in more detail. We describe the four primary data sources used to examine our research question. Finally, we present our results and discuss the implications of our findings for future investigations of how legal environments matter for workplace behavior related to equal opportunity protections more generally.

THE LEGAL REGULATION OF WORKPLACE RIGHTS

Institutional theorists have argued that workplaces pay attention to and shape their EEO-related behavior in response to the legal rules and norms in their external environments (see Stainback, Tomaskovic-Devey, & Skaggs, 2010, for a review). Federal and state-level laws and policies regulating employment are an integral component of the external environment in which work establishments operate. The former has been the primary focus of empirical investigation, but as we explain, studying the latter type of legal environment – created by and enforced at the state level – is an important place of inquiry and influence. In addition, a convincing body of literature suggests that although organizations may adopt workplace EEO policies, the policies themselves often function perfunctorily, such that they are adopted but implemented without procedural change or oversight mechanisms. In the discussion below, we discuss how legal environments relate to both the adoption and elaboration of EEO-related policies in contemporary workplaces.

Federal Legal Environment

Although their impact has been uneven and inconsistent over time, federal EEO-related laws have influenced the experiences of U.S. workers (Kalev & Dobbin, 2006). Federal laws like Title VII of the 1964 Civil Rights Act and related legislation reduced occupational sex segregation, minimized sex pay gaps, and reduced employment discrimination (albeit for some groups more than others, and differently across time), in part, by exerting regulatory pressure on workplaces to comply with laws governing worker's rights (Stainback & Tomaskovic-Devey, 2012). This regulatory function of federal employment law is exercised largely through federal agencies, including the EEOC and Office of Federal Contractor Compliance Programs (OFCCP), and the federal courts. The EEOC and federal courts serve as the arbiters of workers discrimination claims against their employers, and the OFCCP, the agency responsible for overseeing federal contractors' compliance with federal employment law, can perform workplace audits to check for legal compliance, require record-keeping, and reporting (Stainback & Tomaskovic-Devey, 2012).

In the case of SH, the federal government's regulatory role is especially prominent. Since federal law established SH as an illegal behavior at work, workplaces have paid especially close attention to the associated laws partly because of the "politics of fear" surrounding SH in the United States (Saguy, 2003; Zippel, 2006, p. 5); employers fear risk of litigation stemming from allegations of SH because SH allegations violate the ideal image of a "sexually sanitized" and efficient, rational workplace (Schultz, 2003). This suggests that the fear or threat associated with SH litigation may prompt workplaces to create SH training programs. Yet at the same time, relative ambiguity surrounds the issue of SH in federal law and the courts. In response, organizations may institute policies to reduce uncertainty and render the law less ambiguous. Indeed, as Edelman et al. (1999) pointed out, federal courts have historically considered the presence of anti-harassment policies to stand as evidence that a workplace attempts to eliminate SH discrimination and organizations may not be held liable for it if they have a "reasonable and effective" grievance procedure (Edelman et al., 2011). In other words, the courts defer to organizational policies.

We conceptualize the federal legal environment in three ways. First, we consider the federal appellate court circuit in which an establishment is located. Court location may influence an establishment's attention to matters of SH because federal appellate courts provide a legal context in which establishments operate with regard to equal employment, and appellate court ideology has been found to influence lower court behavior and individual awareness of political issues (Guthrie & Roth, 1999a, 1999b; Skaggs, 2009). Appellate circuits exert pressure through legal decisions that signal their likely response to future-related decisions, but also by shaping the environment of support for sex-based rights at work (Skaggs, 2009). Establishments located in federal circuits known to be more progressive or liberal with regard to equal employment issues may respond to anticipated legal decisions in favor of sex-based rights and a normative expectation for these rights by having HR policies, including SH training programs.

The second way we capture an establishment's federal legal environment surrounding the regulation of sex-based rights at work is by considering OFCCP oversight of an establishment. The employment practices and policies of establishments with federal contracts are subject to greater oversight by the OFCCP compared to non-contractors. Specifically, federal contractors with at least $50,000 and 50 full-time workers are required, by federal law, to prepare and maintain affirmative action plans and are subject to review of these plans and on-site reviews of employment policy (U.S. Department of Labor, 2014). This oversight represents a very real form of federal legal pressure for workplace involvement in the regulation of sex-based rights (including the regulation of SH).

A third form of a work establishment's federal legal environment is its past experience with formal discrimination claims, namely formal charges of employment discrimination filed under Title VII of the Civil Rights Act of 1964 with the EEOC against a workplace. These past experiences with discrimination charges may be especially instructive for how workplaces specifically regulate SH because judicial interpretations of SH follow an individual-perpetrator model. This means that the EEOC and the courts identify an individual or group of individuals (rather than the employer) as the perpetrators in SH cases. As such, employers can avoid liability in SH cases if they demonstrate workplace policies and procedures are in place to discourage employees' from engaging in SH and they provide an internal remedy should SH complaints arise (Nelson, Berry, & Nielsen, 2008). Thus, unlike other forms of discrimination, employers are actually immune to legal liability for SH charges if they are not seen as complicit in the alleged perpetrator's acts or behavior. The elaboration of SH training policies, then, is a key way for employers to demonstrate good faith efforts to educate employees, discourage SH, and avoid liability for it. We expect employers with a past record of Title VII charges to be especially likely to pursue such policy elaboration. Because past charges of any kind raise awareness of diversity issues and legal liability for employers, we examine employers' previous experience with all Title VII charges involving various bases of discrimination (i.e., sex, race, color, national origin, religion) and issues (hiring, promotion, termination, harassment, pay), rather than charges raising specific claims; this allows us to capture establishments' entire record with civil rights challenges.

State-Level Legal Environment

Workplaces are also subject to a second, more localized legal regime: the state-level legal environment. Following the passage of Title VII, some states expanded federal enforcement of workplace gender equality

(Guthrie & Roth, 1999a, 1999b). The state legal environment is an especially salient part of establishments' legal environment when it comes to sex-based workplace issues, and U.S. states may have greater discretion in regulating matters of gender equality at work for several reasons. The first is related to the relative ambiguity with which the federal courts have treated matters related to SH. The ambiguity allows for different interpretation over meaning and enforcement of SH. For example, in a 1993 New Jersey state Supreme Court case involving workplace SH, the court determined that harassment need not be sexual in nature but instead, the defining characteristic is that the harassment happened because of the victim's sex (see Saguy, 2003). In addition, the U.S. political system limits the extent to which the federal government can address issues of gender equity (Abramovitz, 1996; Schneider, 2012) and some states have adopted more expansive EEO laws related to the regulation of sex-based rights at work than those required by the federal government and these state-level laws tend to be more explicit about sex-based protections than those at the federal level (see Kmec & Skaggs, 2014). Furthermore, state-level courts provide workers with greater access to legal recourse regarding workplace rights than federal courts because it is frequently easier, faster, and less expensive for a worker to pursue a discrimination claim in a state-level court than in a federal one (Redish & Muench, 1976). The federal EEOC even relies on the findings of the state in employment discrimination cases in the enforcement of federal employment laws (Roscigno, 2007). So when it comes to matters related to enforcing sex-based rights at work, the state has real legal regulatory authority, as demonstrated by past studies showing that state laws impact women's employment (Espinola-Arredondo & Mondal, 2009), the gender pay gap (Beggs, 1995; Ryu, 2010), and managerial sex composition (Guthrie & Roth, 1999b; Kmec & Skaggs, 2014).

SH TRAINING PROGRAM CONTENT

Most existing research exploring the workplace characteristics associated with the presence or adoption of HR-related policies has conceptualized policy outcomes with a dichotomous variable denoting the presence or absence of a policy rather than a measure of the features of the policy (see Dobbin et al., 2011; Kelly & Dobbin, 1999). Since not all policies are equally effective at achieving their goals (Kalev et al., 2006), studying the mere presence of a policy is instructive for understanding the presence of policies, but limited in the capacity to determine how legal environments affect the type of policies that organizations adopt. Studying the content of SH training programs helps us distinguish between policies that are largely ceremonial and those that are accompanied by procedural changes and accountability mechanisms (and presumably more effective). Specifically, our analysis examines SH training programs that are geared largely toward educating employees about SH and their rights, programs that also involve altering existing policies or making personnel changes, and programs that additionally involve follow-up or oversight mechanisms. In doing so, we are able to gauge the extent to which various aspects of federal and localized legal regimes might lead some organizations to adopt symbolic policies − which are likely to be decoupled from actual gender relations and practices − and other organizations to adopt more elaborate policies, tied to existing procedures and oversight mechanisms.

In light of what we know about state legal environments surrounding EEO and sex-based rights more generally, studying the content of SH policies also helps us identify mechanisms for why states may matter more, or in addition to federal legal regimes. Given that state-level law pertaining to equal employment tends to be less ambiguous and in some cases more expansive than federal laws, in addition to state courts providing easier access to plaintiffs, we expect state environments to be especially influential in the protection of gender-based rights at work, generally, and the elaboration of SH policies, in particular.

Additional Factors

In addition to the legal climate, we consider establishment and state-level factors associated with workplace policies to regulate SH. First, an establishment's size is expected to factor into the presence and content of SH programs as larger establishments tend to have more formal human resource-related policies than smaller ones, and may have a legal office or in-house counsel trained to write SH training policies. Second, prior research has shown that industry "climate" related to gender is relevant to analyses examining workplace inequality (Skaggs, 2008, 2009; Stainback & Tomaskovic-Devey, 2012). Of particular interest is the overall representation of women in an establishment's industry, a frequently used indicator of gender equity (see Kmec & Hirsh, 2016), and possibly an indicator of both greater regulatory scrutiny and the diffusion of equal employment practices in the industry (see Joshi, Son, & Roh, 2015). At the same time, in industries historically closed to women or with few women in management, increasing levels of diversity may incite incidences of SH which, in turn, give rise to the development of SH training programs. Finally, research suggests the importance of a state's broader gender climate in shaping workplace opportunities and outcomes (Beggs, 1995). In states with more support of gender egalitarianism and liberalism, in general, greater attention may be given to issues of fair employment such as those pertaining to SH.

DATA AND METHODS

We compiled data from four sources to test our research question. We used the first data source, the 2012 Human Resource Survey (HRS), for information on private establishments' SH training programs. From fall 2011 through winter 2012, the first two authors employed a survey research center to conduct a mixed mode survey of human resource representatives in private U.S. establishments; these are the actual locations where work is performed and also the site where court decisions get translated into employment practices (Saguy, 2003). To generate a sample for the survey, we randomly selected roughly 900 private U.S. establishments that filed an EEO-1 report in 2011. Annually, private employers with 100 or more employees, or federal contractors with 50 or more employees (or first-tier federal subcontractors involving agreements worth $50,000), are required to file an EEO-1 report describing the racial/ethnic and sex composition of employees in nine of the establishment's occupational categories. These reports are then utilized by the EEOC to ensure employer compliance with federal laws prohibiting employment discrimination. Overall, EEO-1 reports commonly serve to measure establishment-level segregation in private firms because of their accuracy, relatively high response rate, national scope, and over-time consistency in measurement of occupations and sex and race/ethnic make-up of employees (see Stainback & Tomaskovic-Devey, 2012).

For the HRS, a survey research center initially contacted work establishments to obtain a name, email address, and title of someone in the Human Resource department to whom they could direct our questionnaire. Following this prescreening phase, the survey center invited the identified person to participate in either a web-based or telephone survey who then provided information regarding workplace policies on SH, diversity, equal employment opportunities, and affirmative action. Overall, 170 of the eligible 900 establishments completed a questionnaire yielding a 19 percent completion rate. Although the completion rate is comparatively lower than other recent establishment surveys (see Kalev et al., 2006; Kelly, 2000), our data offer a unique opportunity to highlight the relevance of legal environments at work. Although we do not make claims about generalizability, the data utilized in analyses allow us to explore if and how state-level and federal regulation of workplace rights play out for specific SH policies. Thus, our approach trades a large, less detailed sample of HR policies for a smaller sample of more specific knowledge regarding the content of SH policies and establishments' past record with Title VII charges. The need for these kinds of data is critical given that we have virtually no collection of information on the content of SH procedures in the United States with which to study their antecedents, nor has anyone, to our knowledge, explored the way involvement with past employment discrimination matters for such policies. The insights drawn from these analyses, then, can be used to model research designed to represent a wider range of work establishments.

We gathered formal discrimination charge data from a second source, the EEOC's Charge Handling Database (CHD). We matched our sample of establishments to all Title VII charges filed against each establishment during the observation period, 1989−2010. A twenty-year observation period should be sufficient to capture any influence discrimination charge experience may have on a workplace. Since most charges filed with the EEOC prior to 2010 do not identify the accused employer by a unique number, we had had to match each employer in the establishment sample to charges contained in the EEOC's CHD; this required a matching of the accused establishment's zip code, name, and address with that in the database. Since automated strategies to perform this matching severely compromised the reliability of the data (in a comparison of automated to manual matching strategies, most of the automated matching algorithms only extracted about 50 percent of the charges filed against each establishment) we performed manual matching to ensure that our strategy captured all discrimination charges filed against each establishment in our sample. The EEOC retains information (e.g., protected class of the complainant, employment issue raised in the allegation, and employer name and location) on each formally filed discrimination complaint in the EEOC CHD. Due to data restrictions, we currently have access to the number of charges per establishment, not the issues, protected classes, or remedial actions taken. Yet still, we can capture an establishment's entire record with formal Title VII discrimination charges and are among the first to assess how prior charge activity affects policy elaboration. Because prior charges − of all kinds — raise awareness of diversity issues and legal liability for civil rights violations, they are an important feature of establishments' federal regulatory environments.

For data on state-level employment laws, we drew on a third data source: the privately maintained CCH State and Federal Employment Law database (CCH Wolters Kluwer, 2012). The database contains a comprehensive, up-to-date description of U.S. state's employment laws. Specifically, the database provides detailed information on fair employment practices, record-keeping, labor relations, penalties, and wage-hour state-level laws. Of specific interest to us are laws related to the regulation of SH at work.

Finally, we include information about establishments (size, industry, headquarter status, workforce demographic composition) from a fourth data source: 2011 EEOC EEO-1 reports (described above). The authors obtained access to annual EEO-1 reports through an Intergovernmental Personnel Act agreement with the EEOC.

Even with missing data, as we show in Appendix, the attributes of our full sample ($n = 170$), those who responded to the questions regarding SH training ($n = 100$), and our analytic sample ($n = 85$) are not dramatically different. For example, establishments in the overall sample are in states with slightly fewer SH regulations than those in the analytic sample (an average of 1.07 in the former and 1.25 in the latter), but establishments across the board are relatively similar in terms of their location in liberal federal appellate court circuits and with regard to federal contractor status. Recent discrimination charges and overall charge totals since 1989 are similar in the full sample, the sample of establishments that have SH training, and the analytic sample. Establishment size, female share of the workforce, industry location, and state attributes are also all relatively similar across the three. Not shown in Appendix, but also of interest, is how our analytic sample compares to the entire 2011 EEO-1 sampling frame based on a set of common attributes (i.e., federal contractor status, number of employees, establishment percent female, and industry with low representation of white women in management). Our analytic sample is composed of larger establishments, more federal contractors, and more establishments in industries with low representations of white women in management, as compared to the average establishment in the larger EEO-1 data sampling frame. However, our analytic sample is very similar in terms of the overall percent female. In terms of biasing our assessment of SH training program elaboration, this comparison suggests that establishments in our sample may be more likely to have SH training programs, given that it is comprised of larger establishments with more federal oversight based on contractor status. However, as our results show, neither establishment size or federal contractor status are significant predictors of the outcome in our full model, thus we do not believe that bias has been introduced.

Dependent Variables

Of the 170 establishments completing a survey, 100 answered the question pertaining to the presence of a SH training program. Eighty-four percent of these 100 had a SH training program and additional measures in our dataset allow us to capture how the content of these SH training programs differ. As a bit of background, our survey queried employers about features of training programs, drawing on those features discussed in Bendick, Egan, and Lofhjelm (2001), an article that provides a comprehensive snapshot of the features of general diversity training in U.S. workplaces. We modified our survey questions to be specifically about SH training. We created an ordinal measure capturing the content of training programs coded so the higher the score, the more elaborate the training program: (0) = no SH training program, (1) = has SH training program that establishes basic rules related to SH (i.e., describe forms SH can take, or what conduct/comments related to considered to be inappropriate, or who can be the target of SH, or provides instruction on how to raise SH claims in the company, or has a goal to promote organizational change in response to SH, (2) = establishes basic rules and engages in procedural reinforcement of SH training (by combining training with SH-related policy reform, procedural reform, or changes in personnel to achieve SH training goals), or establish basic rules and does post-training follow-up (one example of this is seeking employee feedback regarding the training several days post-training), and (3) establishes basic rules and engages in both procedural reinforcement and has an accountability mechanism (by engaging in post-training follow-up with employees on effectiveness of the training). To simplify discussion, we refer to the levels of the outcome as follows: 0 = absent, 1 = weak, 2 = moderate, 3 = elaborate SH training program.

Focal Independent Variables

Federal Legal Environment
Following previous research (Guthrie & Roth, 1999a, 1999b; Skaggs, 2009), we include a dichotomous variable indicating if the establishment is located

in a *liberal federal appellate court circuit* (i.e., one with a history of EEO-favorable decisions), coded "1" if an establishment is located in a liberal circuit (the second = New York, Connecticut, Vermont, third = Pennsylvania, Delaware, New Jersey, and ninth = Washington, Oregon, California, Idaho, Montana, Alaska, Hawaii, Nevada, Arizona) and "0" if otherwise. To measure an establishment's federal institutional environment, we include a dichotomous variable indicating whether an establishment is a *federal contractor*, and thus subject to greater oversight by the OFCCP (coded "1" if a contractor and "0" if not). To capture establishments' *past employment discrimination charges*, we include two measures. The first is a count of the total number of employment discrimination charges filed under Title VII of the Civil Rights Act of 1964 with the EEOC against establishments between 1989 and 2010, obtained from the EEOC's CHD. Because it is our intention to capture establishments' broad historical record with civil rights legal compliance rather than liability for specific forms of discrimination, we include charges of any basis (e.g., sex, race, color, national origin, and religion) or issue (e.g., harassment, hiring, firing, promotion, and pay) in our count measure. We also include this variable's square term in models to test for one form of nonlinearity.[2] Our second measure of past discrimination experience is a dichotomous variable coded "1" if any of the charges were recent (2005–2010), and "0" if not.[3]

State-Level Legal Environment
We include a measure of state-level SH protections created by summing five dichotomous variables coded "1" if a state's provisions for private and public employers are more comprehensive than specified by federal law with regard to: (1) SH law, (2) prohibited practices related to SH, (3) SH policy distribution requirements, (4) SH training, and (5) posting of SH rights, and coded "0" if otherwise. The measure ranges from 0 to 5 with higher values reflecting more comprehensive state provisions regarding SH. For instance, states such as California extend federal law through provisions related to SH training by specifying a minimum number of classroom hours of interactive education for all supervisors in private and public workplaces with 50 or more employees, along with the requirement to repeat the training every two years. Other states, such as Massachusetts, extend federal law by requiring public and private employers to distribute SH policies in written format to all employees on an annual basis and/or subjecting private and public employers to a monetary fine for failure to post notices of statutory provisions regarding SH, as specified in Connecticut law.

Controls

We include several control variables, derived from establishment's 2010 EEO-1 reports, thought to affect the adoption of SH training programs and the focal independent variables. Specifically, we control for the *establishment size* measured as the natural log of the number of employees in an establishment. Models also include a dichotomous variable coded "1" if an establishment's main industry is one identified by Stainback and Tomaskovic-Devey (2012) as having the lowest representation of white *women in management* and "0" if not. These industries include: manufacturing and construction, trade, mining, utilities, transportation. Third, we include a measure of the *percentage of women in an establishment's workforce* (and its squared term, when significant).

In 1972, Congress passed the Equal Rights Amendment (ERA) guaranteeing equal rights for women. By 1977, 35 states had ratified the amendment, although five states later rescinded (see Crowley, 2006). To capture a broader positive state-level gender climate potentially associated with *state ERA ratification*, we include a dichotomous variable coded "1" if a state ratified (and did not subsequently rescind ratification) and "0" if it did not. Last, we include a general measure of state progressiveness which is referred to as Blue state. Drawing from Honoree, Terpstra, and Friedl (2014), this measure captures "the party of each presidential candidate that successfully carried each state in the 1996, 2000, 2004, and 2008 general presidential elections" (p. 4). States that were carried by a Republican were noted as red, while states carried by a Democrat candidate were labeled blue. Three states were considered "swing" or "battleground" states due to equal identification with Republicans and Democrats (two of the four years with each). For the purpose of our study, these states, along with Republican states were coded as "0" and Democrat states were coded as "1."

Methods

We estimate ordinal logistic regression models because our outcome is an ordered measure and the overall Chi-square from a Brant's test suggests that the assumptions of ordered logistic regression are met. Clustering occurs because the characteristics of U.S. states in which establishments are located do not vary across establishments within each state (see Primo, Jacobsmeier, & Milyo, 2007). Because clustered observations can lead to bias in the standard error estimates (Long & Freese, 2006), we estimate robust standard errors, which correct for bias resulting from clusters. To illustrate the independent relationship between federal and state-level legal environments *and* their joint association with the outcomes, we present a series of models. We present four models: Model A (controls only), Model B (state-level legal environment indicators and controls), Model C (federal-level legal environment indicators and controls), and Model D (state- and federal-level legal environment indicators and controls).

RESULTS

Descriptive Results

The features of SH training programs vary across establishments in our sample. Eighteen percent of establishments report having no SH training program while 39 percent of establishments in our sample have what we classify as a "weak" SH training program, one that merely establishes basic rules pertaining to SH. Slightly less than one-third (20 percent) have a "moderate" SH training program (meaning the training establishes basic rules about SH *and* the establishment engages in procedural reinforcement of the training). Finally, 13 percent have "elaborate" training programs that establishes rules pertaining to SH, reinforces the training, and includes an accountability mechanism regarding the training (Table 1).

In terms of legal environments, 38 percent of establishments are located in a liberal federal appellate court circuit while nearly half (47 percent) are federal contractors (and thus held to higher EEO standards than non-contractors). The typical establishment had an average of approximately 5 charges (with a standard deviation of 11.99 and a range of 0–82) in the 1989–2010 timeframe and 53 percent had a recent charge (i.e., one in the past five years). Establishments are located in states with an average score of 1.17 on the SH coverage measure meaning that expanded SH coverage is on the low end (the score ranges from 0 to 5).

On average, establishments employ roughly 379 workers. Recall, our sampling frame consisted of establishments that employ at least 100 employees, so we do not capture small establishments with our sample. Just over one-third (36 percent) are in industries not historically friendly to women in management, namely manufacturing, construction, trade, mining, utilities, and transportation and the typical establishment has a

Table 1. Descriptive Statistics (*n* = 100).

	Mean/Prop.	SD	Min−Max
Dependent Variable			
SH training program content	1.38	0.94	0−3
Independent Variables			
Federal level			
Liberal federal appellate court circuit	0.38		Dichotomous
Federal contractor	0.47		Dichotomous
EEOC charges (1989−2010)	4.99	11.99	0−82
Recent EEOC charge (2005−2010)	0.53		Dichotomous
State level			
State SH regulation	1.17	1.81	0−5
Controls			
Ln # employees (2010)	5.89	1.34	3.17−9.54
% female	45.81	21.75	1.20−95.24
Industry low rep. of wh. women in mgmt	0.36		Dichotomous
State-ratified ERA	0.75		Dichotomous
Blue state	0.61		Dichotomous

Sources: 2011 HRS, 2011 EEO-1 reports, CCH Wolters Kluwer, EEOC CHD.

workforce that is roughly 45 percent female. Seventy-five percent of establishments are located in states that ratified the ERA. Finally, establishments are located in states with an average sex pay gap in 2009 of roughly 78 percent and 61 percent are located in a Blue state.

Multivariate Results

SH Training Program

Results from ordinal regression analyses, presented in four models, reveal an association between state SH protections and the outcome of interest. Turning first to Model A, a model with control variables only, we observe a positive association between both establishment size (number of employees) and location in a Blue state and SH training program elaboration. The addition of state-level controls in Model B shows that states with comprehensive regulation of SH at work adopt more stringent SH training programs. At the same time, size and location in a Blue state were also associated with SH training programs with more content. One additional control – state ratification of the ERA – had a net negative association with the outcome of interest, meaning that compared to establishments in non-ratifying states, those in ratifying states have less elaborate training programs (collinearity diagnostics not shown here reveal that ERA ratification and Blue state are not so highly correlated so as to measure the same concept and create multicollinearity problems). The model assessing the relationship between federal protections and SH training in work establishments (Model C, Table 2) indicates that establishments located in liberal appellate circuit courts have more elaborate policies than those in more conservative courts. In this model, too, we observe a net negative association between state ERA ratification and policy elaboration. Our final model, Model D, includes controls, along with measures of state and federal-level legal environments. In this model, we still see a positive association between state regulation of SH and the outcome, but previously significant federal legal environment measures are no longer significant. In this model, state ERA ratification is negatively associated with SH training program elaboration, but no other controls are significantly related to our outcome of interest.

DISCUSSION AND CONCLUSIONS

The primary goal of this paper was to investigate the joint connections between federal and state-level legal environments and the content of private work establishments' SH training programs. The use of unique data that combines information on establishment-level SH training presence and attributes, past employment discrimination charges filed against these establishments, and information on state and federal-level legal environments, has allowed us to be the first to explore these associations. Our analyses provide methodological and theoretical insight for future research, both of which we discuss below.

Although we cannot make causal inferences with our cross-sectional data, our analyses suggest that an establishment's legal environment, especially at the state level, is important in understanding how workplaces regulate one aspect of employment discrimination: SH. Because past Title VII discrimination charges, even those in the recent past, are not associated with SH training programs, it appears that workplaces do not simply

Table 2. Odds Ratios from Ordinal Logistic Regression Models Predicting SH Training Program Content.

	Model A	Model B	Model C	Model D
State Legal Environment				
State sex. harassment reg.	—	1.28** (0.09)	—	1.25** (0.11)
Federal Legal Environment				
Liberal federal appellate court circuit	—	—	1.99† (0.86)	1.57 (0.58)
Federal contractor	—	—	0.76 (0.39)	0.75 (0.40)
EEOC charges (1989–2010)	—	—	0.99 (0.02)	0.99 (0.02)
Recent charge (2005–2010)	—	—	0.96 (0.45)	1.11 (0.52)
Controls				
Ln # employees	1.32† (0.21)	1.29† (0.20)	1.33 (0.27)	1.27 (0.25)
% female	0.99 (0.01)	1.00 (0.02)	1.00 (0.02)	1.00 (0.01)
Industry low rep. of wh. women in mgmt	1.36 (0.80)	1.26 (0.78)	1.56 (0.92)	1.40 (0.86)
State-ratified ERA	0.59 (0.21)	0.49† (0.21)	0.51† (0.20)	0.45† (0.19)
Blue state	2.51* (0.92)	1.77† (0.60)	1.81 (0.77)	1.42 (0.59)
Cut 1	−0.20	−0.35	−0.23	−0.50
Cut 2	1.82	1.72	1.80	1.57
Cut 3	3.45	3.40	3.45	3.26
N	85	85	85	85
Log likelihood	−106.61	−104.64	−105.69	−104.29
Pseudo R^2	0.04	0.05	0.04	0.06

Sources: 2012 HRS, 2011 EEO-1 reports, CCH Wolters Kluwer, EEOC CHD.
$^{\dagger}p < .10$, $^{*}p < .05$, $^{**}p < .01$ (all two-tailed tests).
Robust standard errors in parentheses. Standard errors adjusted for state clusters.

respond to the threat or potential threat of legal sanctions or investigation, at least when it comes to creating formal routines for addressing SH. The relevance of state-level legal environments in our sampled establishments who are monitored annually by the federal government (recall, we drew our sample from EEO-1 reporting private U.S. establishments), implies that establishments are attuned to the diffuse legal pressures of their local environments, possibly even more so than the direct threat or fact of sanctions that past employment discrimination charges imply. Specifically, we see evidence of pressure stemming from the legal environment of the state with a positive association between a state's regulation of SH at work and our ordinal outcome. Even after taking into account the presence of past experience with discrimination charges at the federal level, the threat of OFCCP audits (characteristic of federal contractors), and an establishment's appellate court circuit, state legal environments are positively associated with the SH training content.

While further research drawing on a larger, more generalizable sample is needed to fully establish the relationship between the presence and content of workplace SH programs, our findings suggest that establishments in states where attention to the regulation of SH at work is more progressive tend to have features of elaborate SH training programs including broad scope, formalized procedural reinforcement, and an accountability mechanism (follow-up of the training). This suggests that organizations in state legal environments that are more progressive with respect to gender-based rights are more likely to respond with substantive policy adoption than organizations in states with less progressive gender rights. These findings are in keeping with Stainback and Tomaskovic-Devey's (2012) argument that gender rights and inequality vary with localized inequality regimes. That is, the regulation of employment rights is geographically unique. While Stainback and Tomaskovic-Devey's (2012) focus was not the state-level, per se, our analysis suggests that, like industry sector, variation in state law contributes to different localized cultural environments, which in turn, exert uneven pressure on organizations to elaborate gender-based rights at work. A broader implication is that both scholars and policy-makers should consider state-level design and implementation of employment laws, access to the courts, and regulatory pressures as important factors promoting workplace fairness. Our findings also reinforce the idea that in an era of federal retreat from EEO regulation, states can and do wield regulatory control over workplaces.

In terms of an establishment's federal-level legal environment, we find minimal evidence of an association between this form of legal pressure and features of the SH training programs considered in our analyses. In fact, the only aspect of the federal legal environment associated with any aspect of SH training programs is location in a liberal federal appellate court circuit; however, this relationship is not significant in the presence of state SH regulation. Findings regarding the influence of liberal appellate court circuits on SH training program elaboration are in keeping with research looking across a variety of gender-related outcomes in organizations, including the adoption of maternity leave policies, the presence of female CEOs, female managers, occupational sex segregation (see Guthrie & Roth, 1999a, 1999b; Hirsh, 2009; Skaggs, 2008). Appellate court circuits provide an important legal context for structuring organizations' protection of gender-based rights.

Having had recent experience with a discrimination claim filed at the EEOC is not associated with establishments' SH training program. The lack of association between past discrimination and SH training program content in general allows us to rule out the possibility that only establishments with a bad track record of employment discrimination pay attention to the regulation of SH at work. Instead, we think our findings regarding past discrimination claims demonstrate the continued presence of a strong culture of fear surrounding SH litigation (Zippel, 2006). That is, a workplace that has had any past experience with the EEOC in relation to any type of employment discrimination may have SH training programs that they can hold up as evidence of legal compliance in future discrimination claims. Nor do we find an association between federal contractor status and our outcome. This too is consistent with others who have found uneven effects of federal contractor status on outcomes during this period (see Hirsh, 2009; Kalev et al., 2006).

The limited association between our outcome and measures of federal-level legal environments suggests that federal enforcement of workers' rights, at least as they pertain to sex-based protections, may be necessary but not sufficient for the elaboration of workplace-based gender protections. As Stainback and Tomaskovic-Devey (2012) suggested, it may be that federal laws wield influence primarily when buttressed by additional pressures. In our analysis, that additional pressure operates via states. Although statistical interactions (not shown) estimating whether the association between federal-level legal environments and outcome differed across levels of state-level regulation were not significant, we encourage others with larger samples to test this idea. However, it is important to note that our findings may only relate to gender-based rights – a legal arena where many states offer more robust protections than federal law alone. In order to draw firm conclusions regarding the influence of federal legal environments, or lack thereof, future research should examine how state environments might impact workplace management of rights based on additional social statuses, such as race/ethnicity, sexual orientation, or criminal background.

In terms of controls, only one – state ratification of the ERA – is consistently significant in models and remains so net of all controls in Model D. Specifically, state ERA ratification is negatively associated with elaboration in establishment-level SH training programs. This negative association may reflect what Kouchaki (2011) calls "vicarious moral credentialing" or the notion that individuals are more likely to express prejudice when members of their group have, in the past, established non-prejudiced credentials. Applied to the context discussed here, this "moral credentialing" may mean that establishments in ERA ratifying states – and hence, states that have symbolically demonstrated norms toward gender equity – feel free to express little support for gender equity (through SH training programs) because their state legal environment has already done so. Or more simply, establishments in ratifying states might consider their state as being gender equitable; by mere location in the state an establishment may then consider itself to be equitable and have no need for elaborate SH training programs. Alternatively, since awareness of SH began to heighten at roughly the same time as state ratification of the ERA, establishments operating in states that ratified the amendment may have perceived such legal protection to include the regulation of SH, thus failing to see the need to institute their own specific SH training programs.

As with any research, the findings of our study are limited. First, while our decision to draw on a non-randomly selected cross-sectional sample of work establishments gives us purchase on previously unanswered questions, we do not intend for our data to be representative of all private U.S. establishments, nor do we intend for our findings to generalize to all settings. Instead, the advantage of our data is that they allow us to explore multiple legal environments associated with a typical workplace policy: SH training programs. A second limitation is in our measure of experience with formally filed discrimination claims. Because we rely on an aggregate measure of past EEOC charges that does not allow for specification of claim allegations, or the outcome of charges, we cannot directly investigate the association between SH claims and SH training features. For this reason, our estimates of the association between past legal experience and SH training programs are conservative. Nonetheless, any experience with the federal government related to employment discrimination is likely to have at least some influence on the way work-places frame or even react to workers' rights. A third limitation of our study is related to the effectiveness of specific SH training program features. Our data do not allow us to identify the effectiveness of SH training programs at curbing problems of SH at work. For this reason, we cannot address the possibility that these programs merely "window dress" (Edelman, 1990, 1992) or actually minimize workplace SH. Nonetheless, our measure of SH programs offers some advantage over the more typical policy presence indicators. Studying the mere presence of a SH training program would have obscured the variation in types of training programs across sampled establishments.

In conclusion, our study has identified both methodological and theoretical directions for future studies examining the relationship between legal environments and workplace behavior. To begin, we anticipate that research would move in the direction of exploring whether broader findings from this study hold for HR-related policies that extend beyond SH. For example, given the unique culture of fear surrounding SH in the United States, might there be an association between policies related to the elimination of discrimination in the hiring process or pay-setting procedures and an establishment's legal environment? Does the individual-perpetrator model characteristic of SH cases make workplace attention to legal pressures to curb SH different than other forms of discrimination? Along these same lines, others could explore how additional features of workplace settings play into the association between legal environments and HR-related policies. Are the associations between the legal environment and HR-related policies different in workplaces with formal HR offices or in-house council compared to those without? Third, our findings beg further scrutiny of legal environments, perhaps by assessing whether any relevant employment cases were tried in federal or, in particular, state courts in or around the time we collected our sample. Fourth, future studies should seek a larger sample of establishments and from them, data on the timing of HR policy adoption, state law adoption, and discrimination charges to enable closer scrutiny of the relationship between legal environments and policy. Finally, future research might examine the relationship between actual past legal experiences with SH claims and their outcomes (namely, did an establishment win or lose SH claims in the past) and the content of SH training programs in the establishment. In closing, as states take it upon themselves to legislate marriage and drug laws, we encourage researchers to keep a watchful eye on the ways states shape employment and workers' rights.

NOTES

1. Throughout, state-level legal environments refer to the legal environments specific to U.S. states (e.g., Florida, Minnesota).
2. In analyses not shown, alternative dichotomous and categorical measures denoting an establishment had none, one, two, or three or more formal Title VII charges filed against it in the time period were never statistically significant.
3. In analyses not shown, we included a continuous measure of recent charges (i.e., 2005–2010). Findings from this model were no different from one presented.

ACKNOWLEDGMENTS

We wish to thank Ronald Edwards and Bliss Cartwright at the U.S. EEOC's Office of Research for supplying data and statistical coding files and Steve Vallas and anonymous reviewers for helpful comments. An earlier version of this paper was presented at the 2014 American Sociological Association meetings in San Francisco. We also acknowledge the Center for Studies in Demography and Ecology at the University of Washington for data support. This work was supported by a Washington State University College of Liberal Arts Berry Family Fellowship; a grant from Cornell University's Institute for the Social Sciences; and a SSHRC Standard Research Grant [grant number 410-2011-0559].

REFERENCES

Abramovitz, M. (1996). *Regulating the lives of women: Social welfare policy from colonial times to the present*. Boston, MA: South End Press.

Beggs, J. J. (1995). The institutional environment: Implications for race and gender inequality in the U.S. labor market. *American Sociological Review, 60*, 612–633.

Bendick, M., Jr., Egan, M. L., & Lofhjelm, S. (2001). Diversity training: From antidiscrimination compliance to organization development. *Human Resource Planning, 24*, 10–25.

Bisom-Rapp, S., Stockdale, M. S., & Crosby, F. J. (2007). A critical look at organizational responses to and remedies for sex discrimination. *Sex discrimination in the workplace: Multidisciplinary perspectives* (pp. 273–293). Malden, MA: Blackwell Publishing.

CCH Wolters Kluwer. (2012). *State employment laws*. Retrieved from http://hr.cch.com/products/ProductID-141.asp. Accessed on November 28, 2012.

Crowley, J. E. (2006). Moving beyond tokenism: Ratification of the equal rights amendment and the election of women to state legislatures. *Social Science Quarterly, 87*, 519–539.

Dobbin, F., & Kelly, E. L. (2007). How to stop harassment: Professional construction of legal compliance in organizations. *American Journal of Sociology, 112*(4), 1203–1243.

Dobbin, F., Kim, S., & Kalev, S. (2011). You can't always get what you need: Organizational determinants of diversity programs. *American Sociological Review*, *76*, 386–411.

Edelman, L. B. (1990). Legal environments and organizational governance: The expansion of due process in the American workplace. *American Journal of Sociology*, *95*, 1401–1440.

Edelman, L. B. (1992). Legal ambiguity and symbolic structures: Organizational mediation of civil rights law. *American Journal of Sociology*, *97*, 1531–1576.

Edelman, L. B., Kreiger, L. H., Eliason, S. R., Albiston, C. R., & Mellema, V. (2011). When organizations rule: Judicial deference to institutional employment structures. *American Journal of Sociology*, *117*, 888–954.

Edelman, L. B., & Petterson, S. (1999). Symbols and substance in organizational response to civil rights law. *Research in Social Stratification and Mobility*, *17*, 107–135.

Edelman, L. B., Uggen, C., & Erlanger, H. S. (1999). The endogeneity of legal regulation: Grievance procedures as rational myth 1. *American Journal of Sociology*, *105*, 406–454.

Espinola-Arredondo, A., & Mondal, S. (2009). *The effect of parental leave on female employment: Evidence from state policies*. Working Paper 2008-15, School of Economic Sciences, Washington State University, Pullman, WA.

Guthrie, D., & Roth, L. M. (1999a). The state, courts, and maternity policies in U.S. organizations: Specifying institutional mechanisms. *American Sociological Review*, *64*, 41–63.

Guthrie, D., & Roth, L. M. (1999b). The state, courts, and equal opportunities for female CEOs in U.S. organizations: Specifying institutional mechanisms. *Social Forces*, *78*, 511–542.

Hirsh, C. E. (2009). The strength of weak enforcement: The Effect of discrimination charges on sex and race segregation. *American Sociological Review*, *74*, 245–271.

Honoree, A. L., Terpstra, D., & Friedl, J. (2014). Red vs. blue states: Cases of employment discrimination influenced by geography? *International Journal of Business and Social Research*, *4*, 1–11.

Joshi, A., Son, J., & Roh, H. (2015). When can women close the gap? A meta-analytic test of sex differences in performance and rewards. *Academy of Management Journal*, *58*, 1516–1545.

Kalev, A., & Dobbin, F. (2006). Enforcement of civil rights law in private workplaces: The effects of compliance reviews and lawsuits over time. *Law and Social Inquiry*, *31*, 855–903.

Kalev, A., Dobbin, F., & Kelly, E. (2006). Best practices or best guesses? Assessing the efficacy of corporate affirmative action and diversity policies. *American Sociological Review*, *71*, 589–617.

Kelly, E., & Dobbin, F. (1998). How affirmative action became diversity management: Employer response to antidiscrimination law, 1961–1996. *American Behavioral Scientist*, *41*, 960–984.

Kelly, E., & Dobbin, F. (1999). Civil rights law at work: Sex discrimination and the rise of maternity leave policies. *American Journal of Sociology*, *105*, 455–492.

Kmec, J. A., & Hirsh, C. E. (2016). *Signaling gender equality? Managerial sex composition and policy adoption*. Unpublished Manuscript. Washington State University, Pullman, WA.

Kmec, J. A., & Skaggs, S. L. (2014). The 'State' of equal opportunity employment law and managerial gender diversity. *Social Problems*, *61*, 530–558.

Kouchaki, M. (2011). Vicarious moral licensing: The influence of others' past moral actions on moral behavior. *Journal of Personal Social Psychology*, *101*, 702–715.

Long, J. S., & Freese, J. (2006). *Regression models for categorical dependent variables using Stata*. College Station, TX: Stata Press.

McDonald, P. (2012). Workplace sexual harassment 30 years on: A review of the literature. *International Journal of Management Reviews, 14*, 1–17.

Meyer, J. W., & Rowan, B. (1977). Institutional organizations: Formal structure as myth and ceremony. *American Journal of Sociology, 83*, 340–363.

Nelson, R., Berry, E., & Nielson, L. B. (2008). Divergent paths: Conflicting conceptions of employment discrimination in law and the social sciences. *Annual Review of Law and Social Science, 4*, 103–122.

Primo, D. M., Jacobsmeier, M. L., & Milyo, J. (2007). Estimating the impact of state policies and institutions with mixed-level data. *State Politics and Policy Quarterly, 7*, 446–459.

Redish, M. H., & Muench, J. E. (1976). Adjudication of federal causes of action in state court. *Michigan Law Review, 75*, 311–361.

Roscigno, V. (2007). *The face of discrimination: How race and gender impact work and home lives*. Lanham, MD: Rowman Littlefield Publishers.

Ryu, K. (2010). State policies and gender earnings inequality: A multilevel analysis of 50 U.S. states based on U.S. Census 2000 data. *The Sociological Quarterly, 51*, 226–254.

Saguy, A. (2003). *What is sexual harassment? From Capitol Hill to the Sorbonne*. Los Angeles, CA: University of California Press.

Schneider, L. U. (2012). *Reactive policy and the perpetuation of the gender wage gap*. Unpublished Manuscript. Grand Valley State University, Allendale, MI.

Schultz, V. (2003). The sanitized workplace. *The Yale Law Journal, 112*, 2061–2193.

Skaggs, S. (2008). Producing change or bagging opportunity? The effects of discrimination litigation on women in supermarket management. *American Journal of Sociology, 113*, 1148–1182.

Skaggs, S. L. (2009). Legal-Political pressures and African American access to managerial jobs. *American Sociological Review, 74*, 225–244.

Skrentny, J. (2006). Law and the American state. *Annual Review of Sociology, 32*, 213–244.

Stainback, K., & Tomaskovic-Devey, D. (2012). *Documenting desegregation: Racial and gender segregation in private-sector employment since the civil rights act*. New York, NY: Russell Sage.

Stainback, K., Tomaskovic-Devey, D., & Skaggs, S. L. (2010). Organizational approaches to inequality: Inertia, relative power, and environments. *Annual Review of Sociology, 36*, 225–247.

U.S. Department of Labor. (2014). *Office of federal contract compliance programs*. Retrieved from http://www.dol.gov/ofccp/. Accessed on November 18, 2014.

Zippel, K. (2006). *The politics of sexual harassment: A comparative study of the United States, the European Union and Germany*. Cambridge: Cambridge University Press.

APPENDIX

Table A1. Comparison of Descriptive Statistics across Samples (Complete, Establishments with SH Training, Analytic Sample).

	All Responding Establishments (n = 170)	Establishments with SH Training Programs (n = 100)	Establishments in Analytic Sample (n = 85)
SH training program content	na	1.38 (0.94)	1.68 (0.74)
State Legal Environment			
State sex. harassment reg.	1.07 (1.75)	1.17 (1.81)	1.25 (1.91)
Federal Legal Environment			
Liberal federal appellate court circuit (%)	37	38	42
Federal contractor (%)	48	47	49
EEOC charges (1989–2010)	5.84 (13.22)	4.99 (11.99)	5.38 (12.69)
Recent EEOC charge (%)	52	53	53
Controls			
Ln # employees	5.87 (1.32)	5.89 (1.34)	5.94 (1.32)
% female	47.48 (25.68)	45.81 (21.75)	44.19 (24.58)
Industry w/ low rep. of wh. women in mgmt (%)	35	36	37
State-ratified ERA (%)	71	75	72
Blue state (%)	58	61	61

Sources: 2012 HRS, 2011 EEO-1 reports, CCH Wolters Kluwer, EEOC CHD.

JOB INSECURITY AND SUBSTANCE USE IN THE UNITED STATES: STRESS, STRAIN, AND THE GENDERING OF PRECARIOUS EMPLOYMENT

Andrew S. Fullerton, Michael A. Long and
Kathryn Freeman Anderson

ABSTRACT

Research on the social determinants of health demonstrates that workers who feel insecure in their jobs suffer poorer health as a result. However, relatively few studies have examined the relationship between job insecurity and illegal substance use, which is closely related to health. In this study, we develop a theoretical model focusing on two intervening mechanisms: health and life satisfaction. Additionally, we examine differences in this relationship between women and men. We test this model using logistic regression models of substance use for women and men based on longitudinal data from the National Survey of Midlife Development in the United States. The results indicate that job insecurity is associated with a significantly higher probability of illegal substance use among women but not men. We interpret this as further evidence of

Research in the Sociology of Work, Volume 29, 241–271
Copyright © 2016 by Emerald Group Publishing Limited
All rights of reproduction in any form reserved
ISSN: 0277-2833/doi:10.1108/S0277-283320160000029026

*the gendering of precarious employment. This relationship is not chan-
neled through health or life satisfaction, but there is evidence that job
insecurity has a stronger association with illegal substance use for women
with poorer overall health.*

Keywords: Job insecurity; substance use; health; gender

Job insecurity is a common feature in the modern workplace. Full-time,
permanent jobs with employment security were the norm in the United
States during the post—World War II period of economic prosperity from
the mid-1940s to the early 1970s (Rubin, 1996). However, long-term trends
in the labor market, including the increasing use of flexible forms of labor,
such as part-time and temporary work, and global outsourcing have con-
tributed to increased levels of job insecurity (Fullerton & Wallace, 2007;
Kalleberg, 2009). In this study, we focus on perceived job insecurity, which
is the subjective evaluation of the likelihood of job loss in the near future.[1]

Job insecurity has both "objective" and "subjective" components.
"Objective" indicators of job insecurity include the probability of involun-
tary job loss during a period of organizational downsizing. However, recent
studies show that "subjective" evaluations of the insecurity of one's job are
equally or perhaps even more important in terms of key outcomes such as
health. Workers who feel insecure in their jobs suffer poorer physical and
mental health as a result (Burgard, Brand, & House, 2009; Ferrie,
Kivimäki, Shipley, Smith, & Virtanen, 2013; Ferrie, Shipley, Marmot,
Stansfeld, & Smith, 1995; Fullerton & Anderson, 2013; László et al., 2010).
Additionally, fears of future job loss are grounded in "objective" conditions
(Klandermans, Hesselink, & van Vuuren, 2010), and they are good predic-
tors of future job loss and wage growth (Campbell, Carruth, Dickerson, &
Green, 2007; Stephens, 2004). Therefore, we refer to these evaluations as
job insecurity, which is consistent with previous research.

Although the negative consequences of job insecurity for health and psychological well-being are well-known, its potential relationship with illegal
substance use (hereafter, substance use) remain relatively unexplored (for
an exception, see Frone, 2008). This gap in the literature is surprising given
the rising problem of substance abuse in the United States in general
(NIDA, 2015), and particularly the recent increase in opiate use in the

United States (Manchikanti et al., 2012). In this paper, we define substance use as using illegal substances, or using a legal substance without a prescription, in larger amounts than the physician prescribed, or for a longer period of time than the physician prescribed. The substances included in this study are: sedatives, tranquilizers, stimulants, painkillers, depression medication, inhalants, marijuana/hashish, cocaine/crack, hallucinogens, and heroin. Previous studies have shown that illicit drug use is higher among unemployed workers (Manchikanti et al., 2012, p. 19), which suggests that the threat of unemployment may also increase one's risk of substance use.

Job insecurity is a psychosocial stressor (Ferrie et al., 2013; Geuskens, Koppes, van den Bossche, & Joling, 2012) and a source of strain. Workers who feel insecure in their jobs may be more likely than others to use illegal substances in order to deal with the stress associated with job loss expectations. Furthermore, job insecure workers not only expose themselves to the negative health consequences of substance use, they are also breaking the law. The stress associated with insecure employment, then, may be negatively associated with a person's health and as a result put one at an increased risk of engaging in criminal behavior. We test a theoretical model of the relationship between job insecurity and substance use focusing on two intervening mechanisms: health and life satisfaction. Additionally, we provide a theoretical and empirical justification for the expectation of differences in this relationship between women and men. The results from this study indicate that job insecurity is associated with a significantly higher probability of substance use for women, but not for men. We interpret this result as further evidence of the gendering of precarious or insecure employment and its consequences for workers.

BACKGROUND

The Health Consequences of Job Insecurity for Workers

Research on the consequences of job insecurity has linked it to a variety of both physical and mental health outcomes. For example, a number of studies have found an association between job insecurity and negative self-rated general physical health (Burgard et al., 2009; Cheng, Chen, Chen, & Chiang, 2005; Ferrie, Shipley, Newman, Stansfeld, & Marmot, 2005; Ferrie, Shipley, Stansfeld, Smith, & Marmot, 2003; Fullerton & Anderson, 2013; László et al., 2010).

Others have demonstrated a relationship between job insecurity and specific physical ailments, such as an increased risk of coronary heart disease for women (Lee, Colditz, Berkman, & Kawachi, 2004), physical energy and fatigue (Cheng et al., 2005), long-standing illness (Ferrie et al., 2003, 2005), specific physical symptoms (Cheng et al., 2005; Heaney, Israel, & House, 1994), and short-term and long-term physical health effects (Schreurs, van Emmerik, Notelaers, & De Witte, 2010). Finally, and perhaps more related to our focus on substance use, several studies have shown an association between job insecurity and mental health outcomes. This line of research includes mental health issues such as depressive symptoms (Burgard et al., 2009; Rugulies, Bültmann, Aust, & Burr, 2006), increased help-seeking for psychological distress (Catalano, Rook, & Dooley, 1986), minor psychiatric morbidity (Ferrie et al., 2003, 2005), and negative emotional states (Cheng et al., 2005). Thus, this literature has demonstrated a number of both physical and mental health manifestations related to the experience of job insecurity.

Substance Use

In this study, we focus on an important yet under-studied potential consequence of job insecurity: substance use. The causes of substance use have been studied in great detail (see Spooner, 1999, for review). Interestingly, researchers have found that variables that predict substance use in adolescents (Spooner, 1999) are sometimes different than those that predict substance use in adults (Blazer & Wu, 2009). As we are primarily interested in studying the association between job insecurity and substance use,[2] we will focus here on reviewing the predictors of adult use. Here we review the findings of a few recent studies to highlight the importance and conflicting findings related to the relationships between socio-demographic variables and substance use.

Substance use patterns have been linked to socio-demographic variables (Kandel, 1991). In numerous studies of adult populations, demographic variables have a significant relationship with substance use. In a study of Detroit, Boardman, Finch, Ellison, Williams, and Jackson (2001) found that whites (compared to African-Americans), younger adults, men, and unmarried respondents were more likely to engage in substance use. Education, income, and employment status were not

associated with substance use. However, in a study on the gender difference in alcohol use of adults over 50 years old, Blazer and Wu (2009)
found that several socioeconomic indicators were significant predictors
of substance use. Specifically, men who had a college degree were more
likely to drink alcohol than those that did not, men that were employed
drank more than those that were not, and those that had higher
incomes also reported drinking more alcohol than those whose
incomes were lower. The results for women were similar to men. Frone,
Cooper, and Russell (1994) also found that age and race were consistently significant predictors of adult substance use in New York State.
These are but a few of the many studies of substance use that focus on
adult populations in the United States, however reporting the results of
these studies demonstrates that (1) inclusion of socio-demographic
variables as controls in prediction models of substance use is necessary,
and (2) the importance of individual socio-demographic variables has
been mixed.

In addition to socio-demographic predictors of substance use, researchers have studied the impact of physical and mental health problems on substance use (Briggs & Pepperell, 2009; Davis, 1994; Ettore & Riska, 1995;
Patton et al., 2002; Unger, Kipke, Simon, Montgomery, & Johnson, 1997).
For example, researchers have found that female substance users often
have more physical and mental health issues compared to non-substance
users (Briggs & Pepperell, 2009; Davis, 1994; Ettore & Riska, 1995).
Similarly, other studies have uncovered links between mental health issues
and substance use (Patton et al., 2002; Unger et al., 1997), suggesting that
perhaps individuals with mental health problems self-medicate with alcohol
and drugs.

Self-esteem and the degree to which a person is satisfied with his or her
life has also found to be correlated with substance use (Bogart, Collins,
Ellickson, & Klein, 2007; Rudolf & Watts, 2003; Zullig, Valois, Huebner,
Oeltmann, & Wanzer Drane, 2001). There is some debate however, on the
casual ordering of the relationship. Some researchers have found that substance use predicts the degree of life satisfaction (Bogart et al., 2007;
Rudolf & Watts, 2003; Zullig et al., 2001), while others (e.g., Boardman
et al., 2001) have found that lower levels of self-esteem predict increased
substance use. Due to the unresolved issues of the causal order of these
variables, in our empirical models we address this through the use of longitudinal data.

Stress Process and Strain

As a theoretical framework for this study, stress process theory provides a model for how external stressors can affect health outcomes and health-related behaviors. Pearlin, Menaghan, Lieberman, and Mullan (1981) describes three main components to the stress process: the stressors, mediators, and outcomes of stress. First, stressors refer to the various sources of stress that may impact an individual, which may be chronic features of daily life or major life events which can produce stress (Pearlin, 1989; Pearlin, Schieman, Fazio, & Meersman, 2005). Next, mediators, such as personal and economic resources or social support, can mitigate the effects of such stressors (Aneshensel, 1992; Pearlin et al., 1981). Conversely, the lack of such mediating resources may exacerbate the effects of stress and lead to negative coping mechanisms (Pearlin et al., 1981). Finally, stressors may lead to a variety of manifestations (Pearlin et al., 1981). Previous research has demonstrated the negative effects of social stressors on a variety of mental and physical health outcomes (Aneshensel, 1992; Pearlin et al., 2005; Turner, Wheaton, & Lloyd, 1995).

Relatedly, criminological theories of social strain trace their roots back to Merton (1938) and his influential argument that deviance results from strain that occurs when individuals cannot obtain the universally held goal of material success through the socially accepted conventional means (i.e., hard work). Due to structural factors that prohibit many individuals from attaining economic success through work alone, some turn to deviant and criminal activities (e.g., robbery, burglary, etc.) as an alternative to conventional methods for achieving their goal. More recently, Agnew (1992, 2001) reconceptualized Merton's argument to focus on strain that is the result of individual-level phenomenon, like divorce or family financial problems, instead of the structural focus preferred by Merton. Agnew's general strain theory (GST) suggests that "strain occurs when others 1) prevent or threaten to prevent you from achieving positively-valued goals, 2) remove or threaten to remove positively-valued stimuli that you possess, or 3) present or threaten you with noxious or negatively-valued stimuli" (Agnew & White, 1992, p. 476). Strain often leads to anger and frustration, which can lead people to engage in deviant behavior. Crime or deviant behavior, including illegal substance use, may help individuals reduce or cope with strain (Agnew, 2001).

Job Insecurity and Substance Use

As it pertains to the present research, we emphasize the external or structural sources of stress as highlighted in social stress and strain theories (Agnew & White, 1992; Aneshensel, 1992). In particular, we examine one source of social stress or strain: perceived job insecurity. The prospect of losing one's job can be stressful for individuals as most people cannot pay for their housing, food, etc. without income from a job. Research on social stressors suggests that it is likely that high job insecurity would lead to stress/strain. Using this theoretical framework, we argue that perceived job insecurity acts as a social stressor which can lead to adverse outcomes. In this case, we argue that the stress/strain from job insecurity will lead to a negative and illegal coping mechanism, substance use. We also account for a variety of personal characteristics, such as sex classification,[3] age, ethnicity, marital status, number of children, education, income, self-rated health, and life satisfaction, which could lessen or mediate the likelihood of turning to substance use as a coping mechanism. In sum, the stress process provides an account for how job insecurity may be linked to substance use. Specifically, we posit that perceived job insecurity as a social stressor will be associated with a higher probability of substance use after controlling for mediating resources.

Empirically, little is known about the link between job insecurity and substance use, but a few exceptions exist. Studies have found an association between job insecurity and prescription antidepressant and psychotropic drug use (Kivimäki, Vahtera, Flovainio, Virtanen, & Siegrist, 2007; Rugulies, Thielen, Nygaard, & Diderichsen, 2010). Frone (2008) uncovered an association between job insecurity and alcohol and drug use around the work day. However, Frone's (2008) study was based on cross-sectional data, focused on legal and illegal substances, and did not examine differences in this relationship between women and men. Although there are only a few studies linking job insecurity to substance use, based on the literature on social stressors and GST, these two concepts may be related. Therefore, we expect that job insecurity will be positively associated with the probability of substance use.

The Gendering of Precarious Employment

Drawing on the discussion of the social stress process above, we might expect to find that the relationship between perceived job insecurity and substance use differs for men and women. Women on the whole experience a marginalized social status which may contribute to greater social stress, and this is particularly the case for women's work arrangements. For instance, women are more likely to be employed in contingent and flexible work arrangements, which are less desirable and more insecure (Hatton, 2011; Kalleberg, 2000, 2011; Smith, 1998). Further, women are more likely to be in marginalized work positions, such as low-wage work, and are less rewarded for similar work in these fields (Fernandez-Mateo, 2010; Fernandez-Mateo & King, 2011). Given these compounded marginalized social identities, we would expect women to be more likely than men to experience negative consequences as a result of perceived job insecurity. Recent research in other fields has demonstrated an intensified effect of multiple marginalized statuses on a number of different social stress and mental health outcomes (Calabrese, Meyer, Overstreet, Haile, & Hansen, 2015; Etherington, 2015; Perry, Harp, & Oser, 2013; Seng, Lopez, Sperlich, Hamama, & Reed Meldrum, 2012). Thus, we can draw a parallel from this related to work to our specific case of job insecurity.

Furthermore, the job insecurity and health literature provides empirical evidence of different effects of job insecurity for women and men. Specifically, previous studies have found a gendered relationship between job insecurity and several health outcomes, including self-rated general health (Rugulies, Aust, Burr, & Bültmann, 2008; Bauer, Huber, Jenny, Müller, & Hämmig, 2009) and psychological distress (De Witte, 1999). Additionally, research suggests that there are different patterns in the social determinants of health for women and men. For example, family structure and social support are stronger determinants of health for women than men (Denton & Walters, 1999; Matthews, Manor, & Power, 1999). Bildt and Michélsen (2002) suggest that work stressors should have different effects for men and women given the persistence of occupational sex segregation. However, the results are inconsistent with respect to the direction of these differences.

The increasing prevalence of "objective" and "subjective" forms of job insecurity in recent decades is closely linked to the flexible turn in employment relations in response to the economic crises of the early 1970s (Rubin, 1996; Fullerton & Wallace, 2007; Kalleberg, 2011). Employer demands for increased flexibility translated into an increasing reliance on non-standard and contingent forms of labor, such as temporary, part-time, and on-call workers (Kalleberg, 2000). Although research suggests that the consequences of non-standard work for job insecurity varies cross-nationally (Fullerton, Dixon, & McCollum, 2016), in the U.S. workers in non-standard jobs are often in more insecure or precarious employment arrangements (Kalleberg, 2009, 2011). The neoliberal discourse promotes flexible (and thus insecure or precarious) employment arrangements as an "opportunity" for self-fulfillment and frames chronic unemployment as individual, moral failures (Bourdieu, 1998, p. 95; Butler, 2015a, p. 14; Vallas & Prener, 2012, p. 339, 347). As a central component of the neoliberal discourse, flexibility and precarity may be seen as politically induced and part of a new system of worker control rather than simply a new work arrangement arising in response to changing employer needs (Butler, 2015b, p. vii; Lorey, 2015). Precarity is not an economic inevitability but the result of a political will, and the generalized sense of insecurity induced by precarious employment arrangements serves to manufacture worker consent (Bourdieu, 1998, p. 84; Butler, 2015a, p. 33).

However, this is not to suggest that precariousness is equally distributed throughout the population. Precarious employment in the United States is gendered in terms of the historical development of non-standard forms of work, such as temporary (Hatton, 2011, 2014) and part-time workers (Vosko, 2010). If we define precarity more broadly in terms of vulnerability derived from the politically induced failure of social and economic support networks, then precarious employment is also gendered in the sense that precarity is an essential part of gender performativity (Butler, 2015a, p. 33). Gender and sexual minorities that do not live their genders in intelligible ways are exposed to an increased risk of violence and harassment and therefore exemplify this link between gender and precarity (Butler, 2015a, p. 34).

Due to the persistence of gender as a structural influence in work organizations (see Acker, 1990; Lorber, 1994), precarious employment conditions, and in the social determinants of health, we expect that the relationship between job insecurity and substance use will be different for women and men in the United States. Given women's overall disadvantaged labor market position there is reason to expect a stronger association with substance use due to the stress and strain associated with precarious employment. However, in contrast to typical quantitative studies in the social sciences, we argue that evidence of a stronger association between job insecurity and substance use for women indicates that insecurity is "gendered" but not reducible to the notion of "gender" or a "gender gap." According to Butler's (1990, 2004, 2015a) performative theory, gender is a contingent set of practices drawing on external norms that is inherently relational (i.e., gender is a process of "undoing" connecting us to others; Butler, 2004) and is not limited to the hyper-normative expressions of masculinity and femininity.

Thus, when we reduce the "gender gap" to differences between men and women we render non-normative gender expressions unintelligible and therefore non-existent. We also implicitly assume that "gender" is a direct reflection of the sex classification that the interviewer typically assigns each respondent either at the beginning of a face-to-face interview or at the end of a phone interview (as is the case in the questionnaire for the Midlife in the United States (MIDUS) data used in this study).[4] The binary "gender" variable employed in studies throughout the social sciences is thus an instance of the "theory effect" (Bourdieu, 1991) in which an implicit, binary theory of gender creates the very "reality" it believes to exist. In order to recognize gender as a contingent and complex set of practices operating at multiple levels rather than a fixed, individual characteristic assignable by an interviewer (for recent critiques of this practice, see Fullerton & Raynes, 2016; Westbrook & Saperstein, 2015), we refer to this binary measure as one's "sex classification" and evidence of a group difference as just one aspect of a larger process of the gendering of precarious employment.

DATA AND METHODS

Data

In order to examine the relationship between job insecurity and substance use, we use data from Waves 1 and 2 of the MIDUS study, which is based on a non-institutionalized, nationally representative sample of English-speaking adults in the United States, aged 25–74 (Ryff et al., 2012).[5] Respondents were initially interviewed in 1995–1996 and then again in a follow-up interview in 2005. We limit the sample to respondents who were employed in wage/salary positions (i.e., not self-employed) in Waves 1 and 2 and had complete information for all of the variables in the statistical models. In order to test for potential sex classification differences in the relationship between job insecurity and substance use, we estimate the models separately for women ($N = 764$) and men ($N = 712$). As we previously stated, evidence of different association between job insecurity and substance use for women and men would suggest that job insecurity is gendered while not completely capturing the notion of a "gender gap."

Measures

The dependent variable in our study is substance use, which is a binary indicator of the use of one or more of the following 10 drugs or medications "on one's own" during the past 12 months: sedatives, tranquilizers, stimulants, (prescription) painkillers, depression medication, inhalants, marijuana or hashish, cocaine/crack, hallucinogens, or heroin.[6] We combine the use of these 10 substances into a single, binary measure due to the low usage rates (0.1% to 5.6%). In the binary outcome, respondents that have not used any of these substances are coded as 0 and those that have used one or more substances are coded as 1.

We include measures of the central independent variable in this study, *job insecurity*, at Waves 1 and 2. The original variable is an ordinal measure of cognitive job insecurity, which is the perceived likelihood of job loss in the near future. For both waves, we recode the original variables into binary measures of job insecurity (chances of keeping one's job for the next two years: 1 = poor, fair, good, or very good, 0 = excellent). Given the tendency of workers to exaggerate job rewards, such as job satisfaction, we recoded the original, ordinal measures of job insecurity into binary measures comparing the least insecure workers to those that feel at least somewhat insecure in their jobs. The recoded binary variables provide a better model fit than several alternatives, including the use of binary variables for every category, the original measures, and the binary indicators for insecure at Wave 1 only, Wave 2 only, both waves, and neither wave (see Burgard et al., 2009). Approximately two-thirds of workers indicated that they had an "excellent" chance of keeping their jobs for the next two years. Workers that are not this confident in their ability to keep their jobs over the next two years perceive at least some degree of job insecurity, and the results in our study suggest that this is the most important distinction for substance use. Results using these alternative job insecurity measures are available upon request.

We also include measures of our two key mechanisms, *poor health* and *life satisfaction*, at Waves 1 and 2. Poor health is an additive index combining physical and mental health (Wave 1: alpha = 0.70 for women and 0.67 for men; Wave 2: alpha = 0.70 for women and 0.72 for men).[7] Higher values indicate poorer overall physical and mental health. Life satisfaction is an additive index combining measures of satisfaction with life, control over life, and satisfaction with oneself (Wave 1: alpha = 0.74 for women and 0.69 for men; Wave 2: alpha = 0.71 for women and 0.72 for men).[8] Higher values indicate more control over and satisfaction with life and oneself.

The final key independent variable is a binary measure of *substance use* at Wave 1, which we code in the same manner as the dependent variable. We expect that respondents who used one or more of these substances at Wave 1 will be more likely than other respondents to also be substance users are Wave 2. Controlling for previous substance use will provide a more robust test of the relationship between job insecurity and substance use. We also include a set of binary indicators for *occupation*, including managerial, professional and technical (reference), sales and service, clerical, and other occupations.[9] Finally, we control for several socio-demographic variables, including: *age* in years (Wave 1), *white* (race: white = 1, else = 0), *married* (marital status: married = 1, else = 0 [Wave 2]), *number of children* (Wave 2), years of *education* (Wave 2), and *log household income* (Wave 2).

Analytic Strategy

The dependent variable, substance use, is binary. Therefore, we examine the relationship between job insecurity and substance use using cross-tabulations and logistic regression models (see Long, 1997). We present odds ratios for each independent variable. However, it is important to note that odds ratios are essentially standardized based on the specification of each model and peculiarities of the sample (for more details, see Mood, 2010). Therefore, one cannot compare odds ratios or logit coefficients across samples or different models based on the same sample. It is possible that differences in odds ratios between models (e.g., reduced vs. full models) or samples (e.g., men vs. women) may reflect differences in unobserved heterogeneity rather than the "true effects" (Allison, 1999; Mood, 2010; Williams, 2009, 2010). Therefore, in order to examine group differences (i.e., women vs. men) in the relationship between job insecurity and substance use we also present average marginal effects and graphs based on predicted probabilities.

Average marginal effects are "global" in the sense that the effects of independent variables are averaged across each respondent in the sample. For continuous independent variables, they represent the marginal effect on the predicted probabilities averaged across the sample. For binary independent variables, they represent a hypothetical discrete change (from 0 to 1) for respondents with the same characteristics on the remaining variables and averaged across the sample (see Williams, 2012, p. 326). Average marginal effects are not affected by group differences in unobserved heterogeneity. We also present graphs based on predicted probabilities that also allow us to show how this association varies by one's level of overall health.

RESULTS

Descriptive Statistics and Bivariate Associations

We present descriptive statistics for the dependent and independent variables in Table 1. We include means and standard deviations for continuous variables and percentages for binary variables. In Wave 2, the substance use rate is slightly lower for women than men, but the difference (9% vs. 11%) is not statistically significant. Focusing on the key independent variables, women are significantly less likely than men to use one or more substances, and women's average health is significantly poorer than men's average health (both at Wave 1). There are also several demographic differences between the samples of men and women.

In Table 2, we present the results from cross-tabulations of job insecurity and substance use for men and women, separately. Wave 1 job insecurity has little to no relationship with substance use at Wave 2. Insecure workers have a somewhat higher rate of substance use than secure workers, but the differences are very modest (9.7% vs. 8.5% for women and 11.7% vs. 10.6% for men). Neither cross-tab at Wave 1 has a statistically significant Chi-Square value.

The results for job insecurity at Wave 2 are very similar for men. Men's substance use rates are very similar with insecure and secure workers (10.6% and 11.1%, respectively). However, the association between job insecurity and substance use is considerably stronger for women in Wave 2. For women, the substance use rate is almost twice as large for insecure as secure workers (12.7% vs. 7.1%), which is a statistically significant difference. However, it is possible that this bivariate association is due to other factors such as previous substance use, health, and life satisfaction. Therefore, we will also examine this relationship using logistic regression models.

Table 1. Descriptive Statistics for Variables in Models of Substance Use.

	Mean/Pct.		SD		Range
	Women	Men	Women	Men	
Dependent Variable					
Substance use (Wave 2)	8.901	10.955	–	–	0 to 1
Independent Variables					
Substance use (Wave 1)	11.649	15.449*	–	–	0 to 1
Job insecurity (Wave 1)	35.209	34.831	–	–	0 to 1
Job insecurity (Wave 2)	32.068	29.213	–	–	0 to 1
Poor health (Wave 1)	−0.074	−0.232[#]	1.684	1.693	−2.756 to 5.100
Poor health (Wave 2)	−0.030	−0.068	1.735	1.748	−2.702 to 6.597
Life satisfaction (Wave 1)	−0.059	−0.111	2.425	2.458	−11.587 to 2.029
Life satisfaction (Wave 2)	0.048	0.062	2.347	2.346	−11.783 to 2.045
Age (Wave 1)	41.715	41.319	9.419	9.015	24 to 72
White (Wave 1)	92.277	94.663[#]	–	–	0 to 1
Married (Wave 2)	65.707	78.230***	–	–	0 to 1
Number of children (Wave 2)	2.132	2.319*	1.591	1.658	0 to 17
Education (Wave 2)	14.732	14.996*	2.479	2.602	3.5 to 20
Log household income (Wave 2)	10.843	11.181***	1.826	1.193	0 to 12.612
Occupation (Wave 2)					
Managerial	20.157	25.562*	–	–	0 to 1
Professional and technical (ref.)	33.770	25.562***	–	–	0 to 1
Sales and service	15.183	13.343	–	–	0 to 1
Clerical	23.560	8.006***	–	–	0 to 1
Other	7.330	27.528***	–	–	0 to 1

Notes: Data come from the MIDUS and MIDUS II. $N = 764$ women and 712 men. The significance tests for differences between women and men are based on t-tests for means and z-tests for proportions. Other occupations include farm, mechanics, repairers, construction, mining, operators, manual laborers, and military.
[#]$p < .10$; *$p < .05$; **$p < .01$; ***$p < .001$.

Logistic Regression Models

In Table 3, we present the results from logistic regression models of substance use for women. We include odds ratios in the tables for each independent variable. Additionally, we include average marginal effects for our

Table 2.   Bivariate Association between Perceived Job Insecurity and Substance Use.

		Perceived Job Insecurity (Wave 1)		
Substance use (Wave 2) Secure Insecure Total		Secure	Insecure	Total
No	Women	91.52	90.33	91.10
	Men	89.44	88.31	89.04
Yes	Women	8.48	9.67	8.90
	Men	10.56	11.69	10.96
	Total	100.00%	100.00%	100.00%
		Chi-Square = 0.30 (Women) 0.21 (Men)		

		Perceived Job Insecurity (Wave 2)		
Substance use (Wave 2) Secure Insecure Total		Secure	Insecure	Total
No	Women	92.87	87.35	91.10
	Men	88.89	89.42	89.04
Yes	Women	7.13	12.65	8.90
	Men	11.11	10.58	10.96
	Total	100.00%	100.00%	100.00%
		Chi-Square = 6.26* (Women) 0.04 (Men)		

Notes: N = 764 women and 712 men.
[#]$p < .10$; *$p < .05$; **$p < .01$; ***$p < .001$.

focal variables: job insecurity at Waves 1 and 2. In Model 1, we only include the two measures of job insecurity. In Wave 2, job insecurity is associated with an increase in the odds of substance use by a factor of 1.89 (or 89%), which is statistically significant. However, the job insecurity coefficient for Wave 1 is not significant. The addition of previous substance use only slightly diminishes the effect size for job insecurity among women (see Model 2). The average marginal effect decreases from .055 to .051,[10] but the odds ratio and average marginal effect remain statistically significant. Controlling for previous substance use and job insecurity, feelings of job insecurity at Wave 2 are associated with an increase in the odds of substance use by a factor of 1.86 or 86%.

In Models 3 through 5, we consider poor health and life satisfaction as two potential intervening mechanisms. Health and life satisfaction at Wave

Table 3. Results from Logistic Regression Models of Substance Use at
Wave 2 (Women).

	Model 1	Model 2	Model 3	Model 4	Model 5	Model 6
Odds Ratios						
Substance use		4.483***	4.170***	4.109***	4.045***	3.885***
(Wave 1)		(1.308)	(1.230)	(1.219)	(1.204)	(1.213)
Job insecurity	0.998	1.042	0.938	0.985	0.951	0.831
(Wave 1)	(0.270)	(0.286)	(0.263)	(0.273)	(0.269)	(0.245)
Job insecurity	1.888*	1.862*	1.772*	1.676$^{\#}$	1.677$^{\#}$	1.720$^{\#}$
(Wave 2)	(0.499)	(0.500)	(0.479)	(0.461)	(0.462)	(0.489)
Poor health			1.133		1.050	1.039
(Wave 1)			(0.097)		(0.098)	(0.100)
Poor health				1.227*	1.200*	1.231*
(Wave 2)				(0.102)	(0.109)	(0.115)
Life satisfaction			0.966		0.984	0.979
(Wave 1)			(0.053)		(0.060)	(0.062)
Life satisfaction				0.992	1.002	1.035
(Wave 2)				(0.055)	(0.062)	(0.068)
Age (Wave 1)						0.989
						(0.016)
White (Wave 1)						0.890
						(0.432)
Married (Wave 2)						0.864
						(0.259)
Number of children						0.948
(Wave 2)						(0.089)
Education						1.038
(Wave 2)						(0.068)
Log						1.036
household income						(0.086)
Average Marginal Effects						
Job insecurity	0.000	0.003	−0.005	−0.001	−0.004	−0.013
(Wave 1)	(0.022)	(0.021)	(0.021)	(0.021)	(0.021)	(0.021)
Job insecurity	0.055*	0.051*	0.047*	0.042$^{\#}$	0.042$^{\#}$	0.043$^{\#}$
(Wave 2)	(0.025)	(0.024)	(0.023)	(0.023)	(0.023)	(0.024)

Table 3. (*Continued*)

	Model 1	Model 2	Model 3	Model 4	Model 5	Model 6
Model Fit						
Pseudo R^2	0.013	0.063	0.071	0.080	0.081	0.108
AIC	458.802	437.821	438.093	434.184	437.737	445.102
BIC	472.717	456.375	465.924	462.015	474.846	528.596

Notes: N = 764 women and 712 men. The odds ratios are unstandardized. The numbers in parentheses are standard errors. The models also include a constant. The McFadden Pseudo R^2 is reported in the table. Model 6 also includes a set of four binary variables for occupation (reference = professional).
[#]$p < .10$; *$p < .05$; **$p < .01$; ***$p < .001$.

1 are not significantly associated with substance use (see Model 3), and the coefficient for job insecurity at Wave 2 is not diminished. The average marginal effect only decreases from .051 to .047. However, health at Wave 2 is significant. A one unit increase in poor health is associated with an increase in the odds of substance use by a factor of 1.23 or 23%. However, the coefficient for life satisfaction remains non-significant. Additionally, after controlling for health and life satisfaction at Wave 2 (see Model 4), the relationship between job insecurity and substance use is somewhat weaker. The average marginal effect is now only .042, which represents an 18% decrease from Model 2. Additionally, the odds ratio and average marginal effect for job insecurity are now only marginally statistically significant ($p < .10$). Combining the measures of health and life satisfaction from both waves in Model 5 produces very similar results. The workers that have the greatest odds of using one or more substances are those that have a history of substance use, feel insecure in their current jobs, and presently are in poor health.

In Model 6, we add the socio-demographic control variables and occupation to the model (the results for occupation are available upon request). Job insecurity is once again associated with an increase in the odds of substance use by a factor of 1.72 (or 72%). Additionally, the average marginal effect for job insecurity is approximately the same. The relationship between job insecurity and substance use is virtually the same for women with or without controls for broad occupational groups, which indicates that this association is not simply a function of the concentration of women in secondary labor market jobs.[11]

In Table 4, we present the results from logistic regression models of substance use for men. There is a very weak, positive association between job

Table 4. Results from Logistic Regression Models of Substance Use at
Wave 2 (Men).

	Model 1	Model 2	Model 3	Model 4	Model 5	Model 6
Odds Ratios						
Substance use		9.859***	9.809***	9.788***	10.132***	9.720***
(Wave 1)		(2.592)	(2.600)	(2.585)	(2.717)	(2.761)
Job insecurity	1.149	1.019	1.017	0.963	0.979	0.956
(Wave 1)	(0.297)	(0.281)	(0.284)	(0.268)	(0.276)	(0.279)
Job insecurity	0.910	0.802	0.798	0.716	0.722	0.687
(Wave 2)	(0.252)	(0.236)	(0.238)	(0.218)	(0.221)	(0.215)
Poor health			1.016		0.946	0.958
(Wave 1)			(0.084)		(0.091)	(0.095)
Poor health				1.091	1.123	1.130
(Wave 2)				(0.085)	(0.101)	(0.105)
Life satisfaction			1.002		1.032	1.038
(Wave 1)			(0.058)		(0.068)	(0.069)
Life satisfaction				0.958	0.941	0.941
(Wave 2)				(0.057)	(0.062)	(0.066)
Age (Wave 1)						0.997
						(0.016)
White (Wave 1)						0.574
						(0.282)
Married (Wave 2)						0.656
						(0.210)
Number of children						1.069
(Wave 2)						(0.082)
Education (Wave 2)						1.002
						(0.064)
Log household income						0.965
						(0.092)
Average Marginal Effects						
Job insecurity	0.014	0.002	0.001	−0.003	−0.002	−0.004
(Wave 1)	(0.026)	(0.023)	(0.023)	(0.023)	(0.023)	(0.024)
Job insecurity	−0.009	−0.018	−0.018	−0.027	−0.026	−0.029
(Wave 2)	(0.026)	(0.023)	(0.024)	(0.023)	(0.023)	(0.023)

Table 4. (*Continued*)

	Model 1	Model 2	Model 3	Model 4	Model 5	Model 6
Model Fit						
Pseudo R^2	0.001	0.150	0.150	0.155	0.157	0.171
AIC	497.769	426.319	430.283	427.652	430.842	443.993
BIC	511.473	444.592	457.691	455.060	467.386	526.219

Notes: $N = 764$ women and 712 men. The odds ratios are unstandardized. The numbers in parentheses are standard errors. The models also include a constant. The McFadden Pseudo R^2 is reported in the table. Model 6 also includes a set of four binary variables for occupation (reference = professional).
#$p < .10$; *$p < .05$; ** $p < .01$; ***$p < .001$.

insecurity at Wave 1 and the odds of substance use (see Models 1 and 2), but the coefficient is not statistically significant in any of the models. Poor health and life satisfaction are not significantly associated with the odds of substance use at either wave (see Models 3 through 5). For men, previous substance use is the only variable in the model that is significantly associated with current substance use.

A comparison of the average marginal effects in Tables 3 and 4 reveals that job insecurity has very different associations with substance use for women and men. For women, the perception of job insecurity at Wave 2 is associated with an increase in the predicted probability of substance use by approximately .04 to .06, which is averaged across the entire sample of women. For men, the difference in the predicted probabilities of substance use between secure and insecure workers is negligible. In a combined sample, job insecurity has a non-significant, positive association with the odds of substance use, which is essentially an average of the strong, positive coefficient for women and very weak, negative coefficient for men (results are available upon request).

In order to examine the relationship between job insecurity and substance use in greater detail, we calculated predicted probabilities for secure and insecure workers at different levels of health in both samples (see Fig. 1).[12] For women and men, poorer health is associated with a higher probability of substance use. However, the association is stronger for women than men. For women that feel insecure in their jobs, an increase from the lowest to highest level of poor health is associated with a .20 increase in the predicted probability of substance use (from .04 to .24). However, for men it is only associated with a .05 increase (from .03 to .08).

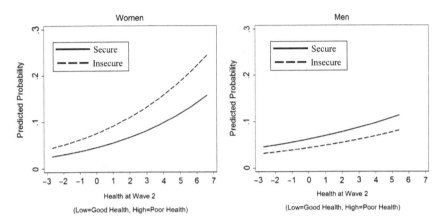

Fig. 1. The Association between Job Insecurity and Substance Use at Different Levels of Physical Health for Women and Men in the United States.

In other words, there is a stronger link between poor health and substance use for women than men.

The graphs in Fig. 1 also highlight the substantially different relationships between job insecurity and substance use for women and men. In the middle of the health range, job insecurity is associated with a .043 increase in the predicted probability of substance use for women compared to a .022 decrease for men. Additionally, the strength of the relationship varies by the level of health. There are no interaction terms in the model, but non-linear probability models are inherently interactive on the probability scale (Long, 1997). Job insecurity displays a stronger association with substance use at the poorest levels of health. For women with the "best" health (i.e., lowest value for poor health), job insecurity is only associated with an increase of .02 in the predicted probability of substance use. However, for women with the poorest health, job insecurity is associated with an increase of .09 in predicted probability of substance use. Poor health may not explain "why" job insecurity is related to women's substance use, but the results suggest that it may exacerbate the consequences of job insecurity for women.

Supplementary Analyses of Intervening Mechanisms

We also examined the links between job insecurity, health, and life satisfaction given the importance of these latter two mechanisms in our theoretical model. The results from OLS regression models of poor health and life satisfaction do not provide much support for the importance of health and life satisfaction as intervening mechanisms (see Table A1). Controlling for previous health and other socio-demographic variables, job insecurity is significantly associated with poorer health for men but not women. However, job insecurity is significantly associated with lower overall life satisfaction for men and women. Given that job insecurity is only associated with an increase in the odds of substance use for women and life satisfaction is not significant in the substance use models for women, these findings suggest that other intervening mechanisms are potentially responsible for the association between job insecurity and substance use for women in the United States. However, our results do suggest that poor health plays a moderating role among women (see Fig. 1). Although job insecurity is related to substance use for women in both good and poor health, the insecurity gap in the probability of substance is much greater for women in poor health than for those in good health.

DISCUSSION AND CONCLUSIONS

This study provides evidence of a link between job insecurity and substance use for women in the United States. The use of one or more illicit substances is likely in response to the stress and strain associated with feeling of job insecurity, but the association between insecurity and substance use persists even after controlling for potential intervening mechanisms such as poor health and low life satisfaction. However, the results do suggest that poor health shapes the relationship between job insecurity and substance use for women. The association between job insecurity and the probability of substance use is more than four times stronger for women with the poorest level of health compared to women with the best health. In other words, good mental and physical health may act as a buffer against the increased risk of substance use that is associated with job insecurity for women.

Our results also suggest that the consequences of job insecurity are gendered in the United States. Differences between women and men in the social determinants of health are well established in the literature (Bauer et al., 2009; Bildt & Michélsen, 2002; De Witte, 1999; Denton & Walters, 1999; Matthews et al., 1999; Rugulies et al., 2008), but the limited amount of previous research on job insecurity and substance use did not examine the potentially gendered nature of this process (e.g., Frone, 2008). Job insecurity is associated with poorer health and lower life satisfaction for men, but this does not translate into an increased risk of substance use.

Although women are less likely to use illicit substances in general compared to men (Briggs & Pepperell, 2009), our results demonstrate that job insecurity is only associated with an increase in substance use for women. This result, though, is fitting with the stress process framework used to guide this research. In this case, job insecurity and women's marginalized social status in general and in the workplace, place them in a more precarious position when compared to men. More specifically, women who report experiencing job insecurity are exposed to more than one type of chronic social stress due to their marginalized position as women and due to the experience of job insecurity (Pearlin, 1989; Aneshensel, 1992). These multiple exposures put them at greater risk for engaging in negative coping mechanisms, such as substance use (Pearlin et al., 1981). Thus, from these greater and multiple stress exposures, we find that women are more likely than men to engage in illicit drug use, which we conceptualize as a negative stress coping behavior using the stress process framework.

The greater life stressors women face can compound and contribute to certain negative consequences as a result. Here, we find that being in poor health, an additional stressor, also contributes to a greater likelihood of substance use for women and to a far lesser degree for men. Additionally, job insecurity has the strongest association with substance use for women experiencing poor health. Thus, poor health may influence substance use both directly and indirectly by moderating the relationship between job insecurity and substance use. Our measure accounts for both mental and physical health, which may both play a strong role in the desire to use illicit substances. It has long been observed that women in the workplace still experience an undue burden of domestic work and child rearing despite their role as family breadwinners as well (Hochschild & Machung, 2003). Recent qualitative work demonstrates that this situation may be worse under conditions of economic insecurity, where women tend to place extra emphasis on the family and intimate relationships in the face of workplace uncertainty, which in turn, produces greater stress and poor mental health outcomes for such women (Pugh, 2015). As such, the culmination of these life situations may contribute to poorer overall health and a greater likelihood of turning to substances in order to cope.

The association between job insecurity and illegal substance use will likely persist. In addition to the increase in precarious work, substance use continues to be widespread in the United States. For example, a recent trend in the country is a major surge in opiate use. Recent figures suggest that over five million U.S. citizens are opiate users and this number is increasing (Manchikanti et al., 2012). As job insecurity continues to be a reality for many U.S. workers, some will turn to substance use as a coping mechanism. This includes opiates which are highly addictive and often causes users to commit other crimes to obtain money to satisfy their addiction (Fischer, Medved, Kirst, Rehm, & Gliksman, 2001). The impact of job insecurity on these peoples' lives, then, can be staggering as some job insecure workers become substance users which place their health at risk. In addition, they become "criminal" because they are frequently engaging in an illegal behavior (substance use), and in some cases they become addicts and may need to turn to criminal behavior (e.g., burglary, larceny) to satisfy their addiction. While most substance users will not turn to criminal activity to fund their addiction, there are clearly numerous negative consequences from substance use.

Limitations

Despite the contributions of this study, it also has several limitations. First, there is a 10-year lag between Waves 1 and 2 in the MIDUS data. Although the use of two time points allows us to control for previous job insecurity and substance use, panel data with three or more waves administered in shorter intervals (e g., three to five years apart) would provide a more robust test of the relationship between job insecurity on substance use. It would also help rule out the possibility of reverse causality (i.e., substance use leading to an increase in job insecurity). Second, the data only contains a single measure of cognitive job insecurity. It is possible that affective job insecurity (i.e., worrying about potential job loss) would increase the risk of substance use for women and men. However, this is a common data limitation in surveys with multiple indicators of substance use and health. Finally, a weakness of the stress process approach is that there are hundreds of potential sources of stress in a person's life and identifying those that are actually influencing an individual's decision to engage in substance use can be difficult (Agnew, 2001; Pearlin et al., 1981). However, given that our results demonstrate that job insecurity is significantly associated with substance use in all of the models for women indicates that it is likely that we have captured an important source of stress/strain in the prediction of substance use for women.

Future Research and Conclusion

Future research in this area should incorporate more detailed questions about job insecurity. In particular, it is unclear whether it is the perceived likelihood of job loss or the extent to which workers worry about this potential job loss that is associated with an increase in the likelihood of substance use. Using Waves 1 and 2 of the MIDUS dataset we found a significant relationship between job insecurity and substance use for women, whereas a similar relationship for men is non-existent. We interpret this as evidence that precarious employment is gendered, while acknowledging that differences between men and women do not completely capture "gender differences" or the "gender gap" in precarity. One's sex classification is gendered to the extent that we rely on gender norms when classifying others on the basis of perceived sex, but it is not reducible to gender without relying on a heteronormative framework that views sex and gender in essentialist terms and non-normative gender expressions as unintelligible (Butler, 1990, 2004). Gender and precarity are interconnected phenomenon and also serve as the potential basis for coalition building to resist recent efforts to extend the reach of the neoliberal discourse (Butler, 2015a, p. 58). Future research should explore other facets of the gendering of precarious employment and potential intersections with race and ethnicity. The association between job insecurity and substance use has vastly different potential consequences for racial and ethnic minorities given the systematic racial biases in the U.S. criminal justice system (Alexander, 2010).

The key finding in this study also contributes to the literature on job insecurity and the consequences of stress and strain for men and women. There are many different types of stressors and causes of strain that affect individuals. Job insecurity is an important, yet often overlooked, one in the substance use and criminological literature. In contemporary society, a large portion of the population faces one form of job insecurity or another on a regular basis. Understanding the repercussions of job insecurity is important as the rapidly changing landscape of the global economy will most likely continue to create work environments in which job insecurity is a reality for many workers.

NOTES

1. The perceived likelihood of future job loss is a measure of "cognitive job insecurity" (Anderson & Pontusson, 2007). Researchers have also examined other types

of worker insecurity, including affective job insecurity (i.e., worrying about the threat of job loss) and labor market insecurity (i.e., perceived difficulty in finding a comparable job if one were to become unemployed).

2. Studies of job insecurity are typically based on samples of adult workers. Although job insecurity and substance use among adolescents is a topic worthy of investigation, it is beyond the scope of this study.

3. We use the term "sex classification" rather than "gender" or "sex" due to the way in which this information is recorded during the survey interview, which we discuss in the section "Data and Methods."

4. Self-reported "sex" is also a (self-)classification if one is forced to choose one of two categories (male or female).

5. Wave 1 response rates are 70% for the phone interview and 87% for the self-administered questionnaire. The longitudinal retention rates at Wave 2 is 65% for the phone interview sample, and 80% of phone interview respondents at Wave 2 completed the self-administered questionnaire.

6. "On one's own" means that the respondent either used the substance without a prescription, in larger amounts than the physician prescribed, or for a longer period of time than the physician prescribed. The substance use rates by drug at Wave 2 are: sedatives (2.6% of women, 2.3% of men), tranquilizers (1.1% of women, 1.7% of men), stimulants (0.4% of women, 0.6% of men), painkillers (3.4% of women, 3.2% of men), depression medication (1.8% of women, 0.6% of men), inhalants (0.1% of women, 0.0% of men), marijuana/hashish (2.2% of women, 5.6% of men), cocaine/crack (0.4% of women, 0.7% of men), hallucinogens (0.1% of women, 0.1% of men), and heroin (0.1% of women, 0.0% of men).

7. The original measures were on 5-point scales (poor to excellent in Wave 1 and excellent to poor in Wave 2). We reversed the category order in Wave 1, created z-scores, and then summed the z-scores at each wave.

8. In Wave 1, the original measures were on 4-point scales ("a lot" to "not at all"). In Wave 2, the original measures were also on 4-point scales but with slightly different category labels ("very" to "not at all" for satisfaction with life and self and "a lot" to "none at all" for control over life). We reversed the category order, created z-scores, and summed the z-scores at each wave.

9. Other occupations include farm, mechanics, repairers, construction, mining, operators, manual laborers, and military. We control for occupation in the "full" models but do not present the logit results in the tables.

10. We compare average marginal effects rather than odds ratios across samples and models given the problems associated with such odds ratio comparisons (see Mood, 2010).

11. The results are virtually the same using a more detailed occupational coding scheme as well (with 10 categories).

12. For the predicted probabilities in Fig. 1, we hold the remaining variables constant at the same values for the male and female samples: substance use at Wave 1 = 0, job insecurity at Wave 1 = 0, poor health at Wave 1 = −0.15, poor health at Wave 2 = −0.045, life satisfaction at Wave 1 = −0.055, life satisfaction at Wave 2 = 0.02, age = 42, white = 1, married = 1, children = 2, education = 15, log income = 11, all occupation variables = 0, and wage/salary worker = 1. These values represent approximate averages of the group-specific means for each continuous variable.

ACKNOWLEDGMENTS

The authors presented a previous version of this paper at the 2013 meeting of the Midwest Sociological Society in Chicago, IL. The authors thank Jeff Dixon for his comments on a previous draft.

REFERENCES

Acker, J. (1990). Hierarchies, jobs, bodies: A theory of gendered organizations. *Gender & Society, 4*, 139–158.

Agnew, R. (1992). Foundation for a general strain theory of crime and delinquency. *Criminology, 30*, 47–87.

Agnew, R. (2001). Building on the foundation of general strain theory: Specifying the types of strain most likely to lead to crime and delinquency. *Journal of Research in Crime and Delinquency, 38*, 319–361.

Agnew, R., & White, H. R. (1992). An empirical test of general strain theory. *Criminology, 30*, 475–499.

Alexander, M. (2010). *The new Jim Crow: Mass incarceration in the age of colorblindness.* New York, NY: The New Press.

Allison, P. D. (1999). Comparing logit and probit coefficients across groups. *Sociological Methods and Research, 28*, 186–208.

Anderson, C. J., & Pontusson, J. (2007). Workers, worries and welfare states: Social protection and job insecurity in 15 OECD countries. *European Journal of Political Research, 46*, 211–235.

Aneshensel, C. S. (1992). Social stress: Theory and research. *Annual Review of Sociology, 18*, 15–38.

Bauer, G. F., Huber, C. A., Jenny, G. J., Müller, F., & Hämmig, O. (2009). Socioeconomic status, working conditions and self-rated health in Switzerland: Explaining the gradient in men and women. *International Journal of Public Health, 54*, 23–30.

Bildt, C., & Michélsen, H. (2002). Gender differences in the effects from working conditions on mental health: A 4-year follow-up. *International Archives of Occupational and Environmental Health, 75*, 252–258.

Blazer, D. G., & Wu, L.–T. (2009). The epidemiology of at-risk and binge drinking among middle-aged and elderly community adults: National survey on drug use and health. *American Journal of Psychiatry, 166*, 1162–1169.

Boardman, J. D., Finch, B. K., Ellison, C. G., Williams, D. R., & Jackson, J. S. (2001). Neighborhood disadvantage, stress, and drug use among adults. *Journal of Health and Social Behavior, 42*, 151–165.

Bogart, L. M., Collins, R. L., Ellickson, P. L., & Klein, D. J. (2007). Are adolescent substance users less satisfied with life as young adults and if so, why? *Social Indicators Research, 81*, 149–169.

Bourdieu, P. (1991). *Language and symbolic power.* Cambridge, MA: Harvard University Press.

Bourdieu, P. (1998). *Acts of resistance: Against the tyranny of the market.* New York, NY: The New Press.

Briggs, C. A., & Pepperell, J. L. (2009). *Women, girls and addiction.* New York, NY: Routledge.

Burgard, S. A., Brand, J. E., & House, J. S. (2009). Perceived job insecurity and worker health in the United States. *Social Science & Medicine, 69,* 777−785.

Butler, J. (1990). *Gender trouble: Feminism and the subversion of identity.* New York, NY: Routledge.

Butler, J. (2004). *Undoing gender.* New York, NY: Routledge.

Butler, J. (2015a). *Notes toward a performative theory of assembly.* Cambridge, MA: Harvard University Press.

Butler, J. (2015b). Foreword. In I. Lorey (Ed.), *State of insecurity: Government of the precarious* (pp. vii−xi). London: Verso.

Calabrese, S. K., Meyer, I. H., Overstreet, N. M., Haile, R., & Hansen, N. B. (2015). Exploring discrimination and mental health disparities faced by black sexual minority women using a minority stress framework. *Psychology of Women Quarterly, 39,* 287−304.

Campbell, D., Carruth, A., Dickerson, A., & Green, F. (2007). Job insecurity and wages. *The Economic Journal, 117,* 544−566.

Catalano, R., Rook, K., & Dooley, D. (1986). Labor markets and help-seeking: A test of the employment security hypothesis. *Journal of Health and Social Behavior, 27,* 277−287.

Cheng, Y., Chen, C.-W., Chen, C.-J., & Chiang, T.-L. (2005). Job insecurity and its association with health among employees in the Taiwanese general population. *Social Science and Medicine, 61,* 41−52.

Davis, S. (1994). Effects of chemical dependency in parenting women. In R. R. Watson (Ed.), *Addictive behaviors in women* (pp. 381−413). Totowa, NJ: Humana Press.

De Witte, H. (1999). Job insecurity and psychological well-being: Review of the literature and exploration of some unresolved issues. *European Journal of Work and Organizational Psychology, 8,* 155−177.

Denton, M., & Walters, V. (1999). Gender differences in structural and behavioral determinants of health: An analysis of the social production of health. *Social Science & Medicine, 48,* 1221−1235.

Etherington, N. (2015). Race, gender, and the resources that matter: An investigation of intersectionality and health. *Women & Health, 55,* 754−777.

Ettore, E., & Riska, E. (1995). *Gendered moods: Psychotropics and society.* London: Routledge.

Fernandez-Mateo, I. (2010). Cumulative gender disadvantage in contract employment. *American Journal of Sociology, 114*(4), 871−923.

Fernandez-Mateo, I., & King, Z. (2011). Anticipatory sorting and gender segregation in temporary employment. *Management Science, 57*(6), 989−1008.

Ferrie, J. E., Kivimäki, M., Shipley, M. J., Smith, G. D., & Virtanen, M. (2013). Job insecurity and incident coronary heart disease: The Whitehall II prospective cohort study. *Atherosclerosis, 227,* 178−181.

Ferrie, J. E., Shipley, M. J., Marmot, M. G., Stansfeld, S., & Smith, G. D. (1995). Health effects of anticipation of job change and non-employment: Longitudinal data from the Whitehall II study. *British Medical Journal, 311,* 1264−1269.

Ferrie, J. E., Shipley, M. J., Newman, K., Stansfeld, S. A., & Marmot, M. (2005). Self-reported job insecurity and health in the Whitehall II study: Potential explanations of the relationship. *Social Science and Medicine, 60,* 1593−1602.

Ferrie, J. E., Shipley, M. J., Stansfeld, S. A., Smith, G. D., & Marmot, M. (2003). Future uncertainty and socioeconomic inequalities in health: The Whitehall II study. *Social Science and Medicine, 57,* 637−646.

Fischer, B., Medved, W., Kirst, M., Rehm, J., & Gliksman, L. (2001). Illicit opiates and crime: Results of an untreated user cohort study in Toronto. *Canadian Journal of Criminology and Criminal Justice*, *43*, 197–217.

Frone, M. R. (2008). Are work stressors related to employee substance use? The importance of temporal context in assessments of alcohol and illicit drug use. *Journal of Applied Psychology*, *93*, 199–206.

Frone, M. R., Cooper, M. L., & Russell, M. (1994). Stressful life events, gender and substance use: An application of Tobit regression. *Psychology of Addictive Behaviors*, *8*, 59–69.

Fullerton, A. S., & Anderson, K. F. (2013). The role of job insecurity in explanations of racial health inequalities. *Sociological Forum*, *28*, 308–325.

Fullerton, A. S., Dixon, C. J., & McCollum, D. B. (2016). *The institutionalization of part-time work: Cross-national differences in the relationship between part-time work and perceived insecurity*. Paper presented at the annual meeting of the American Sociological Association Annual Meeting, Hilton San Francisco Union Square, San Francisco, CA.

Fullerton, A. S., & Wallace, M. (2007). Traversing the flexible turn: US workers' perceptions of job security, 1977–2002. *Social Science Research*, *36*, 201–221.

Fullerton, A. S., & Raynes, D. (2016). *Undoing sex classification in survey research*. Working Paper.

Geuskens, G. A., Koppes, L. L. J., van den Bossche, S. N. J., & Joling, C. I. (2012). Enterprise restructuring and the health of employees: A cohort study. *Journal of Occupational & Environmental Medicine*, *54*, 4–9.

Hatton, E. (2011). *The temp economy: From Kelly girls to permatemps in postwar America*. Philadelphia, PA: Temple University Press.

Hatton, E. (2014). Mechanisms of gendering: Gender typing and the ideal worker norm in the temporary help industry, 1946–1979. *Journal of Gender Studies*, *23*, 440–456.

Heaney, C. A., Israel, B. A., & House, J. S. (1994). Chronic job insecurity among automobile workers: Effects on job satisfaction and health. *Social Science and Medicine*, *38*, 1431–1437.

Hochschild, A. R., & Machung, A. (2003). *The second shift*. New York, NY: Penguin Books.

Kalleberg, A. L. (2000). Nonstandard employment relations: Part-time, temporary and contract work. *Annual Review of Sociology*, *26*, 341–365.

Kalleberg, A. L. (2009). Precarious work, insecure workers: Employment relations in transition. *American Sociological Review*, *74*, 1–22.

Kalleberg, A. L. (2011). *Good jobs, bad jobs*. New York, NY: Russell Sage Foundation.

Kandel, D. B. (1991). The social demography of drug use. *The Milbank Quarterly*, *63*, 365–414.

Kivimäki, M., Vahtera, J., Elovainio, M., Virtanen, M., & Siegrist, J. (2007). Effort-reward imbalance, procedural injustice and relational injustice as psychosocial predictors of health: Complementary or redundant models? *Occupational and Environmental Medicine*, *64*, 659–665.

Klandermans, B., Hesselink, J. K., & van Vuuren, T. (2010). Employment status and job insecurity: On the subjective appraisal of an objective status. *Economic and Industrial Democracy*, *31*, 557–577.

László, K., Pikhart, H., Kopp, M. S., Bobak, M., Pajak, A., Malyutina, S., … Marmot, M. (2010). Job insecurity and health: A study of 16 European countries. *Social Science and Medicine*, *70*, 867–874.

Lee, S., Colditz, G. A., Berkman, L. F., & Kawachi, I. (2004). Prospective study of job insecurity and coronary heart disease in US women. *Annals of Epidemiology, 14*, 24–30.

Long, J. S. (1997). *Regression models for categorical and limited dependent variables.* Thousand Oaks, CA: Sage.

Lorber, J. (1994). *Paradoxes of gender.* New Haven, CT: Yale University Press.

Lorey, I. (2015). *State of insecurity: Government of the precarious.* London: Verso.

Manchikanti, L., Helm, S., Fellows, B., Janata, J. W., Pampati, V., Grider, J. S., & Boswell, M. V. (2012). Opiate epidemic in the United States. *Pain Physician, 15*, ES9–ES38.

Matthews, S., Manor, O., & Power, C. (1999). Social inequalities in health: Are there gender differences? *Social Science & Medicine, 48*, 49–60.

Merton, R. K. (1938). Social structure and anomie. *American Sociological Review, 3*, 672–682.

Mood, C. (2010). Logistic regression: Why we cannot do what we think we can do, and what we can do about it. *European Sociological Review, 26*, 67–82.

National Institute of Drug Abuse (NIDA). (2015). *Drug facts: Nationwide trends.* Retrieved from https://www.drugabuse.gov/publications/drugfacts/nationwide-trends. Accessed on March, 16, 2016.

Patton, G. C., Coffey, C., Carlin, J. B., Degenhardt, L., Lynskey, M., & Hall, W. (2002). Cannabis use and mental health in young people: Cohort study. *British Medical Journal, 325*, 1195–1198.

Pearlin, L. I. (1989). The sociological study of stress. *Journal of Health and Social Behavior, 30*(3), 241–256.

Pearlin, L. I., Menaghan, E. G., Lieberman, M. A., & Mullan, J. T. (1981). The stress process. *Journal of Health and Social Behavior, 22*(4), 337–356.

Pearlin, L. I., Schieman, S., Fazio, E. M., & Meersman, S. C. (2005). Stress, health, and the life course: Some conceptual perspectives. *Journal of Health and Social Behavior, 46*, 241–256.

Perry, B. L., Harp, K. L. H., & Oser, C. B. (2013). Racial and gender discrimination in the stress process: Implications for African American women's health and well-being. *Sociological Perspectives, 56*, 25–48.

Pugh, A. J. (2015). *The tumbleweed society: Working and caring in an age of insecurity.* New York, NY: Oxford University Press.

Rubin, B. A. (1996). *Shifts in the social contract: Understanding change in American society.* Thousand Oaks, CA: Pine Forge Press.

Rudolf, H., & Watts, J. (2003). Quality of life in substance and dependency. *International Review of Psychiatry, 14*, 190–197.

Rugulies, R., Aust, B., Burr, H., & Bültmann, U. (2008). Job insecurity, chances on the labour market and decline in self-rated health in a representative sample of the Danish workforce. *Journal of Epidemiology & Community Health, 62*, 245–250.

Rugulies, R., Bültmann, U., Aust, B., & Burr, H. (2006). Psychosocial work environment and incidence of severe depressive symptoms: Prospective findings from a 5-year follow-up of the Danish work environment cohort study. *American Journal of Epidemiology, 163*(10), 877–887.

Rugulies, R., Thielen, K., Nygaard, E., & Diderichsen, F. (2010). Job insecurity and the use of antidepressant medication among Danish employees with and without a history of prolonged unemployment: A 3.5-year follow-up study. *Journal of Epidemiology & Community Health, 64*, 75–81.

Ryff, C., Almeida, D. M., Ayanian, J. S., Carr, D. S., Cleary, P. D., Coe, C., ... Williams, D. (2012). *National survey of midlife development in the United States (MIDUS II), 2004–2006)*. ICPSR04652-v6. Ann Arbor, MI: Inter-University Consortium for Political and Social Research [distributor]. 2012-04-18. doi:10.3886/ICPSR04652.v6

Schreurs, B., van Emmerik, H., Notelaers, G., & De Witte, H. (2010). Job insecurity and employee health: The buffering potential of job control and job self-efficacy. *Work and Stress, 24*(1), 56–72.

Seng, J. S., Lopez, W. D., Sperlich, M., Hamama, L., & Reed Meldrum, C. D. (2012). Marginalized identities, discrimination burden, and mental health: Empirical exploration of an interpersonal-level approach to modeling intersectionality. *Social Science & Medicine, 75*, 2437–2445.

Smith, V. (1998). The fractured world of the temporary worker: Power, participation, and fragmentation in the contemporary workplace. *Social Problems, 45*(4), 411–430.

Spooner, C. (1999). Causes and correlates of adolescent drug abuse and implications for treatment. *Drug and Alcohol Review, 18*, 453–475.

Stephens, M., Jr. (2004). Job loss expectations, realizations, and household consumption behavior. *Review of Economics and Statistics, 86*, 253–269.

Turner, R. J., Wheaton, B., & Lloyd, D. A. (1995). The epidemiology of social stress. *American Sociological Review, 60*(1), 104–125.

Unger, J. B., Kipke, M. D., Simon, T. R., Montgomery, S. B., & Johnson, C. J. (1997). Homeless youths and young adults in Los Angeles: Prevalence of mental health problems and the relationship between mental health and substance abuse disorders. *American Journal of Community Psychology, 25*, 371–394.

Vallas, S., & Prener, C. (2012). Dualism, job polarization, and the social construction of precarious work. *Work and Occupations, 39*, 331–353.

Vosko, Leah F. (2010). *Managing the margins: Gender, citizenship, and the international regulation of precarious employment*. Oxford: Oxford University Press.

Westbrook, L., & Saperstein, A. (2015). New categories are not enough: Rethinking the measurement of sex and gender in social surveys. *Gender & Society, 29*, 534–560.

Williams, R. (2009). Using heterogeneous choice models to compare logit and probit coefficients across groups. *Sociological Methods and Research, 37*, 531–559.

Williams, R. (2010). Fitting heterogeneous choice models with OGLM. *Stata Journal, 10*, 540–567.

Williams, R. (2012). Using the margins command to estimate and interpret adjusted predictions and marginal effects. *Stata Journal, 12*, 308–331.

Zullig, K. J., Valois, R. F., Huebner, E. S., Oeltmann, J. E., & Wanzer Drane, J. (2001). Relationship between perceived life satisfaction and adolescents' substance abuse. *Journal of Adolescent Health, 29*, 279–288.

APPENDIX

Table A1. Unstandardized Coefficients from OLS Regression Models of Poor Health and Life Satisfaction at Wave 2.

	Poor Health		Life Satisfaction	
	Women	Men	Women	Men
Poor health (Wave 1)	0.475***	0.517***		
	(0.034)	(0.034)		
Life satisfaction (Wave 1)			0.435***	0.455***
			(0.031)	(0.032)
Job insecurity (Wave 1)	−0.067	0.251*	0.093	0.189
	(0.120)	(0.120)	(0.161)	(0.166)
Job insecurity (Wave 2)	0.183	0.211#	−0.568***	−0.724***
	(0.122)	(0.127)	(0.163)	(0.173)
Age (Wave 1)	−0.008	0.008	0.036***	0.009
	(0.006)	(0.006)	(0.009)	(0.008)
White (Wave 1)	−0.085	0.142	−0.341	−0.668*
	(0.208)	(0.244)	(0.280)	(0.334)
Married (Wave 2)	−0.089	−0.089	0.233	0.490*
	(0.125)	(0.142)	(0.169)	(0.195)
Number of children (Wave 2)	−0.011	−0.037	0.022	0.013
	(0.038)	(0.036)	(0.051)	(0.049)
Education (Wave 2)	−0.078**	−0.046#	−0.041	−0.054
	(0.027)	(0.026)	(0.036)	(0.035)
Log household income	−0.040	−0.068	0.043	0.074
	(0.031)	(0.048)	(0.042)	(0.066)
Model Fit				
Adj. R^2	0.254	0.310	0.261	0.283

Notes: N = 764 women and 712 men. The coefficients are unstandardized. The numbers in parentheses are standard errors. The models also include a set of four binary variables for occupation (reference = professional) and a constant.
#$p < .10$; *$p < .05$; **$p < .01$; ***$p < .001$.